D1451384

CHICAGO

HIROSHIMA

ROTTERDAM

BERLIN

JERUSALEM

Design: Brett Snyder

Editorial coordination at Columbia University:
Salomon Frausto
Copyediting at Columbia University: Stephanie Salomon
Editorial production at Columbia University: Chris Barker

Editorial direction at Prestel: Angeli Sachs
Copyediting at Prestel: Curt Holtz
Production at Prestel: Meike Weber
Lithography: ReproLine
Printing and Binding: Graspo

ISBN: 3-7913-2790-9

© Prestel Verlag, Munich, Berlin, London, New York
and The Trustees of Columbia University in the City of New York, 2002

Library of Congress Control Number: 2002109070

Prestel Verlag
Königinstrasse 9 · 80539 Munich
Tel. +49 (0)89 381709-0 · Fax + 49 (0)89 381709-35;
4 Bloomsbury Place · London WC1A 2QA
Tel. +44 (0)20 7323-5004 · Fax +44 (0)20 7636-8004;
175 5th Ave., Suite 402 · New York, NY 10010
Tel. +1 (212) 995-2720, Fax +1 (212) 995-2733
www.prestel.com

OUT OF GROUND ZERO
CASE STUDIES IN URBAN REINVENTION

Edited by Joan Ockman

**Temple Hoyne Buell Center
for the Study
of American Architecture
Columbia University**

Prestel

Joan Ockman **14 INTRODUCTION**

Kenneth Maxwell **20 LISBON**
The earthquake of 1755 and urban recovery under the Marquês de Pombal

Ross Miller **46 CHICAGO**
Out of the blue: the Great Chicago Fire of 1871

Carola Hein **62 HIROSHIMA**
The atomic bomb and Kenzo Tange's Hiroshima Peace Center

Han Meyer **84 ROTTERDAM**
The promise of a new, modern society in a new, modern city, 1940 to the present

Alan Powers

98 **PLYMOUTH**
Reconstruction after World War II

Hubertus Siegert and Ralph Stern

116 **BERLIN**
Film and the representation of urban reconstruction since the fall of the Wall

Milan Prodanovic

138 **BALKAN CITIES**
Urbicide and chances for the reconstruction of Balkan cities

Kanan Makiya

150 **JERUSALEM**
The symbolism of the Dome of the Rock from the seventh century to the present

Max Page

166 **NEW YORK**
Creatively destroying New York: fantasies, premonitions, and realities in the provisional city

Benjamin R. Barber

184 **EPILOGUE**
An architecture of liberty? The city as democracy's forge

INTRODUCTION

Joan Ockman

The essays in this volume originated as a series of lectures
presented under the auspices of the Temple Hoyne Buell Center for
the Study of American Architecture at Columbia University in the
spring of 2002. Like so many cultural institutions in New York City
and elsewhere, the Buell Center felt the need to respond in some
way to the cataclysmic "events" of the preceding September and the
mountain of rubble and remains in the process of being cleared
downtown at the World Trade Center site, widely referred to as
"ground zero." On the one hand, there was a still palpable sense of
the tragedy's ineffability; on the other, an increasingly clamorous
debate (not least engaging the architectural community) as to how to
rebuild. It seemed that it might be of value to try to put the situation
into some historical and cross-cultural perspective. Presumably
there were lessons to be derived from the example of other cities
and the way they have coped with major disasters.

Indeed, while each of the cases of "urban reinvention" under examination here is unique, it offers a suggestive way of thinking about the situation in New York. It may be cold comfort to know that the magnitude of suffering in Manhattan is no greater than that which has been endured in other places and times. Yet the spectrum of responses exemplified by the following essays offers not just a set of variations on the theme of urban destruction, but a sense of the manifold meanings of urban experience. For the most part, these responses confirm the perennial resilience of cities in the face of drastic events. A couple, however, also offer more cautionary tales.

In the case of Lisbon, the earthquake of 1755 was a truly world-shaking event, as Kenneth Maxwell, a scholar of Portuguese history, relates. Estimated to have registered 9.0 on the Richter scale, the quake and its aftershocks were felt as far east as Venice, where Casanova, imprisoned in the Ducal Palace in Piazza San Marco, seized the opportunity to escape from his cell. In Lisbon, the epicenter, between 10,000 and 15,000 people were killed, and about one-third of the city destroyed. But what is singular about Lisbon among the cases considered here is the emergence of what Hegel would call a "world-historical individual." Stepping in for a weak and fearful monarch, the Marquês de Pombal lost no time in taking charge. Pombal was one of those visionary—and ruthless—personalities through whose agency an entire city was transformed, a figure comparable to a Baron Haussmann or Robert Moses. Under his oversight, Lisbon went from being an aristocratic, Jesuit outpost with a jumbled medieval plan to become a modern bourgeois and commercial city embodying Enlightenment values and boasting functional planning and a fireproof, sanitary system of construction. Almost two hundred fifty years later—as a comparison between the drawings signed by Pombal and contemporary photographs reveals—his intervention remains perfectly legible in the neo-Palladian architecture of the city's principal squares and streets.

Chicago presents the opposite scenario. In the heartland of America, pragmatic opportunism reigned supreme after Mrs. O'Leary's cow kicked over a lantern in 1871. Historian Ross Miller describes the enormous real-estate boom that followed the Great Fire and the frenzy of rebuilding, almost all of it shoddy and undistinguished. Meanwhile, a peculiarly American mix of doomsday prophecy and thinly veiled capitalist celebration combined to give the city a new founding myth as a dynamic, *tabula rasa* metropolis. Just two years later, a national economic depression put a halt to the derricks and further conspired to keep Chicago from erecting any significant buildings. Fascinatingly, however, it was this negative experience of post-fire rebuilding rather than the fire itself that, by the early 1880s, engendered the city's great period of architectural modernism. Architects like John Wellborn Root, Daniel Burnham, and Louis Sullivan witnessed the effects of the speculation-driven construction at a formative moment in their careers, and were inspired to design a different sort of building: high-rise frame structures in the solid, fireproof, and commercial but civic-minded style that would become Chicago's seminal contribution to world architecture.

If the havoc wreaked by natural disasters like earthquakes and fires has ultimately tended to be received with a sense of apocalyptic acceptance, that caused by war and human instrumentality has elicited a rather different range of emotions. These emotions are necessarily inflected, as architectural historian Carola Hein points out with respect to Hiroshima and other cities leveled by bombs during World War II, by the historical outcome—whether the city is on the side of the winners or losers.

In Japan, a certain myth of victimhood coalesced after the loss of the war around the notion that Hiroshima was the first city on which an atomic bomb was dropped. Again, compared to New York, the attack on the Japanese city by the American airplane *Enola Gay*, in August 1945, took a vastly greater toll in human life, not to mention urban fabric: upward of 180,000 people have died as the radiation continues to work its long-term effects even today. Yet the indelible image of the mushroom cloud descending on its civilian target bears comparison to that of the two towers collapsing. If prior to the bombing Hiroshima was not a very well known city, afterward the Japanese ground zero became a universal symbol of this horrific and unprecedented form of modern warfare and the focus of an important project of reconstruction and memorialization. In her essay, Hein dwells on the exceptional nature of Hiroshima's rebuilding and the role played by a visionary young architect, Kenzo Tange. In a country that still has little tradition of monumental or comprehensive urban planning, typically resorting to pragmatic forms of "readjustment" in the wake of frequent fires, earthquakes, and floods, Tange's solution to the competition brief for a "peace city" melded Western concepts of modernism with Eastern (specifically Shinto) forms of commemoration to produce an extraordinary work of architecture. While the full scope of his ambitious master plan went unrealized, and while the rest of Hiroshima has been developed in the intervening years like most other postwar Japanese cities, Tange's urban centerpiece continues today to resonate with poetic dignity.

Rotterdam offers another story. Here the extensive damage inflicted in 1940 by Nazi bombs, which eradicated 11,000 buildings in the center of this antiquated and dense port city, was soon welcomed by forward-looking planners, businessmen, and politicians as an opportunity to rebuild a more modern metropolis. In fact, this had been the objective of many in Rotterdam well before the war. Urban planner Han Meyer traces the debates over modernization in Rotterdam from the late nineteenth century to the present, demonstrating how attitudes toward urban form have repeatedly been revised in accord with ideological imperatives or lived experience. Thus the compact urbanism favored by Rotterdam's first reconstruction architect, W. G. Witteveen, was jettisoned in 1944 for the more modernist and "American" ideas of his successor, C. van Traa, who embraced the functionalist zoning of CIAM (the International Congresses of Modern Architecture) and the type of open, "democratic" space in the city center called for by Sigfried Giedion in the name of a "new monumentality." Among the most innovative and celebrated projects to come out of this approach was the Lijnbaan shopping center by the architects Van den Broek and Bakema, hailed as a model of progressive planning. In subsequent years, however, particularly as postmodernist revisionism set in during the 1960s, Rotterdam's citizens took a dimmer view of the postwar development. In recent decades, a succession of strategies has been adopted to reconstruct the city along more traditionally European or Dutch lines.

In Plymouth, England, the reconstruction undertaken after the air raids of 1941 was an object of disdain almost from the start. Here, under the engineer James Paton Watson, the mayor Waldorf Astor, and the elderly London planner Sir Patrick Abercrombie, an idealistic but neotraditionalist plan was adopted. Largely reflecting Abercrombie's thinking, as architectural historian Alan Powers elaborates, the plan was a loose amalgam of the regionalist ideas of Patrick Geddes, the formality of the American City Beautiful movement, and the Garden City philosophy of Lewis Mumford. Implemented over the next two decades, it suffered from poor-quality execution, compromises with respect to some of its basic features, and a general shift in British taste away from Abercrombie's penchant for the grand axial vista toward the more picturesque English aesthetic of "townscape." Despite efforts to remedy some of the scheme's defects in subsequent decades, the honorific city center has succumbed over the years to banal development. Interestingly, however, as Powers notes, Abercrombie's emphasis on integrating the plan with the surrounding region echoes some of the more audacious discussions that took place early on with respect to the World Trade Center site, and constitutes the plan's chief contribution to urban thought.

Berlin too is a city whose fate was decisively changed by World War II. But the traumatic and hyperaccelerated development on which German filmmaker Hubertus Siegert and architectural historian Ralph Stern focus here has to do with the mammoth building program mounted in that city since its reunification in 1989 at the end of the Cold War. Siegert's film *Berlin Babylon*, completed in 2001 and screened as part of the lecture series presented at Columbia, offers a vision of a city in the throes of reinventing itself. As Stern points out in his introduction to a dialogue with Siegert about the making of the film, *Berlin Babylon* defies the usual "city film" genres. Neither a documentary nor a celebration of architectural achievement as such, it captures in vivid and poetic imagery—as may be seen from the stills reproduced in this volume—the arbitrary, brutal, and frequently banal process of city building. In this process the urban construction worker figures at least as heroically as the municipal planner and architect (think of New York City's firefighters and policemen as playing a similar role). Siegert's view of urban processes and protagonists, more curious than cynical, is personified by Walter Benjamin's angel of history, who is evoked in a voice-over in the film, helplessly being blown backward into the future. The film's central metaphor of Babel/Babylon further dramatizes the mythic dimensions of the city's reconstruction and its architectural hubris.

In the case of Balkan cities, Belgrade architect, educator, and dissident Milan Prodanovic, another eyewitness to recent historic events, provides a more political argument. Diagnosing the situation that led to the collapse of the former Yugoslavia over the past decade, he uses the term *urbicide*, coined by his compatriot Bogdan Bogdanovic, to characterize the hostility to cities and to civic culture harbored by the region's multifarious ethnic groups. This hostility was stoked, with murderous consequences, by corrupt "postmodern dictatorships" armed with a lethal mixture of conventional weapons and modern media technology (in particular television). Whether one speaks of the genocide carried out against the Croat population of Vukovar by Serbs, or the destruction of urban and architectural patrimony in the former Herzogovinian capital of Mostar by Croats (including its renowned sixteenth-century bridge), or the general implosion of urban life instigated in Belgrade by Mafia-like military rulers, all these tragic events have in common a hatred by the perpetrators of urbanity and democratic values and a fundamentalist attitude toward ethnic heritage. In Prodanovic's view, the only chance of overcoming these entrenched prejudices and constructing an open, civil society in the Balkans lies in basic educational reform and a rapprochement between local culture and the new forces of globalization.

Contemporary Jerusalem represents another desperate urban situation today, an intensely symbolic and just as intensely contested place that in recent times has been spared the type of physical destruction experienced by the other cities in this volume, yet whose potential for falling victim to such calamity seems to loom larger each day. In a rather different form of response to the question of urban reinvention, Iraqi-born political writer and former architect Kanan Makiya discusses the ideas behind his recent novel, *The Rock*, a work of historical fiction about the building of the Dome of the Rock. Makiya views this monument, located on a site in Jerusalem sacred to three religions since ancient times, as "a lightning rod for complete and total disaster in the Middle East"—and as such, a place comparable to the World Trade Center. In his novel, Makiya gives an account of the Dome's origins based on the facts available in the historical record, but he takes poetic license where the record is incomplete. In his telling, the monument's construction reveals a complicity and connectedness between ancient Islam and Judaism as it also refutes the claims of either side to primacy. Thus, in the face of intransigent enmity and despair, Makiya gives expression to a hope for coexistence and conciliation, as if, through an act of utopian imagination, it might be possible to change historical destiny. If Benjamin's angel blows backward into the future in Siegert's film of Berlin, Makiya attempts to anticipate what is to come in Jerusalem by renarrating the city's past.

The aesthetic imagination is also the focus of an essay by urban historian Max Page on New York City itself, seen from a broad historical and cultural perspective. Page takes us both back in time and back to the future to remind us that New York has long been the subject of premonitions and fantasies of destruction, and perceived as a city constantly being made and unmade. From serious literature and art to science-fiction films and commercial advertisements, these nightmare visions and exceptionalist interpretations have served, in Page's view, to sublimate an unsettling reality of continuous change, the primary experience in this paradigmatically provisional city of capitalism. New York's collective unconscious has also given its residents a certain sense of inevitability with respect to urban transformations and even—like their fellow Chicagoans—caused them to embrace crises and calamities as opportunities for "creative destruction," that is, for new economic and architectural development. Yet arguing that previous disasters in the city's history like fires and epidemics have ultimately had far less impact on New York's overall trajectory than longer-term shifts, Page reserves judgment on just how fundamentally New York's social, political, and economic structures will be altered by the events of September 2001.

Finally, political theorist Benjamin R. Barber offers a historical—and hortatory—critique of the relationship between cities and democracy that serves here as an epilogue. Tracing the idea of "democratic space" from the Athenian polis through the mercantile town to the capital city and industrial metropolis, Barber defines democracy in terms of the norms of social and political interaction that have emerged during this evolution. With respect to this trajectory he sees the contemporary processes of suburbanization and globalization as constituting a radical rupture. Asking how any notion of citizenship can be sustained in a culture where identity is principally conferred by consumer choices and where public space is confined to gated precincts and sanitized theme parks, he delivers a scathing indictment of the "republic of goods." While slightly more sanguine about the potential of cyberspace to serve as a portal for new forms of democratic interchange, he nonetheless laments that the Internet has rapidly turned into another shopping mall where private profit trumps the public interest. Barber thus identifies yet another variety of urbicide, one closer to home than Prodanovic's, but, he would argue, hardly less pernicious in its violence to accepted ideas of urban life and civic culture.

As these preliminary remarks suggest, there are provocative resonances among the diverse essays that follow. It is instructive, for example, that Barber and Prodanovic, coming from opposite worlds, share so many of the same concerns—with issues of democracy and place, cosmopolitanism and identity, urban and global "citizenship." The convergence in their critiques underscores the fatally interdependent dialectic of "jihad vs. McWorld," as Barber has elsewhere characterized it, which played itself out with such dire consequences in September 2001. Likewise, other major themes that run through this volume—of the respective roles of human agency and chance in the shaping of the city, of the relativity of short- and long-term consequences, of urban and anti-urban mindsets, idealism and pragmatism, lived experience and ideology, physical and mythic construction—open up fertile avenues of thought. All of them lead, however obliquely, back to New York's ground zero, which, at this interim moment in the development of the site, has finally been cleared, an empty center awaiting reinvention.

July 2002

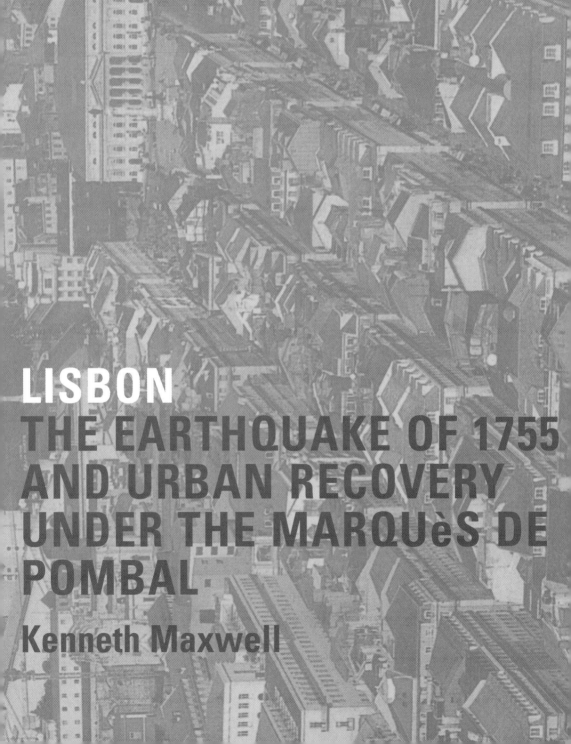

LISBON

THE EARTHQUAKE OF 1755 AND URBAN RECOVERY UNDER THE MARQUèS DE POMBAL

Kenneth Maxwell

An English merchant writing from Lisbon to a friend on November 20, 1755, described the "Late dreadful Earthquake which laid the Capital of Portugal in Ruins…" as "such a Spectacle of Terror and Amazement, as well as the Desolation to Beholders, as perhaps had not been equalled from the Foundation of the World." This essay examines the destruction and subsequent rebuilding of the city of Lisbon.[1]

1755: LISBON
ON THE EVE OF THE EARTHQUAKE

Lisbon is situated on the northern shore of the estuary of the Tagus River. In 1755, the ceremonial and commercial heart of the city was centered on the Royal Palace, built directly on the riverfront. On the eastern side of the palace was a large palace square (Terreiro do Paço). Merchant and retail houses stood along a series of jumbled alleyways and narrow streets constructed over alluvial landfill between steep hills. The other major urban axis was inland to the north, a large public square called the Rossio. In essence, the area between these two urban public spaces, called the Baixa, formed the late medieval city. Lisbon, formerly under Muslim control, had been conquered by Christian knights in 1147 and the Moorish part of the city comprised a series of steep, narrow alleyways built on the sharp slopes to the east of the Baixa under the walls of the old citadel, renamed Saint George's Castle after the *Reconquista*. By the mid-eighteenth century the city had also expanded to the hills to the west and along the riverbank. Here stood many religious establishments and the palaces of the aristocracy.[2]

Lisbon was a great port that took advantage of the sheltered Tagus estuary and its easy access to the Atlantic. After Portugal's establishment of colonial outposts in Asia, Africa, and the Americas over the course of the sixteenth century, Lisbon benefited from the flow of colonial products from Asia and South America as well as from the proceeds gained by early participation in the slave and gold trade in West Africa. The closeness of the royal palace to the sources of Portugal's colonial income—the palace literally abutted the House of India, Customs House, and royal shipyard, the institutions through which streamed spices from the Far East, pepper from India, and sugar, diamonds, and gold from Brazil—led the French, at the height of Portuguese imperial expansion in Asia, to derisively (if enviously) dismiss the Portuguese monarch as the "Grocer King."[3]

In the minds of eighteenth-century Enlightenment thinkers in northwestern Europe, Portugal was also a nation locked in obscurantism. The burnings, so-called "acts of faith" (autos-da-fé) that took place on the waterfront square of Lisbon beside the Royal Palace, provided the best-known images of Portugal for the rest of Europe. Some 45,000 people were investigated by the Portuguese Inquisition between 1536 and 1767, and several thousand condemned and burned in the two centuries prior to the earthquake.[4]

Architectural innovation during the long reign (1706–50) of Dom João V, and his wife, the Archduchess Ana Maria of Austria, had been financed by the gold of Brazil. João V was a devout (if philandering) monarch; he spent huge sums purchasing designs for high Baroque altarpieces and also accumulating books and paintings throughout Europe. João V's major architectural venture was the great palace monastery at Mafra, designed by the Austrian João Frederico Ludovice (Johann Friedrich Ludwig, 1670–1750), and completed in the 1740s based loosely on the model of the Escorial. One French traveler, as he surveyed Mafra, said that only in Portugal would a monarch convert gold into stone.[5]

João V had persuaded Pope Clement XI to grant the title and status of Patriarchate to the city of Lisbon in 1716. It was not until 1737, however, after much Brazilian gold was lavishly spent on Roman patronage, that Dom Tomás de Almeida, who held the position, was made a cardinal by Pope Clement XII. A Patriarchal court modeled on the Roman Curia was created in the Portuguese capital at great expense.[6]

In addition to Mafra, the other major architectural work completed on the eve of the Lisbon earthquake was the magnificently engineered aqueduct that brought water into the capital, constructed under the direction of the Portuguese chief military engineer, Brigadier Manuel da Maia. Both the palace at Mafra and the aqueduct survived the earthquake.[7]

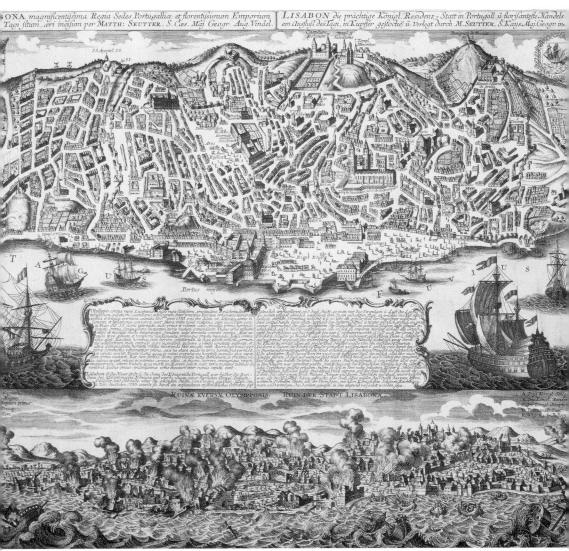

LISBON BEFORE AND DURING THE EARTHQUAKE. ETCHING BY MATEUS SAUTTER, LATE EIGHTEENTH CENTURY. MUSEU DA CIDADE, LISBON

ABOVE RUINS OF THE ROYAL OPERA HOUSE AFTER THE EARTHQUAKE OF 1755. PRINT BY JACQUES-PHILIPPE LE BAS, 1757. MUSEU DA CIDADE, LISBON

BELOW PLAN FOR THE RECONSTRUCTION OF THE CITY OF LISBON IN ACCORDANCE WITH THE NEW ALIGNMENT BY ARCHITECTS EUGÉNIO DOS SANTOS AND CARLOS MARDEL, 1756. INSTITUTO GEOGRÁFICO E CADASTRAL, LISBON

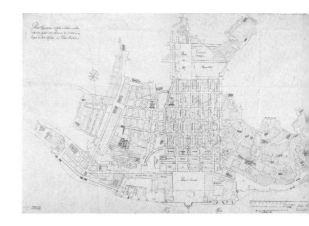

THE EARTHQUAKE

The Great Lisbon Earthquake occurred on All Saints Day, November 1, 1755. The scale of the quake was probably the equivalent of 8.5–9.0 in magnitude on the Richter scale. It led shortly thereafter to a tsunami, a towering tidal wave very rare in the Atlantic Ocean; only three or four such waves in the last three hundred years have struck the Atlantic coast so as to affect the Lisbon area.[8]

Portugal is not considered a high-risk area for earthquakes, and yet there have been very large earthquakes over the course of the centuries in the area of the city, usually at about two-hundred-year intervals. Previously recorded earthquakes in Lisbon occurred in 1344 (probably about 7.0–8.0 on the Richter scale); in 1532 (a likely scale of 7.0–9.0, which also produced a tsunami); in 1755 (approximately a 9.0 scale, with three aftershocks and a tsunami); and most recently, in 1969 (a 6.0 scale).[9]

In 1755, the destruction was enormous: some fifty-five convents and monasteries were severely damaged; the riverfront quay sank and disappeared; and the Royal Palace was destroyed. It is very difficult to ascertain the exact number of dead—contemporary estimates spoke of tens of thousands—but in all likelihood, 10,000 to 15,000 people were killed. The population of Lisbon at the time was somewhere between 160,000 and 200,000. When the earthquake struck on the morning of All Saints Day, people were attending church services, candles were lit on altars, and many churches collapsed onto the congregations during mass.[10]

A British merchant in Lisbon gave a succinct account of his experiences on that fateful morning:

There was I sitting on the first Day of the present Month, about ten of the Clock in the Morning, (the Weather being serene, and the Sky without a Cloud in it,) when I felt the House begin gently to shake; which gradually increased with a rushing noise, like the Sound of heavy Carriages, driving hard at some Distance, and such I at first imagined the Cause of the Noise and Shaking I heard and felt. But both of them gradually increasing, and observing the Pictures in my Room to flap against the Walls. I started up, and immediately perceived it was an Earthquake; and having never been sensible of the Shaking of one before, I stood a good while very composedly remarking its Operations; till from waving and shaking, I thought the Room began to roul, which made me run towards an inward one; more to the Centre of the House; but the Motion was then so extremely violent, that I with Difficulty, kept upon my Feet. Every part of the House cracked about me, the Tiles ratled on the Top of it; the Walls rent on every side; the Doors of a pretty large Book-case that stood in my Room, and which were locked, burst open, and the Books fell from the Shelves within it, but not till after I was got into the Room adjoining; and I heard, with Terror, the falling of Houses round about, and the Screams and Cries of People from every Quarter.[11]

The merchant went out into the city and recorded the reactions as the tsunami struck:

Not long after…a general Pannic was raised from a Crowd of People's running from the Waterside, all crying out the Sea was pouring in and would certainly overwhelm the City. This new Alarm, created such Horrors in the agitated Minds of the Populace, that vast Numbers of them ran screaming into the ruinated City again, where, a fresh Shock of the Earthquake immediately following, many of them were buried in the Ruins of falling Houses. This Alarm was, however, not entirely without Foundation. For the Water of the River rose at once above twenty Feet perpendicular, and subsided again to its natural Pitch in less than a Minute's time. I was of the Number that continued where we were, but the Horror and Distraction of the Multitude were so increased by this astonishing Phænomena, that I confess they appeared more shocking to me than even the very Operations of the Earthquake.[12]

He then succeeded in leaving the city and witnessed the third great disaster that befell Lisbon that morning:

…we perceived, by the Clouds of Smoke which we saw arise, that it had taken Fire; and we have since heard, from Persons who were upon Eminences when the Earthquake happened, that the two great Shocks had been over very few Minutes, before they perceived the Ruins had taken Fire at six or seven different Places. The first that was observed, was at the Convent or Church of *St. Domingo's in the Rocio*; The second at the Boa-Hora, near the Palace; The rest at other Parts of the City, which all raging with great Fury, and burning for five or six Days successively, reduced the whole Capital of *Portugal* to Ashes, except a few Houses at the Out-skirts of the Town, which are, however, so much shattered with the Earthquake, as to be unfit for other Service, than by the Help of Props, to afford a present Shelter to Crowds that could otherwise have no Screen at all against the Inclemencies of Weather, which, in respect to Rain and piercing Winds, are frequently extremely severe in this Country during a great Part of the Winter Season.[13]

The British Consul, writing to London two weeks after the earthquake, told a similar story:

The first shock began about a quarter before 10 o'clock in the morning, and as far as I could judge, lasted six or seven minutes, so that in a quarter of an hour, this great city was laid in ruins. Soon after, several fires broke out, which burned for five or six days. The force of the earthquake seemed to be immediately under the city….It is thought to have vented itself at the quay which runs from the Customs House towards the king's palace, which is entirely carried away, and has totally disappeared. At the time of the earthquake, the waters of the river rose twenty or thirty feet…[14]

About one third of the city was totally destroyed by the quake and flood. The British Consul wrote on December 13:

…the part of the town towards the water where was the Royal Palace, the public tribunals, the Customs House, India House, and where most of the merchants dealt for the convenience of transacting their business, is so totally destroyed by the earthquake and by the fire, that it is nothing but a heap of rubbish, in many places several stories high, incredible to those who are not eye-witnesses of it.[15]

The aftershocks caused widespread damage elsewhere in Portugal and were felt as far away as Venice and southern France and also reached Morocco and northern Africa. But it was Lisbon that bore the brunt of the disaster. The tidal wave and the fire destroyed much of the central part of the city between the Rossio and the Palace Square. The alluvial soil there had likely liquefied. The hills on either side of the Baixa, both to the east and to the west, were less affected, and the buildings along the estuary toward the Atlantic—where the Royal Family was in residence at the summer palace at Belém—survived with less damage. The new opera house, which had staged its first performance in March of that year, was also totally destroyed.[16] This damage and that suffered by other major buildings was documented in engravings made by Jacques-Philippe Le Bas in 1757, the most accurate pictures that exist today of post-earthquake Lisbon.

The scale of the Lisbon earthquake shocked Europe. In Britain George II asked the House of Commons to provide "speedy and effectual relief," and the Commons responded allowing the Treasury to appropriate £100,000 in specie and provisions, clothing, and tools.[17] The cultural impact of the disaster was profound.[18] Goethe, six years old at the time, recalled in his autobiography the reaction of his contemporaries: "Perhaps the Demon of Fear had never so speedily and powerfully diffused his terror over the earth."[19] The event was also the subject of anxious church sermons across the Atlantic in New England.[20] The most notorious reaction came from Voltaire. The catastrophe in Lisbon came at a critical moment during the Enlightenment period, as doubts were beginning to be cast upon the overly optimistic belief in humankind's ability to do and achieve. In his "Poem on the Lisbon Disaster or an Examination of the Axiom 'All is well,'" Voltaire took a very pessimistic view of what had happened:

Oh, miserable mortals! Oh wretched earth!
Oh, dreadful assembly of all mankind!
Eternal sermon of useless sufferings!
Deluded philosophers who cry, "All is well,"
Hasten, contemplate these frightful ruins
This wreck, these shreds, these wretched ashes of the dead;
These women and children heaped on one another,
These scattered members under broken marble;
One-hundred thousand unfortunates devoured by the earth
Who, bleeding, lacerated, and still alive,
Buried under their roofs without aid in their anguish,
End their sad days!
In answer to the half-formed cries of their dying voices,
At the frightful sight of their smoking ashes,
Will you say: "This is the result of eternal laws
Directing the acts of a free and good God!"
Will you say, in seeing this mass of victims:
"God is revenged, their death is the price for their crimes?"
What crime, what error did these children,
Crushed and bloody on their mothers' breasts, commit?
Did fallen Lisbon deeper drink of vice
Than London, Paris, or sunlit Madrid?
In these men dance; at Lisbon yawns the abyss.
Tranquil spectators of your brothers' wreck,
Unmoved by this repellent dance of death,
Who calmly seek the reason of such storms,
Let them but lash your own security;
Your tears will mingle freely with the flood.[21]

Rousseau, shocked by what Voltaire had written, reasserted the natural causes of such catastrophes and protested to him in a letter:

You would have preferred that this earthquake had taken place deep in a desert rather than at Lisbon. Is it possible to doubt that they do not occur in deserts? But we do not speak of those because they cause no harm to the Gentlemen Who Live in Cities, the only people we take into consideration. These earthquakes scarcely harm even the animals and the savages who sparsely populate these remote regions and who do not fear falling roofs or collapsing houses. But what is the significance of such a privilege? Does this really mean that the order of the natural world should be changed to conform to our caprices, that nature must be subject to our laws, and that in order to prevent her from causing an earthquake in any particular place all we need do is build a city there?[22]

In jail in Venice, having sorely tested the Venetian bounds of propriety, another contemporary, Casanova, saw opportunity while others discussed philosophy. When the aftershock jolted the Doge's palace where he was detained, Casanova noted that the roof tiles above his cell had been loosened:

While I was immersed in this toilsome sea of thought, an event happened which brought home to me the sad state of mind I was in. I was standing up in the garret looking towards the top, and my glance fell on the great beam, not shaking but turning on its right side, and then, by slow and interrupted movement in the opposite direction, turning again and replacing itself in its original position. As I lost my balance at the same time, I knew it was the shock of an earthquake....Four or five seconds after the same movement occurred, and I could not refrain from saying, "Another, O my God! but stronger."

The guards, terrified with what they thought the impious ravings of a desperate madman, fled in horror. After they were gone, as I was pondering the matter over, I found that I looked upon the overthrow of the Doge's palace as one of the events which might lead to liberty; the mighty pile, as it fell, might throw me safe and sound, and consequently free, on St. Mark's Place, or at the worst it could only crush me beneath its ruins. Situated as I was, liberty reckons for all, and life for nothing, or rather for very little. Thus in the depths of my soul I began to grow mad.

This earthquake shock was the result of those which at the same time destroyed Lisbon.

...It has always been my opinion that when a man sets himself determinedly to do something, and thinks of nought but his design, he must succeed despite all difficulties in his path: such an one may make himself Pope or Grand Vizier, he may overturn an ancient line of kings—provided that he knows how to seize on his opportunity, and be a man of wit and pertinacity. To succeed one must count on being fortunate and despise all ill success, but it is a most difficult operation.[23]

But if the Lisbon earthquake provoked a philosophical debate in Europe, and allowed Casanova to escape using the weakness in the roof that the earthquake had so fortuitously revealed to him, within Portugal itself the reaction was much more prosaic and practical. The king of Portugal in 1755, Dom José I of Bragança, and his wife, Maria Anna Vitória de Borbon, a Spanish infanta, had never shown great interest in government, obsessed as they were with hunting and the opera. The king was utterly and completely paralyzed and terrified by the earthquake. Even though he had been out of Lisbon and in residence at Belém well to the west of the center of the city when the shocks and tidal wave occurred, Dom José was so frightened that for the rest of his life he refused to sleep in any building made of stone.

The royal family moved immediately into the gardens of the Belém Palace into temporary shelters. Later the king and court took up residence on the hill above Belém, living in wooden and canvas houses until the end of the eighteenth century.

With the Portuguese monarch incapable of responding to the crisis during the critical days of confusion and panic, the lead was taken effectively by his powerful and ambitious minister, Sebastião José de Carvalho e Melo (1699–1782), better known by his subsequent title of Marquês de Pombal, granted in 1769.[24]

The first actions of Pombal were to bury the dead and to impose order. The scale of destruction was such that the removal of bodies became absolutely essential to prevent the spread of disease and plague. Pombal persuaded the patriarch of Lisbon to give permission for bodies to be unceremoniously collected, put in boats, sent out into the Atlantic, and dropped into the ocean without the usual funeral rites. He brought in troops from the garrisons in the hinterland of Portugal to contain disorder. He also gave magistrates the power to act instantly in case of looting or murder; and they acted expeditiously. According to one eyewitness account, in addition to the earthquake dead there were soon about eighty gibbets set up throughout the city where those caught looting and committing other crimes were summarily hanged. Pombal's immediate and draconian response was encapsulated in the famous phrase attributed to him, "bury the dead and feed the living." In his singularly spidery handwriting, he gave his own account of the three immediate priorities. The first was to dispose of the dead in order to avoid disease; second, to feed the population (to achieve this and deter speculators Pombal imposed ceilings on the price of bread); and third, to impose public order.[25]

The fact that the destruction of Lisbon offered great opportunities to urban planners was not lost on one ambitious young Scottish architect: Robert Adam (1728–91). In Rome at the time, Adam saw the earthquake as "a heavenly judgment on my behalf." He aspired to be royal architect of Lisbon and produced rough sketches of what he thought the newly reconstructed city should look like, based—it seems—on the Bellini Palazzo and the great piazza outside Saint Peter's in Rome. The sketches included an urban plan that envisioned a great basin opening onto the Tagus River, backed by an area for the houses of the nobility, behind which would be a bourgeois zone, as Adam described it, with public gardens on either side.[26]

Overall, the young Robert Adam's design, with its theatrical Baroque extravagance, was based on the assumption that Lisbon would be rebuilt in an architectural style that reflected half a century of Portuguese patronage in Rome during the reign of João V. But this was not to be. In fact the style that was adopted for the buildings of the reconstructed Lisbon was in many respects much closer to that of the buildings designed by Robert Adam's father, the Scottish architect William Adam. A nun writing to Rome from Lisbon, looking at the ruins of the opera house and describing it as having been "a center of opulence, gala, grandiosity, and vanity," captured more accurately the sober and utilitarian mood in Portugal after November 1755.[27] The interesting story that was to unfold in Lisbon represented in some sense a conscious rejection of "vanitá," that is, the baroque and rococo extravagances so preeminent under Dom João V, and the embrace of "virtú," the more modest, commercial, practical, pragmatic, neo-Palladian image that came to be associated with the regime of Pombal.[28]

RECONSTRUCTION

The crucial decision that was to have an enormous impact on the reinvented city Pombal envisioned came very early on, when the all-powerful minister turned over the planning process to military engineers. The Portuguese thus did not call in Italian, Austrian, or French architects, as they had done so often for their great public buildings during the first half of the eighteenth century; nor did they set up a competition among international architects, as the young Robert Adam had hoped. In an emergency situation that required quick reaction, Pombal instead immediately brought in Portugal's own military engineers. Three in particular were to play key roles: Manuel da Maia (1677–1768), who in 1755 was almost eighty years of age, the chief military engineer of the country, and had been a tutor in mathematics and physics to Dom José; Eugénio dos Santos (1711–60), who was in his mid forties and a colonel in the engineering corps; and Carlos (Karoly) Mardel (c. 1695–1763), a Hungarian émigré in his late fifties who had served in the Portuguese military engineering corps since 1733, when he came to Portugal to work on the Lisbon aqueduct under Manuel da Maia's supervision.

All three men were experienced professionals, accustomed to overseeing the construction of large-scale civil and military buildings and fortifications, and the management of resources and manpower this involved. Pombal gave to Maia the job of drawing up what he called a "dissertation," detailing the fundamental issues to be addressed, and how these, once defined, might be handled most efficaciously. In the meantime, Pombal introduced legislation prohibiting any building, action, or sale of property before the master plan had been devised. Maia quickly turned in his observations to Pombal, on December 4, 1755.

Maia's dissertation examined a series of propositions regarding the possible options for reconstructing a city after a catastrophe such as the earthquake.[29] These included whether the debris should be used to build up the lowland areas, what size buildings ideally should be in relation to the streets in front of them, and the provisions that should be made to accommodate water run-off in lowland areas, so as to make construction on the landfill free from the risk of inundation at times of tidal flooding. Maia recommended that any rebuilding should be prohibited until a plan was formulated and approved. He looked into the option of moving the city entirely; whether, for example, Lisbon should be relocated to the west toward the area of Belém where the subsoil was stronger and buildings had resisted the quake. He argued that the principal streets should be on a grid pattern and designated for commercial purposes, reflecting the importance of gold and silver within the commerce of Lisbon. As a consequence of their commercial use, these streets should in addition be constructed without covered arches in order to improve security. He also cited two models of rebuilt cities he considered important: Turin and London. In each of these cases he looked back at the rebuilding histories—in Turin, where a new city had been constructed as an extension and adjunct to the old; and Christopher Wren's plans for the rebuilding of London after the fire of 1666.[30]

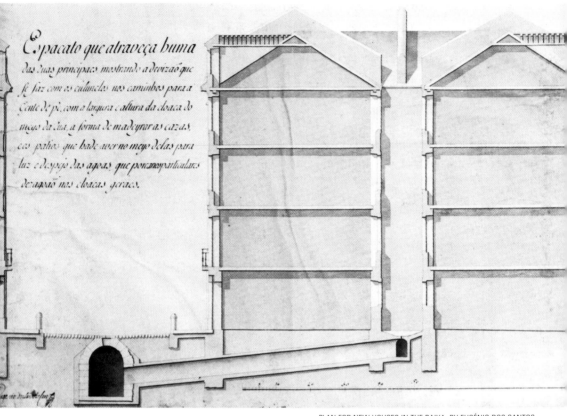

Espacato que atraveça huma das suas principaes mostrando a devizaõ que se faz com os cadueclos nos caminhos para a Gente De pé, com a largura e altura da cloaca do meyo da Rua, a forma De madeyrar as cazas, ces patios que hade aver no meyo delas para luz e despejo das agoas que por meyo particulares deraguaõ nas cloacas geraes.

PLAN FOR NEW HOUSES IN THE BAIXA, BY EUGÉNIO DOS SANTOS, SHOWING STREET ELEVATION AND SANITATION AND CISTERN ARRANGEMENTS, CIRCA 1757–59. SIGNED SEBASTIãO JOSÉ DE CARVALHO E MELO (POMBAL)

The key in the case of Lisbon, Maia observed, was that the king had not insisted that the Royal Palace be reconstructed on its previous site. The king, of course, took this position less for reasons of architectural purity than because he was frightened at the thought of spending any time at a palace within the earthquake zone. But his decision relieved the urban planners of an enormous impediment. If the king was prepared to give up prime real estate, then it would be difficult for anyone else not to do so. Maia's plan was approved quickly. Centering on the rebuilding of the city on its previous site, it avoided what had happened in London where, despite Wren's ambitious plans, property rights and old street lines were not superseded.

With these general principles elaborated, six detailed projects were drawn up, some less radical than others.[31] In the end, however, it was the most radical grid pattern that was approved and adopted, the fifth plan drawn up by Eugénio dos Santos and Carlos Mardel. This involved a total reinvention of the city's core with a complete overriding of previous street patterns and property lines.

The plan substituted the old royal square with a new square of commerce, the Praça do Comércio. This waterfront square was to have identical buildings on three sides, with ground-floor arcades and double pilasters. The north side was broken by a triumphal arch.[32] Two three-story end pavilions of *pedra lioz* (a pseudo-marble limestone long used in Portugal), one of which was to house the merchants' exchange, anchored the east and west arcades on the river side. The arcaded facades also made use of the contrast between the white *pedra lioz* used for the standardized stone window frames and the colored plastered walls.[33] The art historian Robert Smith has written that this extensive use of *pedra lioz* gave "Lisbon a glittering appearance not unlike Venice."[34]

Four main streets, with cross-streets set at right angles, ran inland from the Praça do Comércio toward two newly reconstructed parallel squares of identical buildings, the Rossio and the Praça da Figueira. Facing the streets, identical four-story blocks of dwellings were to be built with shops at ground level. Ochre-colored walls were framed at each end by wide-angled pilasters set flat. The buildings were surmounted by double-hipped roofs. A unit of continuous architecture was thus created at the heart of the city—an area 1,800 by 1,250 feet that, according to Smith, comprises one of the "greatest uniform architectural undertakings of the age of the Enlightenment."[35]

Legislation was passed in May 1758 to provide for the assessment and reallocation of property rights. Geometric measurements were substituted for actual locations so that property owners could be compensated for the land, houses, and old street space reallocated under the new urban plan. Loans were provided to people who needed them, and those who took on new property were given five years to complete the construction of the new buildings. All this was achieved with remarkable rapidity.

The new buildings were to follow standardized and uniform dimensions. Most important, they were to be made earthquake proof by means of a pioneering anti-earthquake flexible wooden cage, or *gaiola*, formed of diagonal trusses reinforcing a horizontal and vertical wooden frame. The reinforced buildings were in turn set on piles made of green pine topped by cross-hatched pine staves and mortar pads. All the buildings in the Baixa were to be constructed in this manner. Each building was provided with a cistern in the back courtyard between the buildings. From here rainwater run-off was directed toward a central cistern under the street.[36]

31

GAIOLA, EARTHQUAKE-PROOF FRAME REQUIRED FOR BUILDINGS CONSTRUCTED IN LISBON AFTER 1756

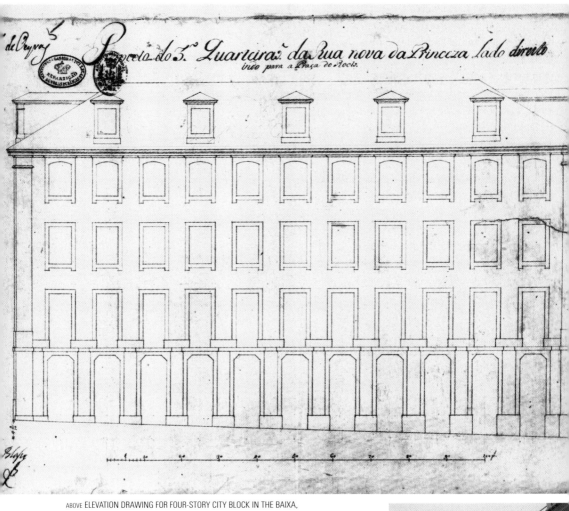

ABOVE ELEVATION DRAWING FOR FOUR-STORY CITY BLOCK IN THE BAIXA, CIRCA 1759–60. SIGNED CONDE DE OEIRAS (POMBAL)

RIGHT FOUR-STORY BUILDING IN THE BAIXA (RUA AUGUSTA) TODAY. PHOTO BY TOMÁS AMORIM

The planners of the new Lisbon thus aimed to create a more sanitary and healthy urban environment. Pombal had called on the assistance of a Portuguese "new Christian" then resident in Paris, António Nunes Ribeiro Sanches (1699–1783), a student of the great Dutch chemist, botanist, and clinician H. Boerhaave (1661–1736).[37] The "new Christians" were descendants of forcibly converted Jews. Some, such as Ribeiro Sanches, reclaimed their Jewish heritage after they had been forced to leave Portugal to escape the Inquisition. Ribeiro Sanches had fled to London in the 1730s and later moved to Vienna where he had been Pombal's personal physician during the period Pombal had served as Portuguese ambassador to the court of Maria Theresa. He subsequently moved to Russia where he worked with the Russian czar and, very impressed by Russian saunas, introduced saunas to Western Europe, arguing that it was very good for people to wash and clean themselves. Ribeiro Sanches was employed by Pombal as a paid consultant and Pombal published his thesis on sanitation and the need for light and air in order to make the inhabitants of urban areas less vulnerable to disease and illnesses.[38]

As with secular property, the question of how to treat ecclesiastical landholdings, churches, and parishes also had to be settled—whether to keep churches in the same place or move them. It was decided that they should be rebuilt in new locations appropriate to the overall city master plan. More decoration was permitted than for the secular buildings, but none of the new Pombaline churches had towers.[39]

The new Praça do Comércio retained a royal presence in the form of a bronze statue commissioned to stand at its center, with Dom José on a horseback. The statue, inaugurated in 1775, was designed by the court sculptor, Joaquim Machado de Castro (1731–1822), and was based on the monument to Louis XIV (1660) published by Jacques François Blondel in *Architecture Française* (1752–56).[40] This did not mean that the reinvented Lisbon had recreated a "Place Royale," however. The royal presence was symbolic. The essence of the new center was that it was to be a place of government, of commerce, of the customs house, and of the stock exchange.

In 1756, the Casa do Risco das Reais Obrás Públicas, a school of architecture and drawing, was established to produce the blueprints for the new buildings that would stand on the principal squares and streets. The school functioned until 1760 under the direction of Eugénio dos Santos, when he was succeeded by Carlos Mardel. The plans drawn up under the supervision of dos Santos and Mardel—every design, every facade, down to the smallest detail—bore Pombal's signature.[41] Maia had recommended that the buildings lining the streets of the Baixa be three stories high, proportional thereby to the width of the streets and a precaution against the eventuality of future earthquakes. Eugénio dos Santos added an extra floor. Over the course of the nineteenth century two extra floors were added.[42]

ABOVE ELEVATION DRAWING FOR BUILDING IN PRAÇA DO ROSSIO
BY CARLOS MARDEL, CIRCA 1759–60. SIGNED CONDE DE OEIRAS (POMBAL)
RIGHT PRAÇA DO ROSSIO TODAY. PHOTO BY TOMÁS AMORIM

All the new buildings were provided with fireproof walls subdividing the roofs; windows and doors were standardized; and no one was allowed to build in any manner other than according to the approved designs. To prevent monotony, subtle variations of door shapes and iron balconies were permitted, and Maia recommended that people might be allowed the freedom to paint windows and the doors different colors in different areas. This process of rebuilding led to the creation of an extensive infrastructure for the prefabrication of standardized stone facings, uniform ironwork, and uniform cut lumber for the *gaiolas*, as well as for the production of mortar and tiles. As a consequence, the reconstruction of Lisbon was directly linked to the government's aim to stimulate an industrial artisan class in Portugal, and thereby aid Portugal's overall economic development.[43]

The principal squares in Lisbon, the Rossio and the Praça do Comércio, as well as the connecting streets, were all constructed according to the Pombaline plan. They remain to this day almost exactly as they were envisioned in the drawings that Pombal approved so assiduously.[44]

PRECEDENTS

Where did the concepts for the style adopted by Pombal for the reinvented city come from? The Portuguese art historian José-Augusto França has drawn attention to the influence of the ideas of proportion and harmony promoted by Blondel in *Architecture Française*.[45]
The prints of the Lisbon earthquake by Le Bas were also published by Blondel (1705–74), founder of the Ecole des Arts in Paris.[46] In addition, the illustrations in Blondel's book clearly provided the model for the statue of the king placed at the center of the Praça do Comércio.

França argues, however, that no European models directly influenced the urban planning of Pombal's Lisbon.[47] It is certainly true that there was a very strong tradition of Portuguese military and civil engineering to which both Manuel da Maia and Eugénio dos Santos belonged. Much of this expertise had been acquired building border fortifications and in colonial town planning. There was also great originality in the solutions these military architects devised to solve the structural dilemmas posed by the need to build well-lit, healthy, earthquake-proof and fireproof buildings in the Baixa of Lisbon and to provide them with cisterns and sewers.[48]

But it is also true that British influence was paramount in this period. The French, in fact, regarded Portugal as little more than a British colony. It should not come as a surprise, therefore, that British influence also might be strong in architecture, or that British models might be adapted to Portuguese circumstances by Pombal. Many of his policies reflected his observations in London and were characterized by subtle borrowing and adaptations to Portugal's national interests and possibilities.[49]

John Harris, one of the leading experts on the neo-Palladian movement in England, considered the Lisbon Praça do Comércio in the mid 1990s and found it remarkably similar to Inigo Jones's designs for Covent Garden published in Colin Campbell's *Vitruvius Britannicus*.[50] In fact, on close examination there is a remarkable coincidence between Eugénio dos Santos's original designs for the monumental north side of the Praça do Comércio and the Piazza designed by Jones with arcaded houses for the north and east sides of Covent Garden arcades. Lord Burlington's design for the Westminster College Dormitory of 1729, illustrated in William Kent's *Designs of Inigo Jones*, as well as the arcaded new gallery wing for Old Somerset House illustrated in volume 1 of *Vitruvius Britannicus* (1715), are also very similar.[51] It is striking how close some of the Lisbon facades are to the British architectural designs engraved at Lord Burlington's initiative by Isaac Ware in his *Designs of Inigo Jones and Others* (1731). Ware was Burlington's assistant in the 1730s and these designs resemble parts of the Covent Garden development. As Harris points out with respect to the derivation of the facades of the Praça do Comércio, the lower arcaded elevations cannot be described as French since such elevations did not exist in France in 1758. They are more accurately described as being Palladian Italianate in style.[52]

Pombal had been the Portuguese ambassador in London between 1739 and 1742, the period when Lord Burlington developed his urban buildings.[53] While in London he became a member of the Royal Society, the premier circle of English Enlightenment thinkers, and, although authoritarian, pursued policies that reflected great rationality, practicality, and utilitarianism.[54]

It is also instructive to compare the design for the Pombaline facades with the designs for a thirteen-bay astylar terrace housing block by John Webb after Inigo Jones. The terrace is not only meant as a facade unadorned by the orders of architecture but also as one that succeeds in a careful balance of voids and wall. This same idea was implemented in the design of the buildings lining the principal streets of the Baixa.[55]

Pombal's Austrian posting from 1745 until 1750 was another important influence on Lisbon's rebuilding. In Vienna Pombal became a close friend of Duke Silva-Tarouca, a Portuguese émigré who had risen high within the Austrian government and was the confidant of Empress Maria Theresa. Silva-Tarouca supervised the remodeling of the summer palace of the Habsburgs at Schönbrunn between 1746 and 1749, and, writing to Pombal about the planned reconstruction of Lisbon, recalled their "delightful conversations" as they had discussed then how Lisbon's "tortuous" and "ugly" and unhealthy "deformities" might best be remedied. Pombal in response described for the duke his legislation and how he planned to finance the rebuilding.[56] Carlos Mardel also brought Central European details to his remodeling of Pombal's country estate at Oeiras. The tiled concave double-hipped roofs used both at Pombal's palace at Oeiras and for the standardized building of the new Lisbon reflect this Austro-Hungarian influence.[57]

ELEVATION OF COVENT GARDEN.
DRAWING BY INIGO JONES, 1640

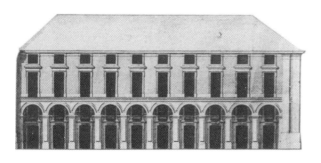

ELEVATION OF PRAÇA DO COMÉRCIO.
DRAWING BY EUGÉNIO DOS SANTOS

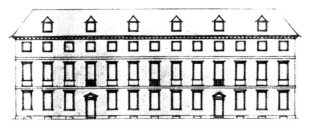

ELEVATION OF ASTYLAR TERRACE HOUSING WITH
TWO ENTRANCES. DRAWING BY JOHN WEBB

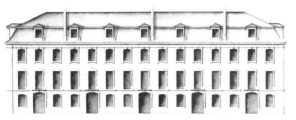

ELEVATION DRAWING FOR A BUILDING IN THE
BAIXA, CIRCA 1759–69. SIGNED CONDE DE OEIRAS
(POMBAL). ARQUIVO HISTÓRICO MUNIICIPÁL

In the mid 1750s, coincident with the post-earthquake planning, Pombal began to confront growing opposition from the old aristocracy and Jesuit order, both extremely influential during the reign of João V but marginalized by Pombal. An assassination attempt against José I in 1758 was carried out in large part because the aristocratic opposition realized that the only way to remove Pombal was to remove the king himself. Dom José was wounded in the attack but recuperated and Pombal used the occasion to turn with total ruthlessness against two of the great aristocratic families of Portugal, the Távora family and the Duke of Aveiro, implicated in the plot, and also took this bungled assassination as an excuse to attack the Jesuits.[58] The removal of two potential sources of opposition within the Church and the aristocracy greatly increased Pombal's authority within the Portuguese state and coincided with the time when the major decisions were being made about the reconstruction of the city. It undoubtedly made possible the radicalism of the solutions adopted, as well as diminished the sources of resistance to the draconian measures imposed on property owners and the Church.[59]

Pombal not only gave attention to the central squares and principal streets; more modest houses were designed and built as well, creating one of the first industrial development zones in a European city. Where the great aqueduct terminated, Pombal placed his industrial suburb with silk manufactories, ceramic works, and cotton textile mills.[60]

Pombal boasted in his "Most Secret Observations," written on June 6, 1775, when the equestrian statue of José I was inaugurated with great ceremony in the Praça do Comércio: "The sumptuous and well built edifices of Lisbon demonstrate the flourishing state of architecture. These things abundantly prove to foreigners that Portugal has no cause to envy them either their draughtsmen, or their painters, or their sculptors."[61]

Unfortunately he was mistaken. Very little of the remarkable urban innovation involved in Pombal's reconstruction of Lisbon was noted outside Portugal. The *philosophes* were more exercised by the earthquake than by the measures taken to deal with its consequences. Pombal's name became notorious in Europe to be sure, but less for his rebuilding of the capital than for his expulsion of the Jesuits, his quarrels with the British over trade, and the gruesome execution of the aristocrats who opposed him.[62] So, it was not the new image of a modern, commercial, and resurgent Portugal that the Europeans saw. Rather unfairly, it was the old image of a land of unreasonable catastrophe and irrational superstition that was reinforced. Voltaire led the pack in *Candide*: "…the Portuguese pundits could not think of any better way of preventing total ruin than to treat the people to a splendid *auto-da-fé*."[63]

The reality, as we have seen, was the opposite. But the Portuguese also were in part to blame. Didier Robert de Vaugondy in 1781 commissioned an article on Lisbon for the *Encyclopédie Méthodique* from the erudite Portuguese natural scientist José Corrêa da Serra. Corrêa da Serra missed the deadline, however, and his article arrived in Paris too late to be published, with the consequence that Enlightenment Europe learned nothing of the new urban invention that had replaced the jumbled medieval city destroyed on November 1, 1755.[64]

CONTEMPORARY OVERVIEW OF THE PRAÇA DO COMÉRCIO AND BAIXA

CONCLUSIONS

There are several points worth emphasizing about the reconstructed Lisbon. The reinvented Lisbon was not a Saint Petersburg or a Brasília; that is, it was not a new city constructed entirely on new lands. This was one of the options Manuel da Maia had delineated; namely, the relocation of the whole city with the abandonment of the old site and the construction of a new city. But Maia also rejected the Turin model because he saw the new city of Turin as merely an adjunct to the old.

What is unique about Lisbon is that it is a new city built on old territory, but one that was also radical in terms of its planning and execution, and therefore not like London. In other words, Christopher Wren had the option of doing in London what Pombal did in Lisbon—overriding property rights and old property lines to radically redesign urban space. In London, however, property rights, parishes, and the location of churches remained, so after the Great Fire London was reconstructed within its old urban configurations.

It is also important to note what is missing in the new Lisbon. There is no new royal palace to dominate the scheme; nor, for that matter, a new cathedral like that of Saint Paul's in London. The Church and the monarchy in this sense are absent. The new Lisbon was intended to be a utilitarian and bourgeois commercial city, a city that was oriented toward economic development and that aimed to modernize Portugal. Pombal's plain, simplified, almost austere, stripped-down and tectonic neo-Palladian city reflected these imperatives.

One of the questions with respect to ground zero is whether New York will follow the London or the Lisbon model. Joyce Purnick of the *New York Times* seems to prefer a Pombal to a Christopher Wren, or at least to an authoritarian like Robert Moses:

> Here it is, the most widely whispered line of the month: "We need a Moses." "We" is New York City; Moses is Robert, the domineering master builder from a less democratic era in the city's history.
>
> Mr. Moses comes to mind increasingly as New Yorkers look to the rebuilding of the World Trade Center site and wonder how it will ever be accomplished, given clashing agendas and a large and ever-growing cast of characters, not one of them a leader with the kind of power and authority it will take to bring order to fragmentation, vision to necessity.[65]

Pombal, of course, exercised an undemocratic and ruthless power that even Robert Moses could only dream about, and there is no doubt that the reinvented Lisbon of the late eighteenth century is indeed very much the product of Pombal's use of state power to create a radically transformed city out of the ashes of the great catastrophe of November 1, 1755.

39

THE BAIXA TODAY (RUA AUGUSTA). VIEW NORTH FROM THE PRAÇA DO COMÉRCIO TOWARD THE PRAÇA DO ROSSIO.
PHOTO BY TOMÁS AMORIM

I am grateful to Joan Ockman for the invitation to participate in the timely series of lectures organized by the Temple Hoyne Buell Center for the Study of American Architecture and to Kenneth Frampton for his thoughtful introduction to my lecture on February 4, 2002, on which this essay is based. I would like to express my appreciation to Dr. Bernardino Gomes, Dr. Luís Santos Ferro, and Mr. Miguel Vaz at the Luso American Foundation for their very welcome assistance in Lisbon; to Dr. Carlos Reis, director of the Biblioteca Nacional, and Dr. Lígia Martins, head of Reservados, for facilitating access to key documents; and, not least, to Tomás Amorim for his research in Lisbon, which helped unravel some key questions I had on this critical event, and for his stalwart assistance in seeing this essay completed.

1. British Historical Society of Portugal, *The Lisbon Earthquake of 1755: British Accounts*, preface by Maria Leonor Machado de Sousa, introduction, translation, and notes by Judite Nozes (Lisbon: British Historical Society of Portugal, 1990), p. 36.

2. For urban plans of Lisbon prior to the Great Earthquake of 1755, see João Nunes Tinoco, *Planta de Lisboa* (1650); Irisalva Moita, ed., *O Livro de Lisboa* (Lisbon: Livros Horizonte, 1994); *Lisboa Antes do Terramoto: Exposição no Castelo de S. Jorge* (Lisbon: Castelo de S. Jorge, 1964); Museu da Cidade, *Cartografia de Lisboa Séculos XVII a XX* (Lisbon: Comissão Nacional para as Comemorações dos Descobrimentos Portugueses, 1997); Maria do Rosário Santos, ed., *Rocio/Rossio: Terreiro da Cidade*, 2nd ed. (Lisbon: Arquivo Municipal, Pelouro da Cultura e Espaços Verdes, Câmara Municipal de Lisboa, Edições ASA, 1998); Augusto Vieira da Silva, *Plantas Topográficas de Lisboa* (Lisbon: Câmara Municipal de Lisboa, 1950); Georgio Braunio Agrippinate, "Olissippo quae nunc Lisboa, civitas amplissima Lusitaniae, ad Tagum, totiq orientis et multarum Insularum et Aphricoeque et Americae emporium nobilissimum," vol. 2 of *Urbium proecipuarum mundi theatrum quintum* (1593; facsimile Lisbon: Câmara Municipal de Lisboa, 1965); J. Couse, "The city of Lisbon as before the dreadful Earthquake of Novembre 1st, 1755" (London: John Bowles, c. 1750; facsimile, Lisbon: Câmara Municipal de Lisboa, 1965); and Dirk Stoop, "Vista do Terreiro do Paço" (Utrecht, c. 1618–81; facsimile, Lisbon: Museu da Cidade, n.d.).

3. For further discussion of Lisbon's role as entrepôt in the distribution of colonial products and bullion, see Kenneth Maxwell, *Pombal: Paradox of the Enlightenment* (Cambridge, U.K.: Cambridge University Press, 1995); Vitorino Magalhães Godinho,"Le Portugal, les flottes du sucre et les flottes de l'or 1670–1770," *Annales* 5, no. 2 (April–June 1950), pp. 184–97; Virgílio Noya Pinto, *O Ouro Brasileiro e o Comércio Anglo-Português* (São Paulo: Cia. Editora Nacional, 1979); Jorge Borges de Macedo, *A Situação Económica no Tempo de Pombal; Alguns Aspectos*, 2nd ed. (Lisbon: Moraes, 1982); Kenneth Maxwell, *Conflicts and Conspiracies: Brazil and Portugal, 1750–1808* (Cambridge, U.K.: Cambridge University Press, 1973); Kenneth Maxwell, "Pombal and the Nationalization of the Luso-Brazilian Economy," *HAHR* 47 (1968), pp. 608–31; and Susan Schneider, *O Marquês de Pombal e o Vinho do Porto: Dependência e Subdesenvolvimento em Portugal no Século XVIII* (Lisbon: A Regra do Jogo, 1980).

4. For background on the Inquisition in Portugal and the differences in the role of the Inquisition in Portugal, Spain, and Italy, see Francisco Bethencourt, *História das Inquisições: Portugal, Espanha e Italia* (Lisbon: Temas e Debates, 1996), p. 361. Also see José Lourenço D. de Mendonça and António Joaquim Moreira, *História dos Principais Actos e Procedimentos da Inquisição em Portugal* (Lisbon: Imprensa Nacional, 1980).

5. For a comprehensive overview, see Angela Delaforce, *Art and Patronage in Eighteenth-Century Portugal* (Cambridge, U.K.: Cambridge University Press, 2002). Also see Rui Bebiano, *D. João V, Poder e Espetáculo* (Aveiro, Portugal: Estante Editora, 1987).

6. See discussion in Delaforce, *Art and Patronage*, pp. 234–35.

7. Joaquim Oliveira Caetano, "O Aqueducto das Águas Livres," in Irisalva Moita, ed., *O Livro de Lisboa*, pp. 293–312. Also see *D. João V e o Abastecimento de Água a Lisboa*, 2 vols. (Lisbon: Câmara Municipal de Lisboa, 1990).

8. For a good selection of eighteenth-century representations of the Lisbon earthquake, many highly fanciful, see Jan T. Kozak and Charles D. James, "Historical Depictions of the 1755 Lisbon Earthquake," *http://nisee.berkeley.edu/lisbon* (Berkeley, Calif.: National Information Service for Earthquake Engineering, 1998).

9. "Impacto sísmico," *Arquitectura e Vida* 2, no. 22 (Lisbon, December 2001), pp. 16–27.

10. For further details and illustrative material, see Maxwell, *Pombal,* pp. 21–35. For a discussion of population figures, see João Pedro Ferro, *A População Portuguesa no Final do Antigo Regime (1750–1815)* (Lisbon: Editorial Presença, 1995); and José Vicente Serrão, "O Quadro Humano," in *O Antigo Regime, 1620–1807,* vol. 4 of António Manuel Hespanha and José Mattoso, eds., *História de Portugal* (Lisbon: Editorial Estampa, 1993).

11. "An Account of the late dreadful earthquake and fire which destroyed the city of Lisbon, the metropolis of Portugal: In a letter from a merchant resident there to his friend in England," in British Historical Society of Portugal, *The Lisbon Earthquake of 1755,* pp. 38–40.

12. Ibid., p. 42.

13. Ibid., p. 46.

14. Cited in C. R. Boxer, *Some Contemporary Reactions to the Lisbon Earthquake of 1755* (Lisbon: Faculdade de Letras, Universidade de Lisboa, 1956), p. 7.

15. Cited in C. R. Boxer, "Pombal's Dictatorship and the Great Earthquake of 1755," *History Today* 5, no. 2 (1955), pp. 727–36.

16. "Recueil des plus belles ruines de Lisbonne causées par le tremblement et par le feu du primier Novembre 1755. Dessiné sur les lieux par M. M. Paris et Pedegache." Published in various editions in English, Dutch, and German.

17. Boxer, *Some Contemporary Reactions,* pp. 10–11.

18. For the earthquake's wide-ranging cultural impact on Europe, see in particular Isabel Maria Barreira de Campos, *O Grande Terramoto, 1755* (Lisbon: Editorial Parceria, 1998); and T. D. Kendrick, *The Lisbon Earthquake* (Philadelphia and New York: J. B. Lippincott, 1955).

19. Boxer, *Some Contemporary Reactions,* p. 18.

20. "The earth delivered from the curse to which it is, at present, subjected: a sermon…preached at the Boston-Thursday-lecture, January 22, 1756. Published by the general desire of the hearers. By Charles Chauncy, D. D., one of the Pastors of the First Church in Boston" (Boston: Printed and sold by Edes & Gill, at their printing office, next to the prison, in Queen-Street, 1756); "An Account of the late dreadful earthquake and fire, which destroyed the city of Lisbon, the metropolis of Portugal: In a letter from a merchant resident there, to his friend in England" (London: printed. Boston; New-England, re-printed and sold by Green & Russell, at their printing-office near the Custom-House, and next to the writing-school in Queen-Street, 1756; also see note 11); and "Two very circumstantial accounts of the late dreadful earthquake at Lisbon: giving a more particular relation of that event than any hitherto publish'd: The first drawn up by Mr. Farmer, a merchant, of undoubted veracity, who came over from the ruined city in the Expedition packet-boat, just arrived at Falmouth. The second related by another gentleman, who came over also in the above packet, and taken in writing from his mouth. Now published from a principle of benevolence, to satisfy the curiosity of the public. To which is added, an account of the antiquity, grandeur, beauty, and extent of the famous city of Lisbon before the earthquake, lately publish'd in London, and came in the last ship" (Exeter, printed. Boston, re-printed and sold by D. Fowle in Ann-Street, and Z. Fowle in Middle-Street, 1756).

21. F. M. A. de Voltaire, *Poèmes sur le Dèsastre de Lisbonne et sur La Loi Naturelle avec des Préfaces, des Notes, etc.* (Geneva, n.d. [1756]), in *Selected Works of Voltaire,* ed. Joseph McCabe (London: Watts and Co., 1911).

22. Jean-Jacques Rousseau, "Cartes à Voltaire de M. J.-J. Rousseau, le 18 août 1756," in *Oeuvres Complètes de Voltaire,* ed. Louis Moland, vol. 39, *Correspondence* (Paris: Garnier, 1877–85), sec. 7.

23. Giacomo Girolamo Casanova de Seingalt, *The Complete Memoirs of Jacques Casanova de Seingalt, 1725–1798,* "a rare unabridged London edition of 1894, translated by Arthur Machen, to which has been added the chapters discovered by Arthur Symons [in 1899]," vol. 2, *To Paris and Prison: Under the Leads.* Available from the Project Gutenberg Literary Archives at: *http://www.gutenberg.config.com/etext01/jculd10.txt.*

24. There is a vast and uneven historical literature on Pombal. See, for example, *Marquês de Pombal: Catálogo Bibliográfico e Iconográfico* (Lisbon: Biblioteca Nacional, 1982); also see the more recent bibliographic essay in Maxwell, *Pombal*, pp. 167–74. The name Pombal is used henceforth anachronistically in this essay, as this is how historians refer to him. For the role of the chief minister in the eighteenth century, see Hamish M. Scott, "The Rise of the First Minister in Eighteenth-Century Europe," in T. C. W. Blanning and David Cannadine, eds., *History and Biography: Essays in Honour of Derek Beales* (Cambridge, U.K.: Cambridge University Press, 1997). The best recent Portuguese edition is Joaquim Veríssimo Serrão, *O Marquês de Pombal. O Homem, o Diplomata, e o Estadista* (Lisbon: Camaras Municipais de Lisboa, Oeiras e Pombal, 1982).

25. "Fragmento, com emendas de Seb. J. De Carvalho e Mello" (manuscript fragment with annotations by Pombal) (Lisbon: Biblioteca Nacional, Colecção Pombalina, codex 696, fl.11–13).

26. A sketch by Robert Adam, found in Sir John Soane's Museum in London by art historian Angela Delaforce, is discussed and illustrated in Angela Delaforce, "The Dream of a Young Architect: Robert Adam and a Project for the Rebuilding of Lisbon in 1755," in Angela Delaforce, ed., *Portugal e o Reino Unido: A Aliança Revisitada* (Lisbon: Fundação Calouste Gulbenkian, 1995), pp. 56–60.

27. Delaforce, *Art and Patronage*, pp. 285–87.

28. See John Gifford, *William Adam, 1689–1748: A Life and Times of Scotland's Universal Architect* (Edinburgh: Mainstream Publishing, 1989); for background, see David Daiches, Peter Jones, and Jean Jones, eds., *The Scottish Enlightenment 1730–1790: A Hotbed of Genius* (Edinburgh: The Saltire Society, 1996).

29. Manuel da Maia's dissertation is published in José-Augusto França, *Lisboa Pombalina e o Iluminismo*, 2nd ed. (Lisbon: Livraria Bertand, 1977), pp. 291–308, as is the principal enabling legislation of May 1758 and June 1758.

30. For the transformation of Turin into a showplace of rectilinear urbanism and the state reforms of Vittorio Amedeo II (1675–1730), which created a complex of purpose-built government offices, see Geoffrey Symcox, "From Commune to Capital: The Transformation of Turin, Sixteenth to Eighteenth Centuries," in Robert Oresko, G. C. Gibbs, and H. M. Scott, eds., *Royal and Republican Sovereignty in Early Modern Europe: Essays in Memory of Ragnhild Hatton* (Cambridge, U.K.: Cambridge University Press, 1997), pp. 242–69; and Robert Oresko, "The Sabaudian Court 1563– c. 1750," in John Adamson, ed., *The Princely Courts of Europe: Ritual, Politics, and Culture under the Ancien Regime, 1500–1750* (London: Weidenfeld & Nicolson, 1999), pp. 231–53; as well as Geoffrey Symcox, *Victor Amadeus II. Absolutism in the Savoyard State 1675–1730* (London: Thames and Hudson, 1983), especially pp. 190–232. For an analysis of Christopher Wren's London, see Adrian Tinniswood, *His Invention So Fertile: A Life of Christopher Wren* (Oxford, U.K.: Oxford University Press, 2002), pp. 147–61. Wren failed to overcome London's problems of land titles, with the result that London retained its medieval configuration despite his comprehensive plan for a new city after the Great Fire of September 1666. Like Pombal later, Wren had planned a commercial city centered on a piazza where the stock exchange would be located with radial vistas and a surrounding complex of commercial buildings. For an illustration of Wren's plan, see ibid., p. 154.

31. The six plans are discussed and illustrated in França, *Lisboa Pombalina e o Iluminismo*, pp. 91–102. Also see Câmara Municipal de Lisboa, *Exposição Iconográfica e Bibliográfica Comemorativa da Reconstrução da Cidade Depois do Terremoto de 1755*, 2nd ed. (Lisbon: Câmara Municipal de Lisboa, 1955).

32. The original design by Eugénio dos Santos for the arch was not built. The present structure was constructed in the nineteenth century.

33. Delaforce, *Art and Patronage*, p. 289.

34. Robert C. Smith, *The Art of Portugal 1500–1800* (New York: Meredith Press, 1968), p. 24.

35. Ibid., p. 105.

36. This drainage and sanitary system functioned until relatively recently. Cistern inspection deteriorated during the course of the twentieth century and many of the cisterns were transformed into cellars and storage rooms, with deleterious effects on the stability of these buildings. See "Baixa Pombalina: Que Futuro?" *Pedra & Cal—Revista do Grémio das Empresas de Conservação e Restauro do Património Arquitectónico* 3, no. 11 (Lisbon: GECoRPA, July/August/September 2001), pp. 1–52; "Dossier Palácio Foz," *Monumentos—Revista Semestral de Edifícios e Monumentos*, no. 11 (Lisbon: Ministério do Equipamento, do Planeamento e da Administração do Território, September 1999), pp. 8–61; "Intervenção no Rossio; A Baixa de Lisboa em Alta," *Arquitectura e Vida* 2, no. 22 (Lisbon, December 2001), pp. 62–67; and "Lisboa: Estado de Alerta," *FOCUS: Semanário de Grande Informação* 118 (January 17, 2002), pp. 12–16.

37. David Willemse, "António Ribeiro Sanches, élève de Boerhaave et son importance pour la Russie," *Janus: Revue Internationale de l'Histoire des Sciences, de la Médecine, de la Pharmacie et de la Technique* 6 (Leiden: E. J. Brill, 1966); José Vicente Serrão, "Pensamento Económico e Política Económica no Período Pombalino: o caso de Ribeiro Sanches," *Ler História* 9 (1986), pp. 3–39; and Ribeiro Sanches, *Dificuldades que tem um reino velho para emendar-se, e outros textos*, ed. Vítor de Sá (Porto, 1972).

38. António Nunes Ribeiro Sanches, *Tratado de conservação da saude dos Povos: obra util, e igualmente necessaria a magistrados, capitaens generais, capitaens de mar e guerra, prelados, abbadessas, medicos e pays de familia* (Paris: n.p., 1756); contains an appendix on earthquakes. Ribeiro Sanches explained that the earthquake was a natural phenomenon, not a divine judgment as had been argued by the Jesuit Gabriel Malagrida in *Juizo da Verdadeira Causa do Terramoto, que padeceu a Corte de Lisboa no primeiro de Novembro de 1755 pelo Padre Gabriel Malagrida da Companhia de Jesus, Missionario Apostolico* (Lisbon: Na Officina de Manuel Soares, 1755). For the fate of Malagrida, see Maxwell, *Pombal*, pp. 82–84.

39. For locations of new and reconstructed churches, see "Planta 77," in Manuel C. Teixeira and Margarida Valla, *O Urbanismo Português: Séculos XIII–XVIII (Portugal–Brasil)* (Lisbon: Livros Horizonte, 1999), p. 304.

40. See discussion in Delaforce, *Art and Patronage*, p. 299.

41. Many of these plans are published in the second volume of the catalogue *Exposição Lisboa e o Marquês de Pombal*, 3 vols. (Lisbon: Museu da Cidade, 1982), which is the most comprehensive iconographic collection relating to Lisbon's reconstruction.

42. The original elevations can be seen in the second volume of *Exposição Lisboa*. For the three-story facades designed by Eugénio dos Santos, for example, see plates 108–11; for his four-story facades, see plates 112–15. All these elevations were personally approved by Pombal. His signature (then as Conde de Oeiras) appears at the top left corner of the blueprints. Pombal used his full name prior to 1759; from 1759 to 1769 he used the title Conde de Oeiras, and after 1769, the title Marquês de Pombal. The drawings illustrating this essay have been dated approximately, based on the manner in which Pombal signed them. Also see the discussion in Maria Helena Ribeiro dos Santos, *A Baixa Pombalina: Passado e Futuro* (Lisbon: Livros Horizonte, 2000), pp. 83–109, which is an excellent and well-illustrated account of the evolution of the street facades and their current status. Also valuable are the brief comments by Teixeira and Valla, *O Urbanismo Português*, pp. 289–93.

43. These industrial activities are well covered in volume 3 of *Exposição Lisboa*.

44. The plans of the new Lisbon superimposed over the old configuration can be seen in Augusto Vieira da Silva, *Dispersos*, 3 vols., 2nd ed. (Lisbon: Biblioteca de Estudos Olisiponenses, Câmara Municipal de Lisboa, 1968), especially vol. 1, pp. 9–22, 386; and vol. 2, p. 212.

45. Especially in França, *Lisboa Pombalina e o Iluminismo*, p. 199.

46. "Recueil des plus belles ruines de Lisbonne causées par le tremblement et par le feu du premier Novembre 1755," cit. note 16.

47. França, *Lisbon Pombalina*, pp. 148–50.

48. Some sixty new settlements and a network of frontier forts were planned in the Amazon region of Brazil, for example, under the direction of Pombal's brother, who was the governor of the area between 1751 and 1759. See José Eduardo Horta Correia, ed., *As Cidades da Amazonia no Século XVIII* (Porto: Faculdade de Architectura da Universidade do Porto, 1998).

49. See in particular Maxwell, *Pombal*, pp. 158–59.

50. John Harris, "A Influência da arquitectura palaciana [sic] inglesa em Portugal no século XVIII," in Delaforce, ed., *Portugal e o Reino Unido: A Aliança Revisitada*, pp. 68–75.

51. William Kent, *The designs of Inigo Jones: consisting of plans and elevations for publick and private buildings/published by William Kent, with some additional designs* (London, 1727; reprinted Farnborough Hants, U.K.: Gregg Press, 1967). For the new gallery wing elevation of Old Somerset House in London, see Pierre de la Ruffinière du Prey, *John Soane, the Making of an Architect* (Chicago: University of Chicago Press, 1982), p. 56, as illustrated in Colin Campbell's *Vitruvius Britannicus*, vol. 1 (1715). Also see the catalogue by John Harris, Stephen Orgel, and Roy Strong, *The King's Arcadia: Inigo Jones and the Stuart Court, a quarter centenary exhibition held at the banqueting house, Whitehall, July 12 to September 2, 1973* (London: Arts Council of Great Britain, 1973), especially p. 398, as well as the illustrations of Covent Garden, pp. 184–85.

52. See Harris, Orgel, and Strong, *The King's Arcadia*, pp. 184–88. For Harris's observation see Delaforce, ed., *Portugal e o Reino Unido*, p. 73. The plans for the new palace of the Duque of Lafões are also remarkably similar to the neo-Palladian London townhouses designed by Lord Burlington in the 1720s. British neo-Palladian influence in the north of Portugal was strong. The close collaboration between John Whitehead, amateur architect and the British consul in Oporto between 1756 and 1802, and João de Almada e Melo, a cousin of Pombal who served as the powerful military and civil governor of the city and who also headed the junta of military works, is well documented. See Flávio Gonçalves, "A Arte no Porto na Época do Marquês de Pombal," in Maria Helena Carvalho dos Santos, ed., *Pombal Revisitado*, 2 vols. (Lisbon: Editorial Estampa, 1984), vol. 2, pp. 103–30. For the striking arcaded design for the proposed new riverfront square in Oporto by Whitehead, see Delaforce, ed., *Portugal e o Reino Unido*, p. 193. In Coimbra, when he was in the process of reforming the university in 1772, Pombal assigned the design of the new science building to Colonel William Elsden, an English military engineer in the Portuguese army, who headed a team of Portuguese architects working in the neoclassical style. See Delaforce, ibid., pp. 180, 184. In the mid 1760s, the British neo-Palladian architect John Carr of York was commissioned to design the new hospital at Oporto; see Giles Worsley, ed., *Life and Work of John Carr of York* (Otley, U.K.: Oblong Creative, 2000), p. 187. The impact of similar architectural influences in British North America and during the early history of the United States is of course well known.

53. See John Harris, *Palladian Revival: Lord Burlington, His Villa and Garden at Chiswick* (London: The Royal Academy, 1995).

54. See, most recently, Roy Porter, *Enlightenment: Britain and the Creation of the Modern World* (London: Allen Lane and Penguin Press, 2000).

55. "An astylar terrace with two entrances, by John Webb (1611–72) after Inigo Jones," in Harris, Orgel, and Strong, *The King's Arcadia*, pp. 187–88, illus. 354; and "Collection of 70 plans for the reconstruction of the city [of Lisbon] after the earthquake of 1755, from the Arquivo Histórico Municipal," *Exposição Lisboa e o Marquês de Pombal*, vol. 2, pp. 57–70.

56. For their fascinating correspondence, see Manuel Teles da Silva [Silva-Tarouca] to Carvalho [Pombal], Vienna, February 22, 1756, and Pombal's response, n.d. "Correspondência entre o duque Manuel Teles da Silva e Sebastião José de Carvalho e Melo," in S. J. Carlos da Silva Tarouca, ed., *Anais da Academia Portuguesa de História*, series 11, vol. 6 (Lisbon: Academia Portuguesa de História, 1955), pp. 356–59 and 417–20. For details on this relationship, see Maxwell, *Pombal*, pp. 8–9. For British diplomatic reports on the projects and progress of the rebuilding, see Public Record Office, "A. Castres to H. Fox, Lisbon. February 11, 1756" (London: State Papers, SP 89/50, folio 200); and "E. Hay to W. Pint. Lisbon, July 23, 1756" (London: State Papers, SP 89/51, folio 296).

57. Very little research has been done on the extraordinary estate Pombal accumulated at Oeiras, which, together with the virtual reconstruction of the Oeiras Palace itself during his rule, also involved the development of extensive pleasure gardens containing a grotto and an agricultural and industrial estate with plantings of vineyards, mulberry bushes, and associated aqueducts, fish ponds, and silk manufactories. Most of these buildings and rural properties were alienated in the twentieth century and fell into disrepair. For a pioneering series of articles on this now largely destroyed eighteenth-century marvel, see José Meco, "O Palácio e a Quinta do Marquês de Pombal em Oeiras: algumas notas sobre a arte no tempo de Pombal," in Carvalho dos Santos, ed., *Pombal Revisitado*, vol. 2, pp. 158–71; and José Meco, "Azulejos Pombalinos," in the catalogue *Exposição Lisboa*, vol. 3, pp. 49–66. Angela Delaforce dates the introduction of the double-hipped roof into Portugal to Mardel's 1734 design for the country house of Leitão Aranha in Junqueira near Belém. See Delaforce, *Art and Patronage*, pp. 243–45 (illus. p. 244).

58. See the description in Maxwell, *Pombal*, pp. 79–86.

59. The confiscated properties of the Jesuits and the aristocratic families condemned for the attempted regicide helped finance many of Pombal's favorite projects. In addition, as the British envoy had rightly observed, the rebuilding of the city "may very easily be accomplished while the gold and diamond mines of Brazil remain unhurt." See Public Record Office, "A. Castres to Sir Thomas Robinson. Lisbon, November 20, 1755" (London: State Papers, SP/50, folio 126). The main source of revenue for the rebuilding of the principal public buildings such as the custom house and the Praça do Comércio came from a surcharge of a four percent tax on all customs duties and a "voluntary" special tax imposed in Brazil. See Fernando Tomaz, "As Finanças do Estado Pombalino, 1762–1776," in *Estudos e Ensaios em Homenagem a Vitorino Magalhães Godinho* (Lisbon: Sá da Costa, 1988), pp. 258–388; and Jacques Ratton, *Recordações e Memórias sobre Occorrencias do seu Tempo*, 2nd ed. (Coimbra: Imprensa da Universidade, 1920), pp. 93, 220–28.

60. Gustavo Matos Sequeira, *Depois do Terromoto: Subsìdios para a História dos Bairros Ocidentais de Lisboa* (Lisbon: Academia das Sciências, 1967); "Regimento do Terreiro da Cidade de Lisboa No Anno de 1777" (Lisbon: Biblioteca Nacional, Colecção Pombalina, codex 456, fl. 57–82 [Lisbon: Regia Officina Typografica, 1777]); Walter Rossa, *Além da Baixa: Indícios de Planeamento Urbano na Lisboa Setecentista* (Lisbon: Ministério da Cultura; Instituto Português do Património Arquitectónico, 1998); and Francisco Santana, ed., *Lisboa na 2a. Metade do Séc. XVIII, Plantas e Descrições das suas Freguesias* (Lisbon: Câmara Municipal de Lisboa, n.d). The most comprehensive listing of occupations in Lisbon in the 1760s is contained in the enumeration of professionals on the tax rolls (*décimas*), "Descriminação, por freguesias, das profissões referidas no pagamento das décimas de manejo na cidade de Lisboa no anos de 1763, 1764, 1768 e 1769," in Jorge Borges de Macedo, *Problemas da História da Indústria Portuguesa no Século XVIII*, 2nd ed. (Lisbon: Querco, 1982), document 31; Nuno Luis Madureira, *Mercado e Privilégios: a Indústria Portuguesa entre 1750 e 1834* (Lisbon: Instituto de Ciências Sociais, 1997); Madureira, *Cidade, Espaço e Quotidiano; Lisboa 1740–1830* (Lisbon: Livros Horizonte, 1982); and Madureira, *Lisboa: Luxo e Distinção 1750–1830* (Lisbon: Fragmentos, 1990). Also see the inventory of the industries established by Pombal in Joaquim Veríssimo Serrão, ed., *História de Portugal*, 5th ed., vol. 6, *O Despotismo Iluminado (1750–1807)* (Lisbon: Editorial Verbo, 1996), pp. 202–03.

61. "Observações Secretíssimas do Marquês de Pombal...sobre a collocação da estatua equestre que enregou a Sua Magestade nesse dia..." (Lisbon: Biblioteca Nacional, Manuscritos, Fundo Geral, Codex 9427.2). For an interesting contemporaneous dissertation on style and urban planning in Portugal duing this period, discovered by Rafael Moreira, see "Uma Utopia Urbanística Pombalina: O 'Tratado de Ruação' de José de Figueiredo Seixas," in Carvalho dos Santos, ed., *Pombal Revisitado*, vol. 2, pp. 131–57.

62. Kenneth Maxwell, "The Spark: Pombal, the Amazon and the Jesuits," *Portuguese Studies* 17 (London: King's College, 2001), pp. 168–83. For European reactions to Pombal, see Franco Venturi, *Settecento Riformatore: la Chiesa a la repubblica dentro i loro limiti (1758–1774)* (Turin: Einaudi, 1976), vol. 2, pp. 3–29.

63. See the discussion of Voltaire in Kendrick, *Lisbon Earthquake*, pp. 198–212 (the quotation from *Candide* is on p. 206). Nevertheless, foreigners who did see the new Lisbon were impressed. A Spanish visitor commented: "Han acavado de arruinarlas, y plantado de nuevo seis calles maestras, y otras seis traviesas todas rectas, sobre las que estan ya construidas quasi todas las casas de una fabrica fuese uniforme, y hermosa, con quantas precauciones ha administrado el discurso para el fracaso de terremotos y fuego; quedando dos plazas perfectamente quadradas, magnificas, y grandes, que dentro de 50 años seran las mejores de Europa." "Carta de Joseph Martínez Moreno a D. Marcos Phelipe de Argáiz, Lisboa, Mayo 12, de 1772," in Fidelino de Figueiredo, *Lisboa em 1772 (Relatório dum Viajante Espanhol)* (Lisbon: Arquivo Histórico de Portugal, 1932), vol. 1, pp. 271–75.

64. Corrêa da Serra was later to become the envoy of the United Kingdom of Portugal and Brazil to the United States and a close friend of Thomas Jefferson. For the *Encyclopédie* lapse, see "Réponse de José Corrêa da Serra au nom de l'Académie des Sciences de Lisbonne à Didier Robert de Vaugondy," annotated by Léon Bourdon; and Catherine Petit, "Notice inédite sur Lisbonne en 1781," both in *Bulletin des Etudes Portugaises et Brésiliennes* 35–36 (Lisbon: Instituto Francês de Lisboa, 1974–75).

65. Joyce Purnick, "Who Can Part the Red Tape? Who Knows?" in "Metro Matters," *New York Times*, February 4, 2002, sec. B, p. 1.

OUT OF THE BLUE
THE GREAT CHICAGO
FIRE OF 1871

Ross Miller

Out of the blue, the planes sliced into the World Trade towers and in an instant New Yorkers were faced with the "inexpressible," the "incomprehensible," the "unthinkable." The volcanic collapse of two of the world's largest buildings was "surreal," "incredible," "unbelievable," more terrifying than war. John Maloney, a director of security for an Internet firm at the Trade Center, told a reporter, "I'm a combat veteran, Vietnam, and I never saw anything like this. I don't know what the gates of hell look like, but it's got to be like this."[1] He was struggling to measure what he had seen, to provide some human scale for what he had experienced. One hundred thirty years earlier, the people of Chicago thought they too were living through nothing less than the end of the world.

The Great Chicago Fire began on the evening of October 8, 1871, on DeKoven Street, on the city's impoverished Southwest Side, and continued unabated until extinguishing itself over Lake Michigan thirty-six hours later. Two thousand acres, 1,800 city blocks, and 18,000 buildings were destroyed; 90,000 residents were left homeless. Although less than three hundred dead were positively identified, many more perished, evaporating in the fire's extreme heat and leaving no identifiable remains.

Eyewitnesses reported that "as if by magic" the Chicago River boiled. Brick and stone melted, lumber crackled and then exploded like mortar shells. A journalist from the *Chicago Post* recalled the "unparalleled sublimity and terror" and remembered feeling the "heat and smoke," hearing the "maddened Babel of sounds." Biblical language learned in childhood provided some consolation for those who awakened to a blasted landscape of giant craters and smoking ruins. How else was one to speak of twisted steel, piles of rubble, bodies entombed? The *Post* reported that even a week after the event, "It required but little imagination to believe one's self looking over the adamantine bulwarks of hell into the bottomless pit."[2]

FIELD, LEITER & CO.'S STORE, CORNER OF STATE AND
WASHINGTON STREETS. PHOTO BY GEORGE N. BARNARD
FROM THE SERIES "RUINS OF CHICAGO" (EARLY 1870s)

The city quickly established a General Relief
Committee to receive and redistribute millions
of dollars in investment and charitable aid.
Within two months of the fire, 5,000 cottages
were completed or under construction to ensure
that Chicago, unlike the majority of American
cities, remained a place where the working poor
would continue to own rather than rent their
homes. As a result of this timely reinvestment,
trade resumed quickly, and real-estate values
soon equaled pre-fire levels. In fact, the thirty-
nine blocks of the Chicago Loop became many
times more valuable without buildings than with
them. Recognizing this oddity before most of
his competition, Potter Palmer, the city's most
flamboyant real-estate speculator, quickly
bought up a mile of property on the east side
of State Street and made his second fortune
building taller, deeper, and wider on what
became Chicago's core downtown blocks. By
October 1872, there was $34 million worth of
new building on the South Side, almost $4
million on the North Side, and nearly $2 million
on the West Side.[3] The city added tens of
blocks to its downtown by turning fire debris
into Lake Michigan landfill. Preachers who had
for years sermonized upon God's displeasure
with the city's wickedness ingeniously
theologized the events of October 8 as a
fortunate fault (*felix culpa*). Putting down their
Bibles, they quoted the newspapers to exploit
the paradox that their sinful metropolis was in
better shape than ever.

Chicago had gone through hell; her people
had suffered. But the city remained
undaunted. That certainly was the message
implied by a famous newspaper photograph
of real-estate agent W. D. Kerfoot. In the
picture, Kerfoot poses only a few days after
the fire in front of his new office, a wooden
shack, indomitably doing a deal. Long before
three firemen raised a flag Iwo-Jima style over
New York's ground zero, the image of an
ordinary businessman reporting for work on a
burned-out downtown block democratized the
heroics of urban survival. Chicago was busy
rebuilding even before the horrifying news of
the city's destruction was reported in national
publications like *Harper's Weekly* and
The Nation. Disaster was big business in
Chicago; that was the real story.

FRONTISPIECE REBUILDING OF CHICAGO. VIEW WEST FROM
WATER TOWER, 1870s. STEREO PHOTO BY COPELIN & SON

RIGHT CLARK STREET, VIEW SOUTH FROM COURT HOUSE.
PHOTO BY GEORGE N. BARNARD FROM THE SERIES
"RUINS OF CHICAGO"

The city had been extensively damaged, yet Chicago's status as the West's dominant commercial and industrial hub remained unchallenged. Saint Louis had ceased to be a serious competitor during the Civil War, when all government trade was permanently diverted north from the border states. According to the Chicago Board of Trade, the city's on-hand supply of grain, lumber, and cattle was 75 to 80 percent intact after the fire, and almost 90 percent of manufacturing, machinery, and production was unaffected by the calamity.[4] Situated on Lake Michigan, at the matrix of a modern canal, river, and railroad transportation network, Chicago's exploitable natural advantages were ever more apparent after the conflagration. Its fiscal position was markedly improved from its pre-fire condition as Boston, New York, and Philadelphia banks underwrote the rebuilding effort. America's financiers understood that Chicago had only begun to develop as a metropolis. Specifically, by having wiped out all the small-time landlords who still held downtown property, the fire did in a couple of days what would have taken many years for land speculators to accomplish. Local Chicago banks, real-estate agents, and landlords made fast fortunes steering millions in outside capital to commercial developers eager to build out their newly consolidated downtown blocks. The evidence that the fire had created an unprecedented opportunity for profit was there to be seen on every street corner. Even the most stubborn doomsayers gave up in the face of such overwhelming civic optimism.

Talk of destruction—actual or allegorical—proved to be no match for the self-congratulatory rhetoric of renewal. On the first Sunday following the disaster, Henry Ward Beecher preached at Plymouth Church that the city "could not afford to do without the Chicago Fire."[5] Before the year was out, Joseph Medill, recently elected mayor on the "Fire-Proof" ticket, ordered a memorial to the battered city. William Le Baron Jenney, a Civil War veteran and Chicago's first modern architect, designed a fire monument built out of safes and columns recovered from the ruins. The mayor, however, refused to build Jenney's tower of ruins because the memorial structure lacked "sufficient dignity." In place of a formal memorial that could stir up disturbing memories of loss and suffering, the city sponsored the Inter-State Industrial Exposition in the fall of 1873.

PROPOSED FIRE MONUMENT BY WILLIAM LE BARON JENNEY, 1872.
PHOTO BY GEORGE N. BARNARD FROM THE SERIES "RUINS OF CHICAGO"

Celebrating the city's material progress, its future and not its past, appealed to politicians. To pile molten lead and iron and situate it in a prominent place would be a daily reminder of the fifteen-hundred-degree convection fires and the pure horror of the day itself. Who needed that? Chicagoans were too hard at work making their city over to mourn. For an Englishman who toured the hastily rebuilt downtown in January 1874, Chicago's pragmatic amnesia was the "concentrated essence of Americanism."[6] Having survived their harrowing test, the brave people of Chicago were encouraged to think of themselves as safely outside of history. There was no need to dwell on bad times or affix blame. As a case in point, all efforts to prosecute Mrs. O'Leary, whose legendary cow, was in fact, determined to be the fire's immediate cause, were abandoned. Such a search for villains would inevitably lead back to the woefully inadequate fire department and to the careless engineers and architects whose buildings and bridges failed to withstand the blaze. Even the best "fireproof" architecture had imploded in the heat. Tens of thousands of lives had been put at risk. Looking back to the near past was simply asking for trouble. So why look back at all?

Before the Great Fire, the city's origins seemed remote, the property of a select group of citizens who had family ties to the earliest Fort Dearborn settlement or to Chicago's incorporation in the 1830s. But after October 1871, Chicago could be considered new again, with a new founding generation. Its heroic rebuilding was a story that all Americans might embrace if it were told well enough. William Bross considered himself just the man to do the telling.

A former Illinois lieutenant governor and eyewitness to the events of October 8, Bross had grown up reading the local novelist Juliette Kinzie's romantic accounts of the city's rough fur-trading and Indian-fighting years in the earlier part of the century. Bross would do her one better by buttressing his romance with facts. Among other things, his *History of Chicago*, published in 1876, documents the transformation of farmland into hundreds of thousands of 25-by-125-foot city lots, its thousandfold population increase in just over four decades, and the drain on municipal services (including fire and police) caused by such meteoric growth.[7] As an amateur historian, however, Governor Bross was more Giuliani than Gibbon. Considering the increasing gap between rich and poor, rentiers and renters, landlords and tenants, he reminds the reader that such class differences were a thing of the past, a sad fact of what he calls "finished" cities like Paris, London, and New York. The horrors of October 8 changed all that. This was not only a poor man's fire. Bross maintained that the most exclusive homes north of the river had been burned along with six hundred businesses, churches, hotels, and theaters. Everything in the path of the flames had been destroyed; the nothing that remained belonged to everyone.

INTER-STATE INDUSTRIAL EXPOSITION BUILDING BY W. W. BOYINGTON, 1873

Boss Bross was offering a new founding myth for the city with a readily available pedigree for proper citizenship. By equating survival with citizenship, his *History* transformed suffering into opportunity. He depicts the new (post-fire) Chicago as a blank slate, a place to make new arrangements, unbounded by class. In the midst of a national financial panic, he advises that "there has not been, for the last twenty years, so good a time for men of capital to start business in Chicago as now. With few exceptions, all can start even in the race for fame and fortune. The fire has leveled nearly all distinctions."[8] Bross's Chicago is an "unfinished" city always open to "men of capital." Even the majority who lack money can profit in such a dynamic place. Chicago is once again a frontier with new pioneers. In his view, "change" is the city's "permanent impulse." While it had taken the oldest American cities centuries, and Chicago initially decades, to change from mud village to metropolis, in Bross's fiction a new Chicago was born of fire in no time at all. He boasts, "It should be noticed that what I predicted would be accomplished in five years was mostly done in three, and much of it in two."[9]

More interested in the recovery's speed than in its quality, Bross omits important details that might easily have dulled his readers' enthusiasm. The governor knew that most of the original rebuilding effort was little more than a peremptory move to get capital flowing into the "Burnt District." Like Kerfoot's office shack in the ruins, the earliest post-fire architecture went up in a hurry because a new building, whatever its quality, was the best way to establish clear title to downtown land. Not much remains of those first structures.

Bross also knew that for the indigenous urban masses opportunity was as remote as ever. The post-fire poor got poorer. Change naturally favored businessmen, the "men of capital" who had developed the city in the first place.

Politicians virtuously re-zoned the urban core to exclude all residential buildings and sidewalks made of wood. Modern fireproofing was required for all structures, including those made of iron and masonry. The cost of new construction was prohibitive. The working poor to whom Bross appealed were effectively excluded from owning businesses or living downtown. Even churches and small businesses that for decades had been located in the Loop were unable to rebuild. Only large offices and manufacturing lofts could exploit expensive land economically by being built taller and wider. Thus architects, engineers, and developers, not the Brossian post-fire everyman, completed the next significant stage of urban reinvention.

It was the city's established architects especially who had the most to gain from a timely rebuilding of the city. The flames were out, but the ferocity of the blaze revealed just how shoddily Chicago had been built previously. Hulks of blackened and scarred buildings emphatically undermined all talk of boundless progress. Building eventually might become the tool and enduring symbol of Chicago's regeneration, but in the fire's immediate aftermath it was possible to come to the opposite conclusion, that cheaply ornamented and hurried architecture, not simply the drunken carelessness of an old woman, had turned an accident into the nation's greatest urban disaster.

The longer the ruins remained, the greater the possibility that survival euphoria might turn to dread. The architectural record was not good. Quality, expense, or material type had little effect on how a building stood up to the conflagration. The *Chicago Tribune*, housed in one of the most modern and elaborate of the city's pre-fire buildings, was, according to a contemporary account,

…the last building in Chicago to survive the general destruction, and its magnificent fireproof building was the last to succumb. The ceilings were of corrugated iron, resting upon wrought-iron "I" beams, while every partition wall in the entire structure was of brick. It was, in all respects, one of the most absolutely fireproof buildings ever erected. That is, it was fireproof up to the date of its destruction.[10]

LA SALLE STREET, VIEW NORTH FROM MONROE STREET. PHOTO BY GEORGE N. BARNARD FROM THE SERIES "RUINS OF CHICAGO"

Compare the fact that on September 11, 2001, buildings designed to withstand the impact of a jetliner and retain structural integrity in eight-hundred-degree heat failed because the planes were bigger and the fires hotter than anticipated. "Buildings had been reduced to ashes, and the wind after scooping rubbish and all in a body hurled it forward in a perfect blinding cloud," one eyewitness to the Chicago fire reported.[11] Another added, "For three days after the fire we walked through the streets, covered everywhere with heaps of debris and parts of walls, and could not help comparing ourselves to ghosts."[12] The disoriented survivors could just as well have been describing Pompeii in 79 A.D. or New York City two millennia later. Such appears to be the universal experience of urban disaster: the mix of astonishment and wonder that in an instant everything can change, the knowledge that nothing is permanent.

Only the rare New Yorker felt a strong attachment to the Trade Towers before September 11. Unlike the Chrysler, Empire State, or even the Seagram Building, the World Trade Center was a realtor's rather than an architect's dream. Its twinned, flat-topped, unornamented metal-and-glass practicality and desolate plaza was just the gargantuan version of the dinosaur modernism still on display in midtown along Third and Sixth avenues—no different really from all the other undistinguished corporate architecture that has obliterated low-rise neighborhoods all over the city since the 1960s. The Port Authority's original rationale for building the two towers was to find a way to package millions of rentable square feet efficiently in one place under single ownership.

For Robert Moses, whose bridges, tunnels, and highways produced a steady flood of cash, these skyscrapers were the biggest tollbooths in the world. But unlike roads and bridges, these engineering marvels had plenty of competition from the private sector. After they were completed in the early 1970s, the skyscrapers proved difficult to rent and expensive to operate. Although undeniably key elements of the city's incomparable skyline, the Twin Towers had no special significance, particularly once they were no longer the world's tallest skyscrapers and simply crowded places to work—nothing much to love or hate, that is, before they were struck down. But the attitude of people toward these buildings changed utterly when, in a matter of seconds, the equivalent of a small town's population, concentrated in just a few acres, was exterminated. Through the revelation of the names and faces of the individuals who perished in the Towers, mass murder was personalized. Now, it seems, no architecture has ever meant more.

Trained as an engineer, Osama bin Laden had a decidedly critical view of modern architecture. He certainly hated the arrogant verticality, the double-the-money preening of the two skyscrapers at the foot of Manhattan, which he first attempted to topple in 1993 with explosives packed into a rented van. There, at the very epicenter of global capitalism—the mecca of godless materialism—the infidel Twin Towers were as odious to him as the giant Buddhas sculpted into the mountains of Afghanistan. Only in their absence do the World Trade towers begin to have the magnitude of significance for Americans that they apparently had all along for Bin Laden and his operatives.

The Chicago Court House was a similar building, whose symbolic value soared as it catastrophically failed. Its well-documented failure became emblematic of the city's vulnerability to fire, and in its ruin it became a rubble-strewn memorial to the unimaginably awful sudden loss of life. An eye-witness Michigan News Company journalist reported, "At 10 minutes past 2 o'clock the court house tower was a glorious sight. It stood a glowing, almost dazzling trellis-work, around which was wrapped a winding sheet—of flame." Hours later when he returned to inspect the damage, he was startled to see that "In some places [the Court House] stone has disappeared altogether. In others it has been gnawed and eaten away, or fallen in great flakes."[13]

CLARK STREET, VIEW NORTH FROM COURT HOUSE.
PHOTO BY GEORGE N. BARNARD FROM THE SERIES "RUINS OF CHICAGO"

While the facade of the Court House flaked, the bell in the oversized cupola broke from its housing and fell through the building's core with the pendulum force of a giant wrecking ball. Floors, ceilings, and walls soon lay in an undifferentiated heap in the basement, atop a friable mountain of fine gray ash. Land records, birth and death certificates—believed to have been vaulted securely in the city's best building—were suddenly incinerated and seemingly unrecoverable. With Chicago's wealth based on real estate and its future dependent on aggressive land trading, permanent confusion over clear title to property appeared to doom the city's recovery. Yet this total, unremediable disaster was averted by a businessman, John G. Shortall, who from his office across the street saw the Court House in flames and immediately calculated what the Chicago fire meant for him, personally.

Like Mr. Kerfoot who got right back to work in the smoking hole where his office had stood the day before, John Shortall figured out, right on the spot, how to turn tragedy around. He was what the real-estate trade of the time called an "abstract man." Like court stenographers who mechanically recorded trials, abstract men prepared copies of land transactions. They were glorified clerks, and before the fire nearly at the bottom of Chicago's business hierarchy. As he watched the Court House burn in a "perfect rain of fire," Shortall realized he could rise to the top—so long as he could manage to preserve forty year's worth of hand-copied abstracts and indexes of Chicago real estate deals before the flames consumed them. He quickly hired two prisoners he saw fleeing from the Court House jail to help him load his personal ledger books onto wagons and drive them to safety. Dressed in a velveteen housecoat and guarding the basis of a billion-dollar monopoly—the future Chicago Title and Trust Company—Shortall waited out the fire at one of Lake Michigan's beaches.

His efforts paid off handsomely. Shortall's abstracts, combined with those of two other firms, were enough to reconstruct a reliable facsimile of the official land records incinerated in the Court House fire. Bypassing the Illinois Burnt Record Act in 1872, the State Legislature made Shortall's copies legal and binding. Looking back in 1891, Shortall reflected on what he had seen on the day the Court House burned to the ground:

The destructibility of all material, the instability of all substance, even the most impervious, shocked me. I saw those walls crumble with the heat, they seemed to melt, slowly, steadily; one could see them moving in the process of disintegration, and presently sink hopelessly down.[14]

But the realization that all material was destructible did not delay him for a second in the tireless recovery of paper that he knew somehow would one day make his fortune. John Shortall instinctively enacted just the sort of accelerated personal recovery, turning tragedy into opportunity, that Governor Bross had in mind for the city as a whole.

Yet any large-scale recovery demanded an army of architects and engineers to rebuild Chicago out of nothing. And architects and engineers certainly came to the burnt city. It was in the two years following the disaster that the history of Chicago offers an especially poignant parallel to the remaking of lower Manhattan—a cautionary tale.

The speed with which the Kerfoots, Shortalls, and Palmers reestablished themselves in better shape than ever proved a seductive model for the majority of Chicago's citizens who were still struggling to get back on their feet. Between 1871 and 1873, so much capital was available for the rebuilding that architects raced from one project to the next. It was not unusual for a building to be finished before the first set of architectural plans was approved. The public was thrilled as the rubble disappeared and the holes pocking the downtown were filled. Speed meant progress. Cheap crackled local stone was sold as marble; cornices fabricated out of pine two-by-fours were painted to look like stone. An instant impression of permanence and solidity—architectural illusions later perfected on the backlots of Hollywood—was all that the politicians and the architects asked of the builders.

By the time Daniel Burnham, John Wellborn Root, and Louis Sullivan—the architects with whom we associate the development of a true modern architecture in Chicago—arrived, much of the city had already been shoddily rebuilt. This hurried first recovery might have gone on longer had not a national economic panic stopped all construction cold in the fall of 1873. In his three-volume *History of Chicago* (1884–86), A. T. Andreas takes an inventory of those structures still standing from the earliest post-fire era, that period of easy money a contemporary writer referred to as "derrick time." He writes, "It was not uncommon to see a building, supposed to be of this [fireproof] class, surmounted by a mansard roof, as flammable as a pile of kindling wood."[15] The architects whom Burnham & Root, among other pioneers of high-rise commercial architecture, would replace had, in Andreas's opinion, a "morbid fondness" for the cheap and unnecessarily dangerous detail. As a result of building too fast, Andreas observes, "many structures, even in the business center of the city, [were] of a character, architecturally speaking, which were discreditable alike to the owners who erected them and the municipal authorities who tolerated them."[16]

In the immediate aftermath of the fire, local architects scrambled madly for attention. Each tried to outdo the other with the empty audacity of his own personal style. A single building might sport an Italianate entrance, a Versailles-like facade, an Empire cornice, and a Bavarian roof. This anarchy of influences, called "cosmopolitan" in the real estate advertisements, failed to impress John Root who was working, in 1871–73, as a draftsman, alongside another newcomer, Daniel Burnham, at Carter, Drake & Wight, one of the long-established local architectural firms. Root and Burnham entered into their own partnership in 1873 just as the city was beginning to feel the effects of a nationwide collapse of credit. The next years were mostly idle for the new firm of Burnham & Root as little new was built in Chicago or any place else in the country.

This lack of immediate employment was to the good, or so Root reasoned. Had the city's building frenzy continued indefinitely, Root speculated, he too might have been seduced by the quick-buck "cosmopolitan" style. On April 29, 1875, he wrote to his sister, "In my own case, I know that if I had been as successful in business as I expected to be when I started, I should have gone to the dickens as fast as my legs would carry me. Now I feel so doubtful of myself that I should very much be tried *with* much money."[17] From his office window high above Washington Street, he had a perfect view of the new architecture built during the two-year post-fire boom, including the new Court House, completed in 1873, which he referred to as "several million dollars' worth of hideousness."

CONSTRUCTION SITE, VIEW SOUTHEAST FROM COURT HOUSE, MID 1870S

John Root was receiving a priceless education in how *not* to be an architect. He thought the young designers were too "green" and "buoyant"; the entrenched A.I.A. crowd was made up of hopeless "fossils." In a letter of March 17, 1873, he reports, "A very costly building of one of the old men is literally falling down of sheer bad construction; another one opposite our office was for several days in such a condition that no one would walk on the same side of the street." He continues incredulously, "There are half a dozen costly buildings in this neighborhood held up by jack-screw, all because of the ineffience [sic] of the architects, who appear daily in the newspapers with cards that talk nonsense about 'bad stone,' 'frost in the walls,' and what not." Yet notwithstanding his growing skepticism, Root still retained some hope that "some of these fine days the people here will wake up to know, if not what good building is, certainly what it is not."[18]

While they restlessly waited for the jobs to arrive, Burnham and Root used the negative example of Chicago's phoenixlike resurrection to prod themselves into more carefully planning what they might build when they finally got their chance. For the first period in his professional life, Root had the time to read books during the day and to draw his ideas without watching the clock. He came to view this unexpected delay in the realization of his ambitions as a "providence." In January 1876, he wrote home to his family:

57

We [he and Burnham] thus have time to cultivate our minds, inasmuch as it saves us from doing much crude work that in after times we should be ashamed of. This compulsory idleness doesn't depress me very much, though it is tedious; for the ultimate success of a professional man is so dependent on his knowledge and industry and in acquiring the knowledge, he feels he can, if necessary, *wait*.[19]

Root somehow understood that to rebuild a modern working city he had to know more. If he was not to replicate the mistakes of the past like all the other architects, he had to prepare carefully and be ready for his opportunity when it arrived.

The wait was longer than he possibly could have imagined. Yet by the late 1870s, land speculators and bankers from all over the country had started to invest their money again in Chicago. As a result of the fire and the failed first rebuilding, most downtown real estate, with the exception of Potter Palmer's barony of hotels and department stores along State Street, was available for development. The size of buildable lots was larger than ever. Even before the fire had completely cooled down, some owners of newly vacant standard 25-by-125-foot lots sold out to professional land traders interested in consolidating contiguous parcels of land. The goal of the real-estate interests was to own as much of a three-acre city block as possible.

By 1880, the worst effects of the national depression were over. Also, since the fire, safe new construction methods had made taller and denser commercial architecture with more rentable square footage practical. This fortunate convergence of capital, technology, and land permitted landlords to multiply the value of their investment as long as they could find architects able to design and execute buildings that were taller and wider than the world had ever seen. Within little more than twenty years, Chicago's central business district would be rebuilt completely a second time. Burnham & Root's Rookery (1884–86), Monadnock (1889–91), and Reliance (1889–91) buildings and Louis Sullivan's Auditorium (1889, with Dankmar Adler), Chicago Stock Exchange (1893–94), and Carson, Pirie, Scott (1899) buildings are only a few of the famous landmarks of the time. Beginning with Burnham & Root's Montauk Building (1881–82), a new breed of local Chicago architects, who had waited their turn to build, took full advantage of their opportunities. John Root and his contemporaries incorporated new inventions like the electric elevator, steel-frame construction, and effective fireproofing into their architecture. They also invented as they went along. Heliotropic, wide-bay "Chicago windows" brought the sun deep into office interiors; abstractly ornamented terra-cotta cladding along the building's spandrels and piers made gigantic structures appear less massive and dwarfing when seen from the street; "raft" foundations of concrete and railroad steel kept skyscrapers stable in Chicago's swampy soil.

The safe and profitable architecture that replaced both the fire-damaged blocks and the Europeanized piles of the first rebuilding represented a permanent break with the past. Had the city's early rebuilding not been aborted by the Financial Panic of 1873—and a subsequent "Little Fire" of July 14, 1874, which also caused millions of dollars' worth of damage—Chicago might well have rebuilt differently. In Switzerland, for example, deep in the Alps, architects and planners have secreted away an exact replica of every town in the country so that in case of disaster rebuilding the country will require no invention at all. Chicago, on the other hand, had to be totally reinvented.

Architects were not the only ones prompted by Chicago's brush with total ruin to overturn accepted formulas for doing things. It is no accident that novelists like Frank Norris and Theodore Dreiser were drawn to the post-fire city. Nor that the University of Chicago, founded in 1893, promoted the scientific study of society. It was also in turn-of-the-century Chicago that Jane Addams rethought the problems of urban poverty. What these innovators had in common was that there was something enduring in the experience of having faced communal annihilation. The acknowledgment of the failure of all that was thought fail-proof, even the language of heroism and defiance that people had relied upon for consolation, radically separated the post-fire generation from the previous one. After touring Chicago in the 1870s, Louis Sullivan warned against the city's tendency to overcome adversity with rhetoric. He wrote, "It is wise to handle words with caution. Their content is so complex and explosive; and in combination they may work beautiful or dreadful things."[20]

What lessons might New York City take from Chicago as it readies its own plans for redevelopment after the recent calamity? It would be wise to keep Sullivan's admonition in mind. Chicagoans too quickly turned away from the awful details and manufactured a myth of rebirth, which they soon adopted as fact. It was not the shock of the original disaster that emancipated Chicago from tired tradition and opened the city to boundless innovation. Rather, it was the secondary failure of the politicians, architects, and builders to move beyond the rhetoric of loss and the mania of revival that prompted the likes of John Root, Daniel Burnham, and Louis Sullivan to start over from nothing. Chicago residents never got around to building a "sufficiently dignified" memorial to the Great Fire. Perhaps those who would rush to rebuild Lower Manhattan should similarly allow the crater at ground zero, now that it is safely emptied of debris, to remain unimproved for a while. If New York is to have any chance of avoiding the fate of Chicago's lamentable first rebuilding, perhaps it too should plan a period of "compulsory idleness" into its program of recovery.

Intentionally allowing a sixteen-acre hole to remain for a while in the heart of downtown New York might just give people time to reflect more on what should be built and what should not. A building moratorium might allow competing interests (public and private) to argue productively about what constitutes "the highest and best use" of this graveyard where thousands were buried under close to two million tons of debris. Only the cleared site—the absence of all that was once so vividly present at ground zero—can fully evoke the awful suddenness of history, can stand as a sufficient memorial to the unnameable thing that came out of the blue on September 11, 2001. The rest is real estate, architecture, and forgetting.

NOTES

1. N. R. Kleinfield, *New York Times,* September 12, 2001.

2. Cited in Joseph Kirkland, "The Chicago Fire," *New England Magazine* 6, no. 4 (June 1892), pp. 726–27, 737.

3. Bessie L. Pierce, *A History of Chicago,* vol. 3 (Chicago: Knopf, 1957), pp. 9, 17.

4. Ibid., p. 10.

5. Elias Colbert and Everett Chamberlin, *Chicago and the Great Conflagration* (Chicago: J. S. Goodman & Co., 1871), p. 445.

6. Pierce, *A History of Chicago,* vol. 3, p. 19.

7. J. W. Sheahan, *Scribner's Monthly* 10, no. 5 (September 1875), p. 529.

CHICAGO LOTS CLEARED FOR REBUILDING. VIEW SOUTHWEST FROM WATER TOWER, 1870s. STEREO PHOTO BY COPELIN & SON

8. William Bross, *History of Chicago* (Chicago, 1876), p. 100.

9. Ibid., p. 101.

10. Charles H. Mackintosh, *The Doomed City: Chicago during an Appalling Ordeal* (Detroit, 1871), p. 31.

11. Ibid., p. 22.

12. Alfred L. Sewall, *"The Great Calamity!" Scenes, Lessons and Incidents of the Great Chicago Fire* (Chicago: A. L. Sewall, 1871), p. 27.

13. Mackintosh, *The Doomed City*, pp. 11, 32.

14. John G. Shortall quoted in Joseph Kirkland, *The Story of Chicago* (Chicago: Dibble Publishing Company, 1892), p. 315.

15. A. T. Andreas, *History of Chicago* (New York: Arno Press, 1975, first published 1884–86), vol. 3, p. 60. Andreas's prime example of rushed and dangerous design was the Grand Pacific Hotel, "the rebuilding of which," he remarks, "was commenced even before the plans were completed." Andreas warns that the Grand Pacific Hotel was not the only building in the Loop to suffer the effects of "this spirit of eagerness."

16. Ibid.

17. Cited in Harriet Monroe, *John Wellborn Root* (Boston and New York: Houghton, Mifflin & Company, 1896), p. 28.

18. Ibid., p. 31.

19. Letter reprinted in ibid., pp. 34–35; emphasis mine.

20. Louis H. Sullivan, *The Autobiography of an Idea* (New York: Dover Publications, 1956; originally published by the American Institute of Architects Press, 1924), p. 199.

HIROSHIMA
THE ATOMIC BOMB
AND KENZO TANGE'S
HIROSHIMA PEACE
CENTER

Carola Hein

When Japan surrendered on August 15, 1945, effectively ending World War II, 215 Japanese cities had been bombed.[1] Among them were the capital, Tokyo, the metropolitan centers of Yokohama, Nagoya, Osaka, and Kobe, and the cities of Hiroshima and Nagasaki. The last two were the first urban centers to suffer mass destruction as a result of single atomic bombs. Apart from Okinawa, where major ground battles had been fought, the Japanese cities had mainly been destroyed from the air.[2] Incendiary bombs in particular caused extensive damage, transforming the densely populated, primarily wooden Japanese cities into wastelands of ashes, with only smokestacks, garden walls, and some reinforced concrete buildings remaining.

The desolation of the urban landscape immediately after the war was an accurate image of the general state of Japanese society. The country was defeated and occupied and its political future unclear. With its economy shattered, people scrambled for shelter, food, and livelihood. Under such conditions, grand reconstruction plans were not the order of the day.

Instead, most of the Japanese cities that rebuilt after World War II focused their efforts on infrastructural improvements like street widening and straightening, leaving the reconstruction of houses to private landowners. But monumental or comprehensive projects were also not part of Japan's way of thinking. In fact, in spite of the regular occurrence of fires, typhoons, floods, and earthquakes, Japan does not have any real tradition of urban reinvention, relying instead on pragmatic planning tools and especially "land readjustment" (*kukakuseiri*), a technique for creating infrastructures and replotting land that includes regulating the number of individual building sites.

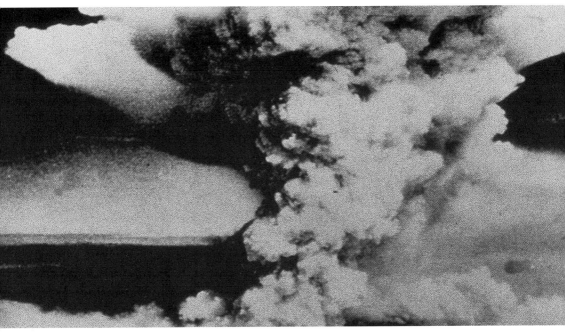

MUSHROOM CLOUD OVER HIROSHIMA. FROM ISHIMARU ET AL., *RECONSTRUCTION OF HIROSHIMA*

This type of reconstruction does not result in particularly compelling architectural and urban visions. As I have also argued elsewhere,[3] the concept of idealistic visions as guidelines for urban transformation is foreign to Japanese thought. This is reflected in the fact that the English word "vision" in its Western sense of future planning does not have an exact equivalent in Japanese. Instead the *katakana* word "bijon," adopted into the Japanese language, tends to be used. During the postwar reconstruction period, Japanese architects thus neither produced competition entries that became icons of architectural history—such as Peter and Alison Smithson's widely published (though never realized) entry in the 1957–58 international urban planning competition for a reunified German capital, which suggested an organic platform system extending over the traditional layout of the city center[4]—nor did they develop coherent large-scale schemes for reconstruction on the model of postwar Rotterdam.[5]

In fact, the only project to come out of this period possessing both symbolic value and iconic character is Kenzo Tange's design for the Peace Center in Hiroshima.[6] Situated in the heart of the city, below the hypocenter of the explosion, the Peace Center was conceived as a public space of assembly and memory, with several urban structures and a cenotaph intended to commemorate the destruction. In order to understand the concept of Tange's Peace Center and its meaning for the city, for Japan, and for the world, it is necessary first to examine the particulars of the city's destruction and then to turn to the specific project of reinventing Hiroshima as "Peace City."

FRONTISPIECE DESTRUCTION CAUSED BY ATOMIC BOMB, INCLUDING (ON RIGHT) THE RUINS THAT WOULD BECOME THE A-BOMB DOME. FROM NORIOKI ISHIMARU ET AL., *RECONSTRUCTION OF HIROSHIMA: PICTORIAL HISTORY OF FORTY YEARS SINCE ATOMIC BOMBING* (1985)

The United States dropped the atomic bomb on Hiroshima on August 6, 1945, at 8:15 in the morning.[7] The beautiful cloudless sky allowed the pilots to hit the target exactly as planned. At the instant the bomb exploded, the pilots observed a mushroom cloud developing in the sky; this came to represent the image most strongly associated with the atomic bomb. For many Americans this image was also the end of the story. The planes veered off, and American observers did not get a closer look at the destruction on the ground until some weeks later. For the inhabitants of Hiroshima, however, the explosion was only the beginning of horrific scenes that would become central to the Japanese experience and representation of the bomb.[8] What people on the ground saw and heard as the bomb exploded was a searing flash of light and a deafening roar. People, animals, and plants closest to the hypocenter of the bomb vanished immediately; only white shadows on the ground testified to their prior existence. The heat set the mostly wooden buildings afire, engulfing people who were trapped.

The number of deaths caused by the bomb cannot be determined exactly. It is estimated that 60,000 to 80,000 people were killed instantly, while many more died painfully by the end of 1945 from extensive burns, radiation, or other wounds, totaling in all up to 140,000 casualties,[9] and numerous survivors would suffer the after-effects for years to come. In fact, the large death toll on the day of the explosion was not unique for an air raid; incendiary bombs dropped on Tokyo on the night of March 10, 1945, killed about 85,000 people. They did not, however, spread radioactive fallout and cause long-term fatalities.[10] By August 6, 1993, the registers underneath the cenotaph at the Peace Center listed the names of 181,836 people who had died of exposure to the bomb. More names have been added since.[11] Many foreigners who were present at the time of the explosion also died, including forced workers from Korea and scholarship students from China and southern Asia; American prisoners of war and Japanese-Americans were also among the victims.[12] Others continue to die from various radiation-related illnesses, and their descendants are at risk for genetic defects—these people are referred to as "temporary survivors" in the film *Hiroshima, mon Amour.*[13]

AERIAL PHOTOGRAPH WITH SHADED ZONE INDICATING AREA OF DESTRUCTION BY ATOMIC BOMB. FROM ISHIMARU ET AL., *RECONSTRUCTION OF HIROSHIMA*

Until the atomic bomb was dropped, the enemy planes that were announced in nightly air-raid warnings had spared Hiroshima, bringing destruction only to neighboring cities. The all-clear had sounded on the morning of August 6. The American B-29 *Enola Gay*, carrying the first atomic bomb (dubbed "Little Boy"), entered Japanese airspace unchallenged, accompanied by two other planes. Not until the moment the bomb was dropped was an air-raid warning sounded,[14] leaving the population no time to reach shelters, which might have afforded them some protection.

At the time, people were on their way to work or to school or were participating in building demolition in the city center, which had been ordered for the creation of "firebreaks"—open spaces ordered by the Japanese government after the Doolittle Raid of 1942, when it became evident that Japanese cities could be attacked from the air, and also after the firestorms in Hamburg. Civilians were mobilized to demolish buildings and create safe areas that would prevent fires from spreading, secure evacuation routes, and create vacant spaces near bridges and important buildings. The city government of Hiroshima put this order into effect in 1944, largely following the master plan for street-widening and construction that it had prepared in 1928, which specified where demolition of buildings was to be carried out. When the atomic bomb fell, about 10,000 houses had already been destroyed for purposes of creating firebreaks and further demolition activities were underway. The firebreaks, however, were insufficient to provide protection against the atomic bomb's heat and radiation.

Having been developed for two years under the code name "Manhattan Project" and tested three weeks before its explosion over Hiroshima, the new bomb was slated for several Japanese cities as possible targets. Kyoto, the historical capital of Japan, was initially selected to be the first. Henry Stimson, the U.S. secretary of war, interceded on behalf of that city, however, arguing that with its centuries-old temples and palaces, it was a historic site that should not be destroyed.[15] Four cities—Hiroshima, Kokura, Niigata, and Nagasaki—were finally recommended for the first attack.[16] Hiroshima, the first city on the list, thus became the target of the first atomic bomb. Three days later, on August 9, the second atomic bomb ("Fat Man") was destined for Kokura. On that day, however, the city was hidden by clouds and the target could not be identified. The planes flew on to Nagasaki, which, as the cloud cover ripped open for an instant, became the target of the second atomic bomb.[17]

Among the reasons given officially for the choice of Hiroshima was the city's military importance. Surrounded by mountains to its north, it had developed on islands formed out of the delta of the Ota River, whose seven (later six) branches flowed through the heart of the city into the Seto Inland Sea. The construction of a castle on the largest island in the delta in 1589 initiated the development of Hiroshima. Under three successive leaders, settlements on the numerous neighboring islands grew into a city, and landfill in the shallow Hiroshima Bay provided even more space for the rapidly increasing population. At the center of the Chugoku region at the western end of the island of Honshu and equipped with a good harbor, Hiroshima soon developed into a military and economic center. In the Sino-Japanese and Russo-Japanese wars it was an important base for army operations. During World War II, the city continued to be a major military headquarters, with a population of 300,000 and about 40,000 troops, and played a major role in operations.[18]

But while Hiroshima was clearly a military city, the target of the bomb was not the military base on the outskirts of the city nor was it an industrial site.[19] Instead, it was the very heart of the city, with the bombardier's marker set on the T-shaped Aioi Bridge just north of the densely built Nakajima neighborhood. The eventual site of the Peace Memorial Park, the Nakajima area was the commercial center of the city until the 1920s. By the 1930s, the area had become less attractive as citizens preferred the Hachobori district closer to the railway station in the eastern part of the city. About 2,600 people, however, were still living in the area when the bomb fell.

Beyond the loss of half of Hiroshima's population and the extent of the destruction, the bomb's unprecedented nature made the reconstruction of the city a unique challenge. Hiroshima quickly came to world attention. Within Japan too, the city took on symbolic meaning as a rallying point for Japanese aspirations to nation-building. In his book *The Victim as Hero*, James Orr discusses the myth of war victimhood that has coalesced in Japan around the notion that it is the only country in the world to have been the object of atomic bombing.[20]

Early reports about Hiroshima gave voice to fears that the city would be barren land for many generations. Many people asked whether it would ever revive. During a round-table discussion organized by the city on February 22, 1946, the feeling that the site of so many deaths was unsuited for reconstruction was expressed by Tomiko Kora, the deputy mayor of the neighboring city of Kure, who suggested that it would be necessary to "search for a new place in the suburbs and construct the new Hiroshima there."[21]

AERIAL VIEW OF THE T-SHAPED AIOI BRIDGE, 1936.
FROM CHUGOKU SHIMBUN, ED., *THE MEANING OF SURVIVAL: HIROSHIMA'S 36-YEAR COMMITMENT TO PEACE* (1983)

The desire to memorialize the event was shared by both the Japanese and the international community, although their points of view were very different. Many leading Japanese citizens were convinced during the period right after the war that a special type of memorial was necessary for Hiroshima. Several publications advocated preserving the ruins as monuments. Ichio Kuwabara, the former president of Asahi Industries, proposed retaining the destroyed area as a monument to and a symbol of world peace, to be surrounded by cultural and religious institutions. The poet Sankichi Toge, who suffered exposure to the radiation and died in 1953 at age thirty-six of a related ailment, proposed a plan for a green, decentralized city. Ultimately international interest in memorializing the destruction was essential to realizing the Peace Center Project and to freeing special funds and obtaining the necessary permits from the postwar occupation army.

The manpower needed to organize the reconstruction of Hiroshima was lacking, however, especially as the mayor and half the members of his administration were among those who had died. Thus the prefectural governor took charge, and by November 1945, the city assembly had organized a reconstruction committee composed of neighborhood representatives. In January 1946, the municipal authorities, city assembly, and residents of Hiroshima worked together on a basic plan for restoration. By 1946, the Hiroshima Reconstruction Bureau was established.[22]

The focus of the reconstruction discussions quickly changed from visionary ideas to pragmatic issues related to rebuilding plans largely conceived during the 1920s and 1930s. Again, this approach was typical for Japan, and occurred in many cases of postwar rebuilding. Thus in Hiroshima the planning of symbolic gestures was combined with the reconstruction of roads, infrastructure, and services. Practical considerations included the future size of the city and its population and economic direction. Many planners thought that Hiroshima could not survive economically without a military industry. In contrast to the prewar population of 420,000 (500,000 including military personnel), some therefore predicted that only about 100,000 people would live in the city. The highest estimates were for 700,000 inhabitants. Yet to the surprise of many, people who had been evacuated before the bombing returned to Hiroshima quickly, while others came back after the war. With many jobs left vacant, a large number of returnees from the former Japanese colonies in East Asia also chose to settle in Hiroshima. Today the city has over one million inhabitants.

SANKICHI TOGE, PROPOSAL FOR THE RECONSTRUCTION OF HIROSHIMA. FROM ISHIMARU ET AL., *RECONSTRUCTION OF HIROSHIMA*

KENZO TANGE, MASTER PLAN FOR HIROSHIMA, 1950

During the same period the central government issued a number of directives for reconstruction. These were intended to serve as guidelines for local administrations. In addition, as the local governments lacked planners, in 1946 the reconstruction office dispatched urban planning experts and architects to several cities, including Hiroshima. These advisers promoted land-use plans rather than the street-use plans that had been the focus of Hiroshima's earlier administration. As part of this program, the national government sent a group of young architect-planners to Hiroshima to give an opinion on the reconstruction. Among them was Kenzo Tange.

Tange predicted a population of 300,000 to 350,000 inhabitants for Hiroshima. In 1947 he prepared a land-use plan. Its main elements were subsequently integrated into the official plan of 1949. The plan included some of the more radical elements that had been proposed for the reconstruction soon after the war, particularly the idea for a Peace Boulevard and Peace Memorial Park.

As mentioned above, firebreaks had already been built throughout the city. One of them, running in an east-west direction, had initially been projected as a 45-foot-wide street, but even before the bomb was dropped, the width of the zone of demolished houses was close to 325 feet. It was this winding space, a firebreak and green strip, that was straightened out and converted into the present-day Peace Boulevard and the symbolic entrance to the Peace Memorial Park. In other words, the physical existence of the firebreak, a military project, ironically served as the background for the realization of Peace Boulevard. But the realization of a street of this width as a mixture of street space and greenery, one of only three such thoroughfares completed in Japan during the postwar period (the other two are in Nagoya), was really possible only because of the city's symbolic value. Hiroshima's reconstruction thus combined the pragmatic need for urban improvement with the symbolic wish to memorialize the destruction.

The search for a new image of the city and the desire to turn the military city into a symbol of peace led in 1949 to the proclamation of the Hiroshima Peace Memorial City Construction Law (Peace City Law). Enacted by the National Diet on August 6, 1949, and requiring the approval of the U.S. occupation forces, it increased funds for rebuilding and enabled the construction of a Peace Center. As summarized by the city's mayor, Shinzo Hamai,

The reconstructed city aspires to become a center of creative peace movements by providing well-equipped facilities for international peace functions and, at the same time, to become an embodiment of peace such as would befit the world wherein complete victory of human wisdom will have ousted war and destruction from humanity to give place to well-being, good will and cultural refinement.[23]

The mayor also noted that a Peace Festival would be held in Hiroshima every year.

Hiroshima was thus exceptional not only as the first city to be destroyed by an atomic bomb, but also in terms of its attempted reinvention. It was the only city in Japan to be reconstructed after World War II in which the local government, with international authorization and support, held a competition for and realized a comprehensive urban project, involving the clearance and rebuilding of a large urban area on expensive real estate in the center of the city for the purpose of a memorial program. Furthermore, the project's urban and architectural design by Tange, the architect selected, was exceptional.

Kenzo Tange is an unusual figure in twentieth-century Japanese architecture. Born in 1913, he studied architecture at Tokyo University, where he became a professor in 1946. Decisively influenced by Le Corbusier, whose project for the Palace of the Soviets he had seen in a foreign art journal while he was still attending Hiroshima High School,[24] as well as by the teachings of his elder colleague Kunio Maekawa, who had worked for two years in Le Corbusier's office, Tange would become identified with public architecture in Japan beginning in the early postwar period.[25] His work was an attempt to synthesize the Japanese spirit with modern architectural influences emanating from the international community. Hiroshima Peace Center was his first major work and brought him international fame when he was only in his thirties.

Tange's design for the Peace Center integrates a park, along with its buildings and memorials, into the city. Besides the Peace Memorial Complex and the cenotaph, the Peace Center consists of a square used for annual peace celebrations and the "A-Bomb Dome," which incorporates the remains of a bombed structure. The whole project is located north of Peace Boulevard. The Memorial Complex comprises three buildings. In the middle is a museum, in which an exhibit about the atomic bomb and its destruction of Hiroshima is on permanent display. Flanking the museum are Peace Hall to the west and the City Auditorium to the east. The simple, reduced forms of the building complex, particularly the museum with its raised floor, flat roof, and concrete construction, reflect the ideas of European and American modernists, but they also are closely tied to traditional Japanese architecture.

KENZO TANGE, GREATER EAST ASIA MONUMENT, TOKYO. COMPETITION DRAWING, 1942

The architect's knowledge of traditional Japanese spaces and Western urban concepts, as well as his ability to combine the disciplines of urban planning, landscaping, and architecture, allowed him to respond convincingly to the program's requirements. The design was celebrated by Western critics as a masterpiece of modernist architecture and an exemplary creation of an urban core. In 1951, Tange would be invited to the eighth meeting of CIAM (the International Congresses of Modern Architecture, and the leading organization of modern architects in the West), held in Hoddesdon outside London, to present the project. The theme of the meeting was "The Heart of the City,"[26] and the exposure of the Hiroshima scheme would propel Tange onto the international stage.

Japan's decision to hold a competition for the design of the Peace Center was an important result of the Peace City Law and another unusual aspect of the project for Hiroshima. Unlike the European countries, especially Germany after World War II, which relied heavily on architectural and planning competitions to effect its rebuilding, Japan had no tradition of competitions (and still does not to this day).[27] Except for some small city-planning competitions, mostly in Tokyo, that did not lead to realization, the Hiroshima competition represents the only such contest of the reconstruction period.

Even before the Peace City Law, though, in 1948, the city of Hiroshima took the unusual step of holding an architectural competition related to the city's projected function as a peace city. The city had been home to thirteen churches before the bombing. As a result of the competition, one of them, in the vicinity of the Hiroshima train station, was rebuilt as the World Peace Memorial Church, with financial support from many countries. A first prize was not awarded in the competition, and the design went to one of the jurors, Togo Murano, whose scheme combined traditional and modern elements.[28] Significantly, however, Tange was one of the participants in this competition.

Despite the relative paucity of competitions in Japan, Tange also participated in several other competitions prior to Hiroshima, and two of his wartime competition entries, in particular, can be seen as forerunners of the design for the Hiroshima Peace Center. In 1942, Tange entered a competition for the design of a monument to "Greater East Asia"—of which Japan was to be the leader and which was an attempt to create a sense of solidarity among the nations of Southeast Asia.[29] Tange's design for this commemorative construction, which he located in the greater Tokyo area, is characteristic of his approach to architecture and urban form. Instead of proposing a high-rise building, which he believed typified Western more than Japanese monumental structures, he drew on the Japanese traditions of natural objects and horizontal development. As a backdrop for the Greater East Asia project, he chose a natural landmark, Mount Fuji.

Tange's ability to shift back forth and back between different styles and between Eastern and Western influences is also demonstrated in a second major wartime competition entry that may be related to the Hiroshima project. This was a traditionalist design for the Japanese Cultural Center in Bangkok (1942). In Germany during and after World War II, where styles tended to be associated with political opinions, such versatility would most likely have been impossible. In Japan, however, it did not provoke debate. One explanation for this cultural difference is that since European architectural styles were imported to Japan only in the mid-nineteenth century, the modern movement in Japan did not develop as a reaction against earlier styles.

Tange submitted his design for the Peace Memorial Complex, one of 145 entries, to the Hiroshima City Reconstruction Bureau in August 1948. According to the competition brief, the project had to be located southwest of the Hiroshima castle on the site of the former Nakajima neighborhood, the entire area of which was to become "a symbol of lasting peace and a place suitable for recreation and relaxation for all people." The brief stipulated that the complex was to be "simple, bringing out the beauty of the environment, and unique, good, contemporary taste."[30] Specified in the program were a Peace Memorial Tower, a Science Memorial Hall, and a cenotaph. The majority of the participants, including the second-place winner, Toshiro Yamashita, and the third-place winner, Ryozo Arai, limited their proposals to Nakajima, framed by the projected 325-foot-wide (or in a symbolically intended metric measurement, 100-meter-wide) Peace Boulevard and by two rivers. Their buildings, although related to one another, did not take into consideration the larger urban context.

In contrast, Tange's prize-winning project, on which he worked in association with Takashi Asada, Sachio Otani, and Tokokuni Kimura,[31] established connections with the immediate surroundings and even projected a network of related facilities for other areas of the city. Reaching beyond the Nakajima neighborhood, it integrated urban design, architecture, and landscaping. Having previously worked on the land-use plan for Hiroshima, Tange was both familiar with the city and its reconstruction needs and cognizant of the larger aim of transforming Hiroshima into a peace city. The visionary scheme exemplifies Tange's approach to monumentality and memorializing, and it serves as a springboard for examining the impact of modern design as well as traditional Japanese form on his work.[32]

To Tange, the Peace City brief was a mandate to reinvent Hiroshima totally, with facilities that "would be of a real service to mankind in its pursuit of peace and happiness."[33] Going far beyond the Nakajima district, the scheme included facilities spread throughout the city, from tourist accommodations like international hotels and dormitories, an aquarium, a seaside park at Ujina, and a hippodrome, to a project for improving the Ota River. At the core of the scheme, he envisioned a park extending north of Peace Boulevard beyond the A-Bomb Dome to encompass the castle and the area west of it, including the riverfront. This vast area was to be divided into the Peace Hall area around the memorial facilities, and what Tange called the Peace Park, to include recreational facilities (such as a swimming pool and a wrestling area) as well as cultural facilities (among them, a library, an art museum, an open-air theater, and a children's center). Also proposed were infrastructure and institutions intended to improve the quality of life of the local population—fireproof housing, public health institutions, schools, and waterworks, and parks and greenery along the rivers.[34] Tange did not want to privilege either housing or memorializing, and argued that housing for

KENZO TANGE WITH TAKASHI ASADA, SACHIO OTANI, AND TOKOKUNI KIMURA, HIROSHIMA PEACE MEMORIAL PARK, 1949.
MODEL OF PRIZE-WINNING SCHEME

citizens and the creation of an international memorial complex had to go hand in hand. A multifaceted urban improvement scheme was thus to be an extension to the memorial park in the former Nakajima neighborhood. This grand project was not realized and instead the city government put up public housing on the Peace Park site. However, the heart of Tange's proposal, for the Peace Center located in the former Nakajima neighborhood, was built.

Drawing on the architectural language of Le Corbusier, the realized project presents three buildings on *pilotis* connected by aerial passageways parallel to the Peace Boulevard.[35] Beyond the Peace Memorial Hall a square provides space for the yearly peace ceremonies. In the center of the area a huge arc frames the view toward the symbolic A-Bomb Dome, located beyond the Motoyasu River. The Dome is the surviving remnant of the former Hiroshima Industry Promotion Hall, a brick-and-steel building located close to the center of the explosion.

KENZO TANGE, NORTHERN SECTOR OF MASTER PLAN
FOR HIROSHIMA PEACE MEMORIAL PARK INCLUDING RIVERFRONT
AND CULTURAL FACILITIES, 1950

Perhaps the most surprising part of Tange's Peace Memorial Park design was his proposal for an arch. This element was subsequently modified in form. As one of the judges, Hideto Kishida, a strong defender of Tange's work, pointed out, the arch appeared to be a direct reference to Eero Saarinen's design for the Saint Louis Gateway Arch (1947–66).[36] It also resembled the projected arch for the failed EUR (Esposizione Universale di Roma) in Rome. Kishida questioned in 1949 why a project that contained so many original ideas had to fall into this kind of quotation. Tange responded to the criticism,[37] stating that he saw three options regarding the memorial tower specified in the competition brief: proposing a tower, proposing an arch, or ignoring the request. Considering the first option, Tange recalled that a British architect had suggested that a pagoda be constructed to commemorate Hiroshima's atomic destruction.[38] Tange, however, felt that a different form was necessary in this context, especially as a pagoda in reinforced concrete had already been built by the architect Chuta Ito to memorialize the Great Kanto Earthquake of 1923.[39]

Thus having decided against a vertical structure, which he considered to exemplify Western monumentality, Tange saw the arch as emerging naturally from the project. But after lengthy discussions, and allegedly the rejection of a proposal by the Japanese-American sculptor Isamu Noguchi, Tange ultimately decided on a saddle-vault cenotaph as the centerpiece of his project. His rejection of the pagoda form was not a rejection of religious models per se, though; indeed, the design of the Peace Center appears to be strongly inspired by Japanese Shinto architecture.

Central to Japanese Shinto belief are the shrines at Ise. A major pilgrimage site in Japan, the Ise shrines are famous for being ritually reconstructed every twenty years. Tange made his earliest official visits to Ise in 1953, and he would publish a book about the shrines in 1965, calling them the prototype of Japanese architecture. While Hiroshima's Peace Park was conceived prior to these visits, it appears that their architecture and spirit influenced his concept of architectural and urban space early on.

This influence at Hiroshima is evident first in Tange's composition of the site. As Kishida points out in his comments on the competition, Peace Park is organized along an axis perpendicular to Peace Boulevard.[40] Rather than employ a monumental Western axis *à la* Versailles or a traditional Chinese axis, though, Tange's design appears to have been inspired directly by the design of the Shinto shrines. At Ise, bridges—which are among the structures that are ritually rebuilt—lead to the shrine precinct. At Hiroshima, bridges are likewise a central element. Tange, for whom Peace Boulevard signified the "Road to Peace," saw them as symbolizing the link between one culture and another. The architect paid particular attention to the details of their design, including commissioning handrails by Noguchi.

In Shinto shrines, visitors enter through the Torii gate, symbolizing the transition from the physical to the spiritual world, before proceeding to a second gate, which is for prayers. The view beyond this gate is obscured and the visitor is not allowed to proceed to the inner precinct. Tange uses this same organizational principle in his design for Peace Park. The Peace Memorial Museum serves as the gateway to the inner precinct, while the cenotaph functions as the place for prayers. Beyond, shaded by the trees of Peace Park and separated by the river, is the sacred space, the A-Bomb Dome.

The similarity to the Ise shrines goes further. The *pilotis*—the piers that carry the central building and are often interpreted as an allusion to those of Le Corbusier—can be seen as deriving from traditional Japanese granaries with raised floors. Differences between Tange's design and Le Corbusier's concept become more evident if one looks at the recent restoration of the Peace Memorial Complex and the rebuilding of the City Auditorium.

ISE SHRINE, NAIKU, JAPAN. AERIAL VIEW LOOKING DOWN ON INNER PRECINCT AND SITE OF FUTURE REBUILDING. FROM KENZO TANGE AND NOBORU KAWAZOE, *ISE: PROTOTYPE OF JAPANESE ARCHITECTURE* (1965)

In the 1950s, when Tange was unable to meet the deadline for finishing the auditorium building, the project was given to another architect. In the 1980s, though, he was given the opportunity to rebuild the auditorium as an international conference center, and was finally able to complete a design closer to his original plan. This permitted him to connect the three buildings by aerial passageways as he had initially projected. Instead of three independent buildings, Peace Hall is now part of a system, linked with the other buildings through elevated corridors in a form characteristic of traditional Japanese architecture. In this way the group of three buildings has gained an even stronger "Japanese" character.

Tange's project thus responded ingeniously to the different concepts of memorializing existing in the West and in Japan. While building educational and memorial structures for foreign visitors, the architect simultaneously established the site as a sacred space. Whereas foreign tourists are invited to understand the effects of the destruction through the exhibits in the galleries of Peace Hall where objects related to the bombing are displayed, this is something many Japanese prefer to ignore. In her novel *The Flowers of Hiroshima*, Edita Morris describes the resistance of the main character, who is Japanese, to visiting the Peace Memorial Museum, which her American guest is eager to see.[41]

It is the cenotaph and the other memorials that seem to speak more to Japanese culture. Consonant with Japanese spiritual tradition, Tange explicitly sought to incorporate the scorched earth at Hiroshima into his peace memorial. The Shinto religion is intimately bound up with natural objects and with the earth or soil. Spirits are believed to be living in stones, rivers, and mountains, and it is thought that when people die they become spirits. The area under the hypocenter of the explosion, then, is understood by the Japanese visitor as filled with spirits, making the entirety of Peace Memorial Park sacred ground.[42]

Further, natural stones bearing inscriptions are more in keeping with Japanese tradition than are figural memorials. Even Japanese inscriptions reflect cultural differences. The inscription on the cenotaph at Hiroshima reads, in one possible translation, "Rest in peace—the mistake will never be repeated."[43] As the sentence does not contain a pronoun—typical for the Japanese language—it is vague or tacit enough to leave room for interpretation (and therefore also for argument). If it said, "We will never repeat...," debate would arise as to who "we" are, demonstrating that there is no universal point of view, no international "we."

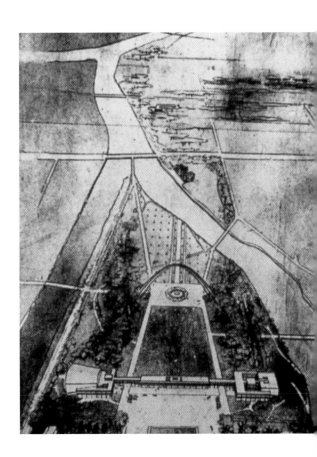

HIROSHIMA PEACE MEMORIAL PARK, EARLY SCHEME WITH ARCH

Another difference specific to the Japanese culture of memorializing is represented by the symbolic meaning accorded to temporary events, such as the custom of floating white flowers down a stream, or the annual lantern festivals. In an earlier passage from Morris's novel, the American guest in Hiroshima wants to break off a flower in a bouquet the main character's sister is holding, not realizing she is planning to float the flowers on the river in memory of those who died during the bombing.[44] These floating memories, typical for a culture that celebrates "Hanami," or cherry-blossom viewing, in honor of the short-lasting blossoms, are extremely meaningful for the Japanese, if not necessarily for the visitor, and they are accommodated in the more ritualistic aspects of Tange's project.

Tange's architectural and urban solution thus fulfills the requirements of a memorial in the first city ever destroyed by an atomic bomb in a variety of ways, responding to the expectations and needs of different groups of people. As such, as he hoped, it is a monument that is not easily forgotten.[45] It offers a site for both information and memorializing. It embraces the past and the future. A spiritual symbol, it nonetheless conveys the message that peace is not bestowed by the gods, but needs to be worked for. Tange himself described the project as both a "symbolic image" and a "factory for peace." The latter characterization is reminiscent of that used for the United Nations headquarters in New York, which was referred to as a workshop for peace.[46] In its idealism, the Peace Center project also falls into the lineage of other projects advocating world peace, such as the proposal by the French Ernest Hébrard and the Norwegian Hendrick Christian Andersen for a World City in 1913, or Le Corbusier's vision for the League of Nations in Geneva in 1928.[47]

Despite the fact that of Tange's sweeping concept for Hiroshima only Peace Memorial Park in the Nakajima district was realized, this in itself was a major victory, given the economic difficulties and general conditions of the period from 1949 to 1955, when it was completed, as well as the challenges of land readjustment and the importance of private land ownership in Japan. Indeed, approximately 30 acres had to be cleared for its construction, including 400 temporary dwellings that had sprung up on the site shortly after the war ended.

79

LEFT A-BOMB DOME SEEN AT NIGHT WITH LANTERNS FLOATING IN THE WATER IN FOREGROUND. FROM MATSUHIGE YOSHITO, ED., *ATOMIC BOMB PHOTO TESTAMENT: A COLLECTION OF PHOTOGRAPHS BY THE PHOTOGRAPHERS WHO SURVIVED THE BOMBING IN HIROSHIMA* (1996)

PREVIOUS HIROSHIMA PEACE MEMORIAL PARK, WITH CENOTAPH IN FOREGROUND, 2001. PHOTO BY ANDREAS PAULY

Peace Park came into existence during the short period of time when the ordinary framework of Japanese urban planning had dissolved, leaving room for new solutions. It stands as a reminder that city planning can include identifiable landmarks and local particularities. Tange stated:

[P]eace park is not that heart of an ideal city to which we have been mentally so attached. It represents an unusual and fortunate opportunity in Japan. For it has been possible to gain the co-operation of various administrative and governing interests and get them to agree to act together as a single body so that the realization of this project may be possible.[48]

Regrettably, this window of opportunity closed again once the local and national administrations were reconstituted in the 1950s.

Another, more ironic factor affecting the re-creation of Hiroshima as a city devoted to peace was the advent of the Korean War in 1950. The same year in which construction on the Peace Memorial Hall began, the American army was placing orders in Japan for matériel like jeeps, trucks, and machine-gun parts. Military equipment was manufactured in Hiroshima's factories. The city's economic revival, which was also aided by the construction of the Peace Center, was thus intimately related to war. Just as Peace Boulevard started out as a firebreak created for military reasons, peace and war continued to be intertwined in the city.

Apart from Peace Memorial Park, as noted, few of Tange's ideas came to fruition. Elsewhere in the city, desperate for housing, Hiroshima's residents quickly constructed flimsy buildings wherever they could, and land that was intended to be reserved for riverside parks and other public amenities was built on privately. It was only in 1966, after a sufficient number of public housing projects were constructed, that the so-called "A-bomb slums" were demolished to make way for parks along the river, thus realizing part of Tange's original scheme.

The Hiroshima of today does not exhibit the beauty, harmony, and elevated quality of life to which those in charge aspired. The peace park, museum, and boulevard exist, but they have been absorbed into an ordinary Japanese city without an overall vision on the scale imagined by Tange, and with few other outstanding architectural landmarks or any general urban response to the city's unique history.[49] All Japanese cities, the ones that were bombed and those like Kyoto that were spared, now resemble one another. The economic forces of the postwar period destroyed as much of the built environment as did the air raids. In fact, many buildings in Hiroshima that the atomic bomb did not obliterate were torn down later. The Peace Center, situated in the center of Hiroshima, thus remains an isolated structure by comparison to ruins of churches and other buildings preserved in German cities, for example, Hamburg's Saint Jacobi or Berlin's Kaiser-Wilhelm-Gedächtniskirche.

HIROSHIMA PEACE MEMORIAL PARK, VIEW NORTH FROM PEACE MEMORIAL MUSEUM ALONG AXIS TO CENOTAPH AND A-BOMB DOME, 2001. PHOTO BY ANDREAS PAULY

A more comprehensive analysis of urban reconstruction and memorializing in the context of the period after World War II would have to take into account whether cities were on the side of the war's winners or losers. Warsaw, a city destroyed by the German aggressors, tried to recuperate its townscape; Rotterdam, on the other hand, while likewise destroyed by the Germans, tried to modernize its urban form. German cities, particularly Berlin, made strong statements about their newly won democracy and their rejection of Nazi politics and the architecture and planning that were associated with it.

The symbolism of Hiroshima and the discussion surrounding the atomic bomb are still very much alive today for local residents who lost loved ones and for those who are still dying, for the Japanese population as a whole, and, finally, for the international community. The United States in particular has struggled—and is still struggling—with its role in Hiroshima, as demonstrated by its efforts to prevent the United Nations from declaring the A-Bomb Dome a World International Heritage Site (the dome was finally added to the register in 1996) and the debate in 1995 over the Smithsonian's exhibition at the National Air and Space Museum featuring the *Enola Gay*, with its subsequent cancellation. The attempts to shut out nuclear memories have thus come back to haunt us.[50]

Yet if most Japanese cities have been rebuilt without obvious traces of the destruction that occurred only fifty years ago and few memorials recall it, Hiroshima remains one of the few cities literally to have undergone a complete change of heart. Tange's Peace Park stands in its midst as a reminder of the horrors of warfare, and particularly of the atomic bomb, but also of the possibilities of urban reinvention.

NOTES

1. This number does not include cities and settlements on the islands of Ryukyu, where battles on the ground and subsequent requisitions by the U.S. Army caused large-scale destruction.

2. One hundred fifteen cities that suffered extended damage were included in the policy statement "War Damage Restoration Planning" (*Sensai Fukko Toshikeikaku*). For the rebuilding of Japanese cities after World War II, see Carola Hein, Jeffry Diefendorf, and Yorifusa Ishida, eds., *Rebuilding Urban Japan after 1945* (London: Macmillan, forthcoming 2003).

3. Carola Hein, "Visionary Plans and Planners," in Nicolas Fiévé and Paul Waley, eds., *Japanese Capitals in Historical Perspective: Place, Power and Memory in Kyoto, Edo and Tokyo* (Richmond, Surrey, U.K.: Curzon, forthcoming 2002).

4. See Carola Hein et al., *Hauptstadt Berlin* (Berlin: Gebr. Mann Verlag, 1991).

5. For the reconstruction of Rotterdam, among many other articles, see Cor Wagenaar, "Rotterdam and the Model of the Welfare City," special issue on reconstruction in Europe after World War II, *Rassegna* 54, no. 2 (June 1993), pp. 42–49; and the essay by Han Meyer in the present volume.

6. English-language publications use the name Hiroshima Peace Center. This name reflects Tange's larger aim to transform the entire city of Hiroshima, with Peace Memorial Park and its buildings and memorials as its core. See Udo Kultermann, ed., *Kenzo Tange, 1946–1969: Architecture and Urban Design* (New York: Praeger, 1970); and Kenzo Tange, *40 ans d'urbanisme et d'architecture* (Tokyo: Process Architecture Publishing, 1987).

7. The reasons the bomb was dropped have been the subject of debate and controversy for many years. One official argument has been that the bomb was necessary to end the war as soon as possible and to avoid massive American casualties. See J. Samuel Walker, *Prompt and Utter Destruction: Truman and the Use of Atomic Bombs against Japan* (Chapel Hill: University of North Carolina Press, 1997).

8. As Laura Hein and Mark Selden point out, "Beginning in 1945, United States officials prevented wide distribution of most images of the bomb's destruction, particularly of the human havoc it wrought, and suppressed information about radiation, its most terrifying effect." Laura Hein and Mark Selden, "Commemoration and Silence: Fifty Years of Remembering the Bomb in America and Japan," in Hein and Selden, eds., *Living with the Bomb. American and Japanese Cultural Conflicts in the Nuclear Age* (Armonk, N.Y.; and London: M. E. Sharpe, 1997), p. 4. For the construction of official narratives by both the Americans and the Japanese, see ibid., p. 5.

9. See Norioki Ishimaru, "Reconstructing Hiroshima and Preserving the Reconstructed City," in Hein, Diefendorf, and Ishida, eds., *Rebuilding Urban Japan*. Also see Walker, *Prompt and Utter Destruction*, p. 77.

10. For the destruction and reconstruction of Tokyo, see Hiro Ichikawa, "Reconstructing Tokyo: The Attempt to Transform a Metropolis," in Hein, Diefendorf, and Ishida, eds., *Rebuilding Urban Japan*; and Walker, *Prompt and Utter Destruction*, p. 28. The destruction of Hiroshima was exceptional in many regards, as a single bomb caused the obliteration of an entire city as well as long-term health problems related to radiation. Another difference between the atomic and conventional bombs was the form and extent of the impact. While conventional bombing left irregular patterns of destruction in other cities, in the case of Hiroshima the destruction was almost circular around the hypocenter.

11. *Hiroshima Peace Reader*, 10th ed. (Hiroshima: Hiroshima Peace Culture Foundation, 1994), p. 47.

12. For a discussion of the fate of American-born children of Japanese immigrants who were in Hiroshima at the time of the atomic bombing see Rinjiro Sodei, "Were We the Enemy? American *Hibakusha*," in Hein and Selden, eds., *Living with the Bomb*, pp. 232–59.

13. The film *Hiroshima, mon Amour* was directed by Alain Resnais from a screenplay by Marguerite Duras, and opened in 1959.

14. *Hiroshima Peace Reader*, p. 30.

15. For the choice of cities as possible targets of the atomic bomb, see Walker, *Prompt and Utter Destruction*, p. 61; and Gar Alperovitz, *The Decision to Use the Atomic Bomb* (New York: Vintage Books, 1995), pp. 515–34.

16. Alperovitz, *The Decision to Use the Atomic Bomb*, p. 526.

17. Ibid., p. 533.

18. According to the *Hiroshima Peace Reader* (p. 30), Hiroshima was the site of the Second General Headquarters, while the First General Headquarters was in Tokyo.

19. Hein and Selden, "Commemoration and Silence," p. 4.

20. Seiji Imahori stated in 1985, "In Japan, every one from successive prime ministers to the Communist Party has repeatedly declared [us] 'the only nation ever to have been atom-bombed' [*yuiitsu no hibakukoku*]," quoted in James J. Orr, *The Victim as Hero: Ideologies of Peace and National Identity in Postwar Japan* (Honolulu: University of Hawaii Press, 2001). p. 1.

21. *Hiroshima Peace Reader*, p. 19.

22. Ibid., p. 44.

23. Quoted in *Peace City Hiroshima* (Tokyo: Dai Nippon Printing Co., n.d.).

24. For Tange's early career and his first encounter with Le Corbusier's architecture, see David B. Stewart, *The Making of a Modern Japanese Architecture, 1868 to the Present* (Tokyo and New York: Kodansha International, 1987), p. 170.

25. See chap. 10, "Tange Kenzo's Tokyo Monuments, New Authority and Old Architectural Ambitions," in William H. Coaldrake, *Architecture and Authority in Japan* (London and New York: Routledge, 1996), pp. 251–77.

26. For a discussion of the 1951 CIAM meeting, see J. Tyrrwhitt, J. L. Sert, and E. N. Rogers, *The Heart of the City* (London: Lund, Humphries, 1952).

27. Carola Hein, "La Culture des concours en Allemagne et au Japon," *A+* 167 (Brussels, 2001), pp. 96–102.

28. See Botond Bognar and Togo Murano, *Togo Murano: Master Architect of Japan* (New York: Rizzoli International Publications, 1996).

29. The competition for the monument to Greater East Asia and its meaning in the creation of Japanese modernism are discussed in Shoichi Inoue, "Fascism and Architecture in Japan," photocopy of lecture presented at the symposium "Architecture and Modern Japan," October 21, 2000, Columbia University; and Shoichi Inoue, *Ato, kicchu, japanesuku: daitoa no pousto modan* (Tokyo: Seidoshi, 1987).

30. *Hiroshima Peace Reader*, p. 45.

31. "Shinsahyo," *Kenchikuzasshi* 10–11 (Tokyo: Architectural Institute of Japan, 1949), pp. 37–39.

32. For a further examination of Tange's attitude toward traditional Japanese architecture, see Cherie Wendelken, "Aesthetics and Reconstruction: Japanese Architectural Culture in the 1950s," in Hein, Diefendorf, and Ishida, eds., *Rebuilding Urban Japan*.

33. *Peace City Hiroshima*, p. 2.

34. Ibid.

35. The buildings were originally planned to consist of a conference hall capable of holding 2,500 people, discussion rooms, offices, a library, and a banquet hall, as well as exhibition galleries for atomic bomb relics and other objects. Ibid., p. 3.

36. Masaki Naka, *Kindaikenchikuka Tange Kenzo ron* (Tokyo: Kindaikenchikusha, 1983), p. 175.

37. Ibid., p. 179.

38. The name of the British architect is given in *katakana* as "Jappe." Ibid., p. 165.

39. Ibid., p. 165.

40. "Shinsahyo," pp. 37–39; and Naka, *Kindaikenchikuka Tange Kenzo ron*, p. 172.

41. Edita Morris, *The Flowers of Hiroshima* (New York: Viking Press, 1959), pp. 40–42.

42. It is worth noting that the occupation army apparently did not object to Tange's design, nor, in general, did it intervene much in religious affairs in Japan during the postwar period. While the emperor was forced to relinquish his deitylike status, places of religious significance related to the Imperial House were maintained.

43. The Japanese inscription reads, "Yasuraka ni nemutte kudasai, ayamachi ha kurikaishimasenkara."

44. Morris, *The Flowers of Hiroshima*, pp. 19–21.

45. Naka, *Kindaikenchikuka Tange Kenzo ron*, p. 165.

46. I would like to thank Joan Ockman for drawing this point to my attention. See Naka, *Kindaikenchikuka Tange Kenzo ron*, pp. 167–68.

47. See Giuliano Gresleri and Dario Matteoni, *La città mondiale: Andersen, Hébrard, Otlet, Le Corbusier* (Venice: Polis/Marsilio Editore, 1982).

48. Paolo Riani, *Kenzo Tange* (London and New York: Hamlyn, 1970), pp. 8–10.

49. N. Ishimaru et al., eds., *Architectural Witnesses to the Atomic Bombing: A Record for the Future* (Hiroshima: Hiroshima Peace Memorial Museum, 1996).

50. Michael Perlman, *Hiroshima Forever: The Ecology of Mourning* (Barrytown, N.Y., and St. Paul, Minn.: Barrytown Ltd. for Station Hill Arts, 1995), p. 79.

ROTTERDAM
THE PROMISE OF A NEW, MODERN SOCIETY IN A NEW, MODERN CITY
1940 TO THE PRESENT

Han Meyer

At first glance it might seem natural to compare New York after September 2001 to Rotterdam after the May 1940 bombing by Nazi Germany. Both cities were the victim of a hostile attack by air that demolished an important part of the inner city. There are many obvious differences between the two events, however. In Rotterdam, the affected area was much larger than the World Trade Center and vicinity. On the other hand, the number of victims in New York exceeded that in the Dutch city.

From an urbanistic point of view, the most crucial difference concerns the respective sociocultural roles of these two places and the cultural expectations relating to their reconstruction. In Rotterdam, German bombs hit an old, partly medieval, poorly built city, which had been criticized for almost a century because of its chaotic structures. City planners and politicians had dreamed for years of cleaning up the old city and creating a brand-new, modern metropolis; the razed area of the center now provided the possibility for a fundamental modernization. Thus the ensuing reconstruction policy was based on the promise of modernity: instead of remaining a backward city, Rotterdam had the chance to become a uniquely modern one. In contrast, the terrorists who struck New York destroyed one of the most important icons of modernism.

On May 10, 1940, the German army invaded the Netherlands, where it was confronted with unexpected resistance from the poorly armed Dutch army. Four days later, on May 14, the Germans bombed Rotterdam in a move to force the Dutch to capitulate. The bombing was a warning: the Germans threatened to bomb Amsterdam if resistance continued. The Dutch government surrendered on May 15. From that day until it was finally liberated by the Allies on May 5, 1945, the Netherlands was subject to German occupation.

During the first years after the bombing, Rotterdam seemed a schizophrenic city. On the one hand, the city had suffered 1,150 deaths; 10,000 people were left homeless; and approximately 6,500 acres of the downtown area were completely destroyed, including 11,000 buildings, among which were 25,000 apartments and many factories, shops, schools, churches, movie theaters, and other structures. This gutting of the city generated enormous horror, fury, and despair—expressed in the Russian-born French sculptor Ossip Zadkine's sculpture for Rotterdam, *The Destroyed City*, in which the figure's rib cage, like the city's heart, is empty. Soon, however, regret and pain were transformed into optimism. The bombing, though itself a nightmare, came to be considered a condition for making the dream of a modern city a reality.

The United States played an important role in the reconstruction of the Netherlands. The Marshall Plan, initiated by U.S. Secretary of State George Marshall in 1947, contributed large amounts of American money to aid the postwar economic recovery. Meanwhile, American urban planning ideals served as inspiration for the development of new urban concepts in Rotterdam. The American city, particularly New York, was considered "the forerunner of the city of a new scale," as Sigfried Giedion wrote in *Space, Time and Architecture*.

The most heavily damaged city in Holland, Rotterdam, was also the one that had the greatest admiration for the American city. This regard had already been evident during the 1930s in debates surrounding urban reconstruction held among local architects, urbanists, business and industrial leaders, and politicians. Architects and urban designers traveled frequently to New York and Chicago and were impressed by American architecture and urbanism. American advisers like Lewis Mumford were invited to Rotterdam; they in turn would proclaim Rotterdam the ideal model of the new modern city following its rebuilding.

AN EXEMPLAR OF THE DUTCH CITY

Before May 1940 Rotterdam typified the traditional Dutch city. For cities in Holland, the relationship between city and water is double-edged: water both benefits the city, permitting fishing, shipping, and trading, and presents a danger to the low-lying land areas during periods of flooding. The structure and parceling of the urban ground plan is directly related to the management of water.

The dike has always been an especially important component of the urban structure. This is, first, because it functions not only as a flood barrier but also as a major traffic artery and, indeed, the city's main street. As in many Dutch cities, the Rotterdam dike is called Hoogstraat (High Street), referring to the high, dry roadway running along its top. Second, the dike divides the city into two different parts: the "polder city," inside the dikes, protected against floods, and the "water city," outside the dikes. During the eighteenth and nineteenth centuries the polder city became the town's neglected backyard, characterized by a structure of small parcels of land, badly constructed buildings, narrow alleys, and a network of canals and ditches with very poor water quality. The result was that public health conditions in the polder city were abysmal, producing three dramatic cholera epidemics during the mid-nineteenth century.

In contrast, the water city developed outside the dikes in Rotterdam since the sixteenth century took advantage of its open access to the river, which provided favorable circumstances for shipping-related activities, as well as better conditions for public health. The only disadvantage was the increased inconvenience, and occasional risk, in times of high tide, but these problems were regarded as acceptable in return for the advantages of an unimpeded relation to the river. The water city grew into the most important part of the city: all major public and commercial buildings, trade offices, including the stock exchange and other financial institutions, were located here. The riverfront quay, called "Boompjes," in

MAP OF ROTTERDAM, 1920

BIRD'S-EYE VIEW OF ROTTERDAM FROM THE SOUTH, 1855.
DRAWING BY CANELLE. MUNICIPAL ARCHIVES, ROTTERDAM

TOP ROTTERDAM CITY CENTER, 1939. AERIAL VIEW FROM THE NORTH WITH THE NEW COOLSINGEL IN THE FOREGROUND.
MUNICIPAL ARCHIVES, ROTTERDAM

BOTTOM ROTTERDAM CITY CENTER, 1945. AERIAL VIEW FROM THE NORTH WITH THE SURVIVING CITY HALL IN THE FOREGROUND.
MUNICIPAL ARCHIVES, ROTTERDAM

particular became the main public promenade and the location of the homes of many wealthy merchants and other prominent citizens. (Its name, meaning "small trees," comes from the fact that it was planted with lime trees.) To this day, the area between the Hoogstraat and the river is still known as the water city. Together, the polder city and the water city constitute the historic center of Rotterdam.

Beginning in the mid-nineteenth century, several plans were set in motion for cleaning up the city. The polder city had been densely built, owing to an increase in its population and the practical impossibility of extending its territory, and it posed a serious threat to public health. Meanwhile, the water city had become a problem in relation to traffic flow. At the same time, Rotterdam was discovered by the rest of Europe as international shipping companies found it an ideal port for the transit of goods between the Atlantic and the industrial German hinterland. By the end of the nineteenth century, new extensions of the city and the port came to be located on the left bank of the Nieuwe Maas River.

The historic city, however, was largely unable to accommodate the increased north-south traffic that accompanied the construction of an elevated rail- and roadway bridging the Nieuwe Maas in the 1860s. The Municipal Board of Rotterdam limited itself to some improvements in the canals and dikes of the polder city. Most of the energy devoted to urban development was focused on the expansion of the port and the city to the south (on the left riverbank) and to the west (toward the mouth of the river). The historic city remained essentially unchanged structurally since its founding.

The first important modernizations of the inner city occurred after World War I. The Coolsingel, the former limit of the historic city, was transformed into a major boulevard and became the new central axis, providing sites for a new city hall, chamber of commerce, and Central Post Office, as well as the main hospital, theaters, department stores, and other buildings. This major intervention marked the beginning of the process of moving the city center—the central business district— northwest of the historic city, from the water city to the Coolsingel. In the 1930s, the construction of a new urban motorway crossing the Nieuwe Maas to the west of the Coolsingel solidified the relocation.

LONGING FOR MODERNITY

Although the transformation of Rotterdam's historic city center had begun—slowly—city planners, politicians, and businesses were anxious to see it truly modernized. The longing for a radical modernization of the city was motivated by several factors. One was the desire for conditions that would allow for economic expansion and mobility. Rotterdam had become a major port, but opportunities for ancillary institutions like offices and banks were lacking. In short, there was no base for the infrastructure necessary to a central business district worthy of a city that by the 1930s had become Europe's largest port.

Moreover, poor circulation impeded mobility. The growing stream of cars and trucks moved through the narrow streets of the old city laboriously. The new Coolsingel and the new cross-river motorway produced some relief, but these were only a beginning.

The desire for modernity was also culturally and ideologically motivated. Since the end of the nineteenth century, debate in Rotterdam among the intelligentsia had been dominated by complaints about the lack of a vigorous intellectual and cultural climate. The city was faced with an increase in population of 10,000 inhabitants each year, mostly peasants coming from the south part of the Netherlands. During the early twentieth century, Rotterdam's image became one of a city of rural poor, living under desperate conditions and struggling to survive in an urban jungle.

FIGURE/GROUND DIAGRAMS OF
THE CITY CENTER
LEFT 1939
RIGHT 1945

The impetus for a radical modernization was thus stimulated by an increasing desire for civic culture, and spearheaded by a group of leading port entrepreneurs and business leaders. During the first few decades of the twentieth century, this group formed a network that was responsible for new urban amenities, such as a zoo, theaters, and museums, but also for public housing. The debate thus joined that revolving around modern architecture and new urban design concepts elsewhere in Europe. Important contributors to this civic culture of the 1930s included C. H. van Leeuwen, director of the Van Nelle tobacco, tea, and coffee company; J. Ph. Backx, head of Thomsen, Rotterdam's largest shipping company; and Karel Paul van de Mandele, director of the Bank of Rotterdam.

TWO CONCEPTS OF MODERNIZATION

While the desire to modernize was generally shared, two different conceptions of modern architecture and urbanism emerged. One view was expressed by Rotterdam's City Architect, W. G. Witteveen, who came out of the tradition of the great European urban transformations and of the Dutch urbanistic experiments of Hendrik Petrus Berlage. Witteveen's idea of modern Rotterdam was a city that would feature monumental urban spaces, like that of the Coolsingel, and have a strong architectural cohesiveness, dominated by boulevards and avenues with closed perimeter urban blocks. Witteveen was responsible for the new cross-river urban motorway, which indeed was designed as a coherent architectural element within the city. His masterpiece was a new residential area in northwest Rotterdam, Blijdorp. All his notions of the modern city are summarized in this design: boulevards in which the architecture of the flanking buildings is strictly regulated, and perimeter blocks with a strong architectonic coherence.

The other approach was represented by the architects of the modern movement, united in the Rotterdam architects' society Opbouw ("Building Up"). Its members included the architects Willem van Tijen, Johannes Brinkman, L. C. van der Vlugt, Johannes Hendrik van den Broek, and others. New concepts of modern residential buildings were developed, breaking with the traditional perimeter block and with the direct relation between streetscape and building. Rotterdam's civic leaders supported this approach. One of the results of this support was the new building for the Van Nelle factory, designed by Brinkman and commissioned by van Leeuwen. Soon the Van Nelle factory became the symbol of the enlightened modernization of Rotterdam.

During the 1930s the latent conflict between the two different approaches became manifest, for instance, in the development of the Blijdorp plan. One of the blocks of this residential district was designed by van den Broek, who wanted to break with the closed perimeter block. The block he designed opens onto an adjacent park, which creates a direct relationship between the park and the interior courtyard of the block. The block was constructed in spite of strong opposition from Witteveen.

RECONSTRUCTION AND CONTROVERSY

The Blijdorp controversy foreshadowed the struggles the design process of Rotterdam's reconstruction would face during the war. Immediately after the bombing of May 1940, Witteveen started to design a new urban plan for the devastated historic center. He completed it in just eight weeks.

Several things obliged Witteveen to work so quickly. First, he wanted to prevent the Germans from intervening in the planning process. During the first months of occupation, the Germans had not yet gained control of all local agencies, and the city administration of Rotterdam wanted to exploit this situation. Second, the clearing of the rubble of the bombed city center required an immediate ban on dumping. Witteveen saw an opportunity to combine this necessity with a response to the longstanding desire to rid the city of its many canals by transforming the archipelago of islands alongside the river into a new dike with an urban motorway. But the third reason for Witteveen's haste was perhaps the most important: to preclude the ideas of the Opbouw architects and the arbiters of civic culture from influencing the debate surrounding reconstruction.

The new design reflected all the elements of Witteveen's approach. The architect attempted to combine restoration of the historic city— respecting the collective memory of the city— with improved traffic circulation and the creation of conditions for the construction of large, representational buildings.

Witteveen was not able to prevent mounting criticism from those anxious to modernize. During the war years, impatient civic leaders founded "Club Rotterdam," which organized secret meetings in the Van Nelle factory and functioned as a shadow administration in the city. In the eyes of Club Rotterdam, Witteveen's plan was not radical enough, especially concerning the new traffic systems. Moreover, the group expressed strong objections to his desire to create monumental and architecturally uniform boulevards and avenues. This meant limiting private initiative, according to Club Rotterdam; they preferred to afford businesses a maximum of architectural freedom so as to stimulate private participation in the reconstruction process. To Club Rotterdam, New York represented an ideal approach, in which there was a clear division of responsibilities between the public and the private sector: the public sector was responsible for the layout of a neutral network of streets, while the private sector had laissez-faire to build.

Finally, at the end of the war, in 1944, Club Rotterdam forced Witteveen to resign. He was succeeded by C. van Traa, the former associate director of the City Planning Department.

THE DESIGN OF A MODERN CITY

Thus four years after the bombing, a brand-new approach to reconstruction design commenced in Rotterdam. Van Traa's ideas were much more radical and at the same time much more pragmatic than Witteveen's design had been. His new plan included a number of important elements.

The first of these was a complete reparceling of land. In 1940, all the privately owned land in the city center had been appropriated by the Dutch government. Van Traa went well beyond the previous moderate parceling, forcing a spectacular increase in the parcels' size. Ninety percent of the parcels in the prewar center were 160 to 325 square feet; in the postwar city eighty percent of the parcels were 650 to 3,250 square feet. Landowners whose parcels were expropriated had first choice in the redistribution of the land, but most of them were forced to buy a larger parcel and at another site than the original one. Owners who were not able to invest in the larger parcel received financial compensation.

In conformance with the ideas of the modern movement, van Traa wanted to create a clear functional zoning of the city center. In his view, the center was not a place for residential districts; only shopkeepers and other businesspeople were supposed to live there. His new design did provide for some apartment buildings, but these were built with the understanding that apartments could be converted into offices as needed over time.

The most important aspect of this functional zoning was the definitive removal of the central business and shopping districts from the historic water city to the area west of the Coolsingel. This consolidated a process that already had begun before the war. As the former water city became a center of river-going vessels, the real center was no longer focused on the river. The increasing estrangement between city center and river that had begun with the destruction of the famous Boompjes waterfront by bombing, and continued with the relocation of the center to the Coolsingel area, was completed by the construction of a new dike along the Boompjes.

Another requirement for a modern city, according to Van Traa, was openness, an expression of the new transparent, democratic society of the future. "Openness is social progress!" was his motto. Open space was to dominate the postwar city center: in the prewar city center fifty-one percent of the surface area was occupied by buildings; in Van Traa's plan for the postwar city, only thirty-one percent.

The new openness represented more than simply a new balance between built mass and open space. It also offered a new system of public spaces and new building typologies. Priority was given to the automobile. The basic framework of the reconstruction plan was an orthogonal grid of motorways, intended to afford maximum free access from the national highways to the city center and vice versa. The Coolsingel assumed the role of central boulevard in this framework and underwent yet another transformation.

The prewar Coolsingel had been modeled on the example of the Parisian boulevard, which was of limited length and closed at the extremities by buildings or statues. The new postwar Coolsingel was inspired by New York's Fifth Avenue, with an unlimited length and an open view to the horizon. Actually, the new openness of the Coolsingel was not intended to give a view of the horizon, but of the river, an expression of the open society and its open relationship to the world. This "window" onto the river was to counteract the estrangement between center and river. To achieve this, one of the most remarkable buildings of the interwar period, the Bijenkorf department store, designed by Willem Dudok, was demolished to make room for a rather abstract idea of openness and relationship to the river.

Another feature of the new relationship between city and river was the urban motorway along the river east of the center. This thoroughfare, the Maasboulevard, was also inspired by American examples like the Henry Hudson Parkway in New York. To this day, this boulevard is regarded as the most beautiful entrance to a city in Holland.

It followed, of course, that the new modern urban plan would be infilled with modern architecture. Rotterdam seemed to become a laboratory for architects of the modern movement. In search of new building typologies, they began to develop new concepts, especially prompted by two factors. First, most of the shops that had been demolished in the devastated area of the center had relocated to its edge. During the first years of the war, the city constructed several such temporary shopping centers. After the war, the shopkeepers felt relatively comfortable in their new locations and avoided returning to the original sites, preferring not to be among the pioneers in a desert that was still euphemistically being called "city center."

93

TOP DESIGN FOR THE RECONSTRUCTION OF ROTTERDAM CITY CENTER BY W. G. WITTEVEEN, 1940. MUNICIPAL ARCHIVES, ROTTERDAM
BOTTOM DESIGN FOR THE RECONSTRUCTION OF ROTTERDAM CITY CENTER BY C. VAN TRAA, 1946. MUNICIPAL ARCHIVES, ROTTERDAM

In order to convince shopkeepers and businesspeople to return, it was necessary to develop collectively organized accommodations for shops and small companies. The second factor encouraging new building typologies was the need for a new balance between pedestrians, through traffic, and the organization of loading and discharge for shops, department stores, and other commercial activities. In the prewar city the combination of these three functions in the same street had resulted in confusion and frustration. Two examples illustrate the search for new typologies: the Lijnbaan shopping center and the Groothandelsgebouw (Collective Trade Building).

The Lijnbaan was designed by Van den Broek and Bakema, based on their study trips to American cities like Chicago and New York. With the Lijnbaan, the team designed the world's first pedestrian shopping center. The central street is lined by shops and integrated into the street grid, but is not accessible by car. Loading and discharge take place in special streets behind the shop buildings. Adjacent large apartment buildings flank the Lijnbaan; their collective gardens open directly onto the public street. The revolutionary aspect of the Lijnbaan ensemble is the new organization of shopping, through traffic, loading and discharge, residential space, and greenery. Whereas in the old city different functions were mixed together in a chaotic way, the Lijnbaan displays a clear new arrangement of urban functions. It became a paradigm of the new, functionalist Rotterdam.

The Groothandelsgebouw is an enormous building by Rotterdam standards: 1,300 feet long and 260 feet wide. The building provides space for numerous trade companies, offices, and small manufacturers, as well as for shops, restaurants, and a movie theater. Here what is revolutionary is that the design concept locates loading and discharge activities in the interior of the block. The street penetrates the building, which seems to be an enormous urban machine.

ROTTERDAM'S
RECONSTRUCTION REVISITED

During the 1950s and early 1960s, Rotterdam was lauded as a courageous and progressive example of postwar reconstruction. The new city was widely considered the outstanding implementation of the ideals of the modern movement. American critics and planners like Lewis Mumford and Edmund Bacon wrote lyrical articles about Rotterdam. According to Mumford, Rotterdam was the most successful example of postwar reconstruction, an enlightened model of Western urbanism.

During the second half of the 1960s, however, doubts and criticism increasingly began to surface. In 1968, the V & D department store commissioned Rob Wentholt to write a book on the new city to commemorate the seventy-fifth birthday of the company and to celebrate the postwar city center. V & D was very interested in the success of the reconstruction as it had been the first department store with the courage to open a new building in the empty city center in 1950.

According to Wentholt, however, there was nothing to celebrate. His book, *De Binnenstadsbeleving en Rotterdam* (The inner-city experience of Rotterdam), was a sharp and critical review of the results of more than two decades of reconstruction. Wentholt criticized the results of the reconstruction as dull and empty, a city still without a heart, without an identity, and without the signs and structures of a collective memory.

The once cultivated openness appeared to him to be simply emptiness, a city without a critical mass, where in the late evening the streets were so desolate that one could shoot a cannon without hitting anyone. In cities of similar size, like Amsterdam and the Hague, the population density in the center was almost ten times that of Rotterdam. This problem increased when, beginning in the mid 1960s, the population of the city started to decrease further because of flight to the suburbs.

A second criticism made by Wentholt had to do with the poor quality of the public space. There was too much of it in the center of Rotterdam; it was difficult to control and to make culturally meaningful. The absence of a clear concept of public space, the use of cheap materials, and the many circulation routes reinforced the impression of urban blight.

What was most significant in Wentholt's attack was what he saw as the absence of history in modern Rotterdam. The triumphant farewell to the historic city during the early reconstruction period, and the conception of the center as a tabula rasa, had ultimately produced a spiritual vacuum, not to mention waves of misplaced nostalgia. As Wentholt pointed out, people increasingly idealized the prewar city center as intimate and inviting and as having character and identity.

Wentholt also especially criticized the disappearance of any relationship between city center and river. According to the concepts of the reconstruction, this relationship should in fact have been intensified by the center's role as a window onto the river. As already suggested, however, this idea appeared to be no more than an abstraction, all the more so with the construction of the high new dike along the river during the 1950s and the disappearance of shipping-related activities from the city center's harborfront during the 1960s.

Wentholt's book served as a wake-up call to the city. For many residents, it reflected what they were already thinking. It also connected with the growing dissatisfaction that was developing internationally in relation to modern architecture and urbanism. The utopia of the modern movement had become unconvincing, and Wentholt's book exposed it as a rigid dogma.

By the 1970s, the postwar approach to Rotterdam's reconstruction was definitively out of date. The city government halted completion of the network of roads, with the result that some traffic routes in the center area are characterized today by strange curves and breaks. The city administration placed priority on expanding the residential function of the city center, and thousands of new apartment buildings were added in the central area. Then, during the 1980s and 1990s, Rotterdam's urban planners shifted their emphasis to improving the quality of public space, and to the quantity and variety of urban functions: new theaters, museums, and other public buildings were constructed.

Last but not least, during the 1990s, much energy was devoted to developing a new relationship between the city and the river. The obsolete harbor area on the left bank of the Nieuwe Maas, "Kop van Zuid" (Head of the South), was reconfigured into a new extension of the city center in an attempt to make the river the center of the city instead of its border. This is still a work in progress, as is the planned improvement of the area occupied by the former water city. In these new developments, the return of the perimeter block is striking.

Thus, after initially attempting to remake itself by following American examples of city planning, Rotterdam has rediscovered its European, and especially Dutch, urbanistic roots. More than fifty years after the design process of postwar reconstruction began, Witteveen's principles and approach have been rehabilitated.

REFERENCES

Andela, Gerrie, and Cor Wagenaar, eds. *Een Stad voor het leven. Wederopbouw Rotterdam 1940–1965* (A city for living. Reconstruction Rotterdam 1940–1965). Rotterdam: 010, 1995.

Bacon, Edmund. *Design of Cities.* New York: Viking, 1967.

Blijstra, R. *Rotterdam, Stad in Beweging* (Rotterdam, city in motion) Amsterdam: Arbeiderspers, 1965.

Bosma, Koos, and Cor Wagenaar, eds. *Een geruisloze doorbraak. De geschiedenis van architectuur en stedebouw tijdens de bezetting en de wederopbouw van Nederland* (A silent bursting. The history of architecture and urbanism during the occupation and reconstruction of the Netherlands). Rotterdam: Nederlands Architectuur Instituut, 1995.

Camp, D'Laine, and Michelle Provoost, eds. *Stadstimmeren: Rotterdam 650 Years.* Rotterdam: City of Rotterdam, 1990.

Gemeente Rotterdam (City of Rotterdam). *Het Nieuwe Hart van Rotterdam. Toelichting op het basisplan voor den herbouw van de binnenstad van Rotterdam* (The new heart of Rotterdam. Explanation of the basic plan for the rebuilding of the inner city of Rotterdam). Rotterdam: City of Rotterdam, 1946.

Giedion, Sigfried. *Space, Time and Architecture: The Growth of a New Tradition.* Cambridge, Mass.: MIT Press, 1941.

Meyer, Han. *City and Port: Urban Planning as a Cultural Venture in London, Barcelona, New York and Rotterdam.* Utrecht: International Books, 1999.

Mumford, Lewis. "The Skyline. Een wandeling door de Rotterdamse city met een lofzang op de Lijnbaan" (A walk through the city of Rotterdam with praise for the Lijnbaan). *Bouw,* November 30, 1957.

Roelofsz, E. *De Wederopbouw van Rotterdam 1940–1950* (The reconstruction of Rotterdam 1940–1950). Rotterdam: VUGA's, 1989.

Rutgers, J. "De herbouw van Rotterdam, in het bijzonder in verband met de grondexploitatie" (The reconstruction of Rotterdam, especially in relation to the exploitation of ground). *De Ingenieur,* February 11, 1955.

van Schilfgaarde, P. *De Wederopbouw van Rotterdam. Stedelijke herverkaveling in de praktijk* (The reconstruction of Rotterdam. Urban reparceling in practice). Gravenhage, the Netherlands: VUGA's, 1987.

van Traa, C., ed. *Rotterdam—de geschiedenis van tien jaren wederopbouw* (Rotterdam—A history of ten years of reconstruction). Rotterdam: City of Rotterdam, 1955.

Wagenaar, Cor. *Welvaartstad in wording. De wederopbouw van Rotterdam 1940–1952* (The welfare city in process of formation.The reconstruction of Rotterdam 1940–1952). Rotterdam: Nederlands Architectuur Instituut, 1992.

Wentholt, Rob. *De Binnenstadsbeleving en Rotterdam* (The inner-city experience of Rotterdam). Rotterdam: Ad Donkers, 1968.

PLYMOUTH
RECONSTRUCTION
AFTER WORLD WAR II

Alan Powers

In his 1998 book *The English*, the broadcaster Jeremy Paxman complains that the English people fail to understand the value of urban life. "The most recent calamity to befall England," he writes, "was for her cities to be half-bombed during the war: the measure of misfortune not so much what was lost as what replaced it. When the Luftwaffe gave the English the opportunity to rebuild their cities more graciously, they merely recreated worse versions of what had been there before."[1] This comment typifies a present disdain for the way that British cities bombed during World War II were reconstructed, very different from the idealism of the planners and architects who engaged in the task. The planners and politicians who worked on the rebuilding of the city of Plymouth aimed for exactly the qualities of "graciousness" that Paxman finds lacking. Their promise that urban living would become more convenient and enjoyable seems not to have come true.

Plymouth is the principal administrative and commercial center of southwestern England, beautifully situated by the sea, but with a protective harbor and anchorage that made it a scene of naval history beginning in Elizabethan times. The city was heavily bombed by German aircraft between July 6, 1940, and May 1941. It was a target because of the strategic importance of its naval dockyard, but the bombing also belonged to the same attempt to reduce civilian morale that was behind the "Moonlight Sonata" raid on Coventry on the night of November 14, 1940. The destruction of Plymouth was less sudden than Coventry's single night of holocaust, but quantitatively greater.

The writer Christopher Sykes describes the experience of the Plymouth bombing on the night of March 20, 1941, in his biography of Nancy Astor, the Virginia-born Member of Parliament for one of the sections of the city, and wife of the Lord Mayor, Waldorf Astor. The Astors had taken the king and queen on a tour of the already damaged city the same day. Two and a half hours after the royal couple left, Plymouth experienced its worst raid, which destroyed most of the city center. Sykes describes what happened to the Astors that night:

A bomb exploded near the house and smashed all the glass on the Hoe side of Elliot Terrace [the Astors' house in Plymouth since 1909]. An air-raid warden came down the street and ordered the inhabitants to go down into the basements. The Astor party obeyed and, as Ben Robertson, an American journalist who was staying with the Astors at the time, related, Nancy "talked about Virginia and her childhood and the tobacco fields and about Rose Harrison, her maid, saying that Rose and she had worked together for thirty years....Someone called in to say that an incendiary was on the roof. 'Come on everybody,' called Lady Astor, 'get the sandbags. Where in hell are the buckets?' From this we were up and down the stairs. Once she stopped by a blasted window to look at Plymouth which for miles was a blazing fire. Her eyes filled with tears, and pushing back her steel hat she said, 'There goes thirty years of our lives, but we'll build it again.'"[2]

In April 1941, 1,500 houses were beyond repair and virtually the whole of the retail center of the city was unusable. If the raids caught the Astors unprepared, the situation for the rest of Plymouth was no better. At first, there was no organized emergency fire service, nor any plans for evacuation. Lady Astor rallied morale by turning cartwheels and somersaults around the room when visiting shelters, and shouting, "Are we downhearted?" but she also described the lack of evacuation plans to the press as "the greatest flop of the war"; only by April 29 were 10,000 school children removed to the country, by which time the worst of the bombing was over.[3] Three hundred thirty-six civilians were killed, including seventy-two in an underground shelter that was hit directly, and there were other casualties, such as the eighty men in a petty officers' block in the Royal Naval Barracks. Bad news was often suppressed for reasons of morale, but, as in the case of Coventry, the commitment to reconstruction seems to have been linked to a guilty sense that more precautions might have been taken.

A number of heroic myths about wartime Plymouth developed, some of which have since been cast into doubt. The most picturesque was the dancing on the Hoe, the elevated grassy plateau overlooking Plymouth Sound, where Sir Francis Drake had coolly continued his game of bowls when told of the advancing Spanish Armada in 1588. In 1941 and for the remainder of the war, a band played on the Hoe in the afternoon, often supplied by visiting U.S. Navy ships and bringing the latest swing tunes. The dancers, however, were apparently not primarily those who were spending the nights huddled in cellars, but people who came in from outlying villages and returned home to safety each night.[4]

Prime Minister Winston Churchill was persuaded to visit the city on May 2 and rallied the citizens by proclaiming, "Your homes are low but your hearts are high." When his eyes filled with tears at the sight of the destruction, however, Lady Astor broke in with, "It's all very well to cry. You've got to do something."[5] The newly appointed Minister of Works and Buildings, Lord Reith (formerly the Director General of the BBC), also came to Plymouth, in July 1941. He urged the city to begin ambitious reconstruction plans, "boldly and comprehensively," as he had already done with the City Architect of Coventry and his team, although in that case planning had begun even before the war and was merely accelerated by the bombing.

FRONTISPIECE STREET IN PLYMOUTH AFTER THE BOMBING. FROM *A PLAN FOR PLYMOUTH*, 1943. COLLECTION OF ALAN POWERS

The promise of future social improvement became one of the unofficial war aims during the blitz.[6] Planning for reconstruction was a way of improving morale and of fulfilling long-held goals on the part of left-wing campaigners. The special issue of *Picture Post* magazine of January 4, 1941, titled "A Plan for New Britain," was one of the exemplars and included proposals for planning town and country along with schemes for a national health service, education, and employment. The article "The New Britain Must be Planned," by the architect Maxwell Fry, depicted an imaginary city center with congested housing that shared many characteristics with prewar Plymouth, and contrasted it with a future city along Corbusian lines, although some of its buildings are more Art Deco in character, resembling some of those built later in postwar Plymouth.[7]

Plymouth had no City Architect in 1941, but, as was more common, a City Engineer—the Scotsman James Paton Watson, appointed in 1938, who had the primary responsibility of producing a reconstruction plan. Others contributed their ideas, which included a scheme for a new commercial area in the form of a ring of shops with a central underground parking lot that was devised by a Mr. G. Holmes, chairman of the Housing Committee. Another proposal was for rebuilding the shopping center farther north to serve the new suburbs.[8] There was some pressure for an international competition, and some for giving Paton Watson sole responsibility, but the Chamber of Commerce favored an outside expert. Paton Watson was therefore joined by Sir Patrick Abercrombie, professor of town planning at London University and the founder-editor of the *Town Planning Review* in 1913.[9] His appointment was predictable, as he was the leader in his small field, although he was already heavily committed during these years to work on the County of London Plan (1943) and the Greater London Plan (1944) which, while similar in intention to the Plymouth Plan, undoubtedly occupied more of his time. Perhaps Abercrombie felt that Plymouth was in good hands with Paton Watson. The latter "considered that much of his own role consisted of keeping his poet-architect partner's feet firmly on the ground."[10]

101

PATRICK ABERCROMBIE, LORD ASTOR, AND JAMES PATON WATSON
WITH MODEL FOR CENTRAL PLYMOUTH. PLYMOUTH CITY LIBRARIES

PROPOSED CENTRAL LAYOUT FOR PLYMOUTH.
FROM *A PLAN FOR PLYMOUTH*, 1943. COLLECTION OF ALAN POWERS

Lord Astor himself was interested in planning issues, believing that planning would help public health. Before the war, as Brian Chalkley and John Goodridge write, "he had gone to considerable lengths to offer better housing to those in the most overcrowded districts, including building a model estate at Mount Gould on the eastern outskirts of the town."[11] Although a Conservative, Astor believed in a high level of state intervention in planning in order to achieve the ends he desired, even advocating the nationalization of agricultural land. *A Plan for Plymouth* was published in book form in 1943. Handsomely produced in quarto, with foldout color maps, architectural perspectives, and black-and-white photographs of the city past and present, it was priced at ten shillings and sixpence, which was considered very good value and implied a high level of subsidy.[12] It included a foreword by the American ambassador, John G. Winant, who asserted, "No place in Britain has firmer historical ties with the New World," and quoted the words of the Mayflower Compact concerning what is "most mete and convenient for the general good."[13]

If most of the hard work for the Plymouth Plan was accomplished by Paton Watson and his staff, the Plan's authorship is seen inevitably as Abercrombie's. Present since the inception of professional town planning in Britain in 1910, Abercrombie combined four different visions of its purpose. Early in his career, he joined the School of Civic Design at Liverpool University at a time when it advocated formal architectural solutions to city centers, inspired by the American City Beautiful movement, yet Abercrombie was also attracted to the very different priorities proposed by Patrick Geddes, whom he met during the same period.

Abercrombie followed Geddes in emphasizing the regional scope of planning; like Geddes he believed in the reciprocity of town and countryside. Abercrombie's personal response to the loss of rural identity in the period following World War I prompted the founding of the Council for the Preservation of Rural England (CPRE) in 1926, with the goal of constructive planning rather than simply reacting against modernization and change. If CPRE united the divergent interests of modernist and traditionalist architects, so also did the writings of Geddes's American disciple, Lewis Mumford, who is quoted several times in *A Plan for Plymouth*. Mumford's book *The Culture of Cities*, first published in England in 1938, had a wide influence on a younger generation of architect-planners working in Coventry, London, and elsewhere during the war years.[14] Abercrombie and most other English planners shared Geddes's belief in the cultural value of old buildings in creating identity and variety in a city, although they often went futher than his practice of "conservative surgery" in their more radical removal of historic urban context.

One of Geddes's themes is the importance of ceremonial spaces in cities, which he interpreted in religious terms. As Volker M. Welter explains in his study of Geddes, *Biopolis* (2002), he often planned a *via sacra* in the form of a processional way, and this idea may be the origin of Plymouth's Armada Way.

The fourth component of Abercrombie's vision, which he shared more with Mumford than with Geddes, may be characterized as a reformed Garden City ideal within a regional context. While Abercrombie deprecated suburban sprawl, he believed that homes of the future should be planned to low densities and set in abundant grass and trees. These would be an improvement on the bleak rows of semi-detached houses that had already started to fill up the hillsides around Plymouth. Abercrombie was conscious of the need to stimulate a sense of community in these new developments by the provision of appropriate communal buildings, as Lord Astor had already attempted in his Mount Gould scheme at Plymouth, begun in 1919, which included an "institute" for tenants intended to create a sense of community.

The *Plan for Plymouth* exemplifies all these aspects of Abercrombie's ideas. The formalism of the proposals made for the city center was a response to a site Abercrombie viewed as a *tabula rasa*, even if the legal issues of ownership and compensation were still inscribed on the slate and took much legal effort to resolve. The regional vision derived from Geddes and Mumford was apparent in strategic thinking about the location of industry and housing, and in the restructuring of the existing suburbs into community neighborhoods.

The preservation of rural England was exemplified by the inclusion of a survey of agricultural land by Dudley Stamp, a noted geographer. Rather than having a formal "Green Belt," such as had been imposed around London shortly before the war, the urban area of Plymouth would include pockets of agricultural land. These would improve the quality of life for farmers by bringing them closer to the city, and retain visible links to the soil for those who worked in industry and other occupations. In addition, at a time before widespread refrigeration, the proximity of farms would ensure a local supply of fresh produce for the city.

The preservation of old buildings was addressed chiefly in the form of the historic area of Plymouth, the Barbican, which although adjacent to the most severe destruction, had largely escaped damage. Here, Abercrombie wanted the existing fishing trade to continue around the historic harbor basin of Sutton Pool, while the best original buildings would be restored and revealed, and the gaps infilled sensitively but without pastiche. The entire quarter would become an attraction for residents and tourists, with restaurants on the quay side in the Continental manner. Abercrombie even proposed rebuilding the old city wall around the Barbican to reinforce its separate identity.

The ideal of low-density development (twelve houses per acre) would be accomplished by reducing population in the city center—something the bombing had already done quite effectively—and controlling the growth both of new suburban settlements and around existing villages. The scope of the plan extended outside the city boundary and across the river Tamar into Cornwall. The Plan shows densities decreasing from 100 persons per acre in those central areas remaining residential to 50 in the inner suburbs and 25 in the outer suburbs. In the central areas, the density had previously been at least 200, rising to 253 in Vintry Ward, the Barbican area.[15]

As "poet-architect," Abercrombie went further than his contemporaries toward creating a specific philosophy for planning, one that might be better described as a poetics of planning. The English cultural geographer David Matless has drawn attention to Abercrombie's interest in the theory of Feng Shui as a means of defining the planner's role as the interpreter of places. Matless writes, "Abercrombie presented Feng Shui as a doctrine of intervention, seeking an evolving functional aesthetic harmony between humanity and environment."[16] Taking the word "harmony" almost literally in a discussion of Feng Shui in 1933, Abercrombie, quoting an unidentified Chinese text, saw the planner as a composer who knows how to reconcile disparate elements according to "the local currents of the cosmic Breath."[17] While Abercrombie was influenced by these ideas, he did not expect others to view them as more than figures of speech, for he wrote, "We can hardly anticipate a practice based on such esoteric principles....But it should be possible to evolve a system of landscape design which will be authoritative enough to prevent brutal outrage on the one hand and a misguided attempt at a bogus naturalism on the other."[18] The apparently eclectic mixture of styles and purposes seen in the Plan for Plymouth seems to bear out this philosophy, and Abercrombie could scarcely have anticipated the popular interest in Feng Shui that developed in the 1990s. For him, the doctrine seems largely to have been relevant as a license to follow his intuitive reading of the site rather than as a set of prescriptive principles.

"A VIEW FROM THE STATION AS IT MIGHT BE."
FROM A PLAN FOR PLYMOUTH, 1943. COLLECTION OF ALAN POWERS

For a visitor to Plymouth today, the commercial center is the most conspicuous evidence of Abercrombie's vision. Apart from being a response to a cleared site, it was intended to redress faults in the largely random evolution of Plymouth's main area of shopping and cultural facilities. Before the war, the city had suffered from severe traffic problems, owing partly to the narrow streets, but also to the wider geographical situation of being a peninsula with few routes in or out. Traffic congestion was the worst in the whole of the south of England outside London, and there was a high accident rate. This was probably the most compelling practical argument for rebuilding the center, but Abercrombie and Paton Watson resisted the return to the previous plan form for other reasons too. They were alert to the confused impression given by Plymouth to new visitors, who would arrive at North Road station wanting, usually, to proceed southward to the Hoe, but finding no clues in the street layout to enable them to do so.

Visitors arriving by rail today can at least thank Abercrombie for resolving this problem. The form he proposed for the center was strictly rectilinear, within a kite-shaped boundary rising from the valley bottom behind the Hoe up a gradual slope toward the station, axially composed around Armada Way. This was Abercombie's *via sacra* and he promoted the idea by dedicating it as a memorial to those who had lost their lives during the blitz. Side streets branch off this spine, and the whole is bounded by a ring road. Most of the buildings proposed within this area were to be of uniform four-story height in perimeter blocks. These were described as "shopping precincts" by Abercrombie, who had also proposed a "precinct" free of through traffic for the university area in Bloomsbury in his County of London Plan. There was some novelty in this partial separation of traffic and shopping, and the Plan states, "We prophesy that the freedom of movement thus engendered will much more than compensate for the alleged loss of advertising value said to be obtained from shop windows facing a street."[19]

The pedestrianization was less radical than the completely pedestrianized shopping street proposed and eventually carried out by Donald Gibson at Coventry, but it belongs to the same early stages of transforming shopping into a controlled and orchestrated experience. The relocation of shops from Union Street to the new central shopping area was particularly contentious. This street connects Plymouth with neighboring Stonehouse, which is close to the Naval Dockyard at Devonport and, until 1914, was an independent borough. Believing that the Dockyard would expand, Abercrombie wanted to convert Union Street entirely to traffic flow.

In order to realize the central area and maintain long-term control of it, the city needed to acquire a large amount of land. This was complicated by a web of competing interests. Plymouth did not receive as much government reconstruction money as it had hoped, and the political priority was for housing and schools rather than for the shopping area. Existing businesses continued in many cases to occupy temporary shops in rows of Nissen huts (barrel-vaulted structures roofed in corrugated iron) during the slow progress of reconstructing the central area. Although the plan was adopted by the City Council in September 1944, it was challenged in the High Court. Even Nancy Astor joined a campaign against the relocation of the central shops, which were felt to have damaged business interests. Lord Astor's advocacy of the Plan was resented by business leaders, and Astor was blocked from running again for Lord Mayor. It appears that getting the Plan adopted at the beginning was easier to achieve than actually implementing it, since the years of peace also brought disillusionment and a loss of idealism.

While Abercrombie was ruthless in sweeping away most of the surviving buildings in the central area, he encouraged the retention of the Gothic Revival Guildhall, situated at the bottom of the valley between the new shopping center and the Hoe. Although he was relatively scathing about its style, he liked its gray limestone construction, and in particular the civic square that already surrounded it. Between the Guildhall and the shopping center, he planned a new east-west street, called Royal Parade, to act as a boundary between zones, with a civic precinct to the south incorporating the old Guildhall with new, enlarged civic offices. These were represented in the Plan as low-rise neoclassical buildings, but when the time came to build them, in 1959, the new city architect, H. J. W. Stirling, proposed a twelve-story block of civic offices to break the monotony of the Abercrombie scheme. The Civic Center and the Magistrate's Court were duly built in this form in 1960 by the firm of Jellicoe, Ballantyne and Coleridge. Royal Parade was the first of the new streets to be laid out, and was opened by King George VI in 1947, amid what was still a desolation of bomb sites. A reproduction of Drake's Drum (a relic of Queen Elizabeth I's naval hero, and a talisman of British invincibility) was positioned at the intersection of the two main axes, forming the base of a flagstaff.

Before there was anything to see on the ground, the Plymouth Plan came to national prominence through a film, *The Way We Live*, scripted and directed by Jill Craigie in 1945. Craigie was drawn to Plymouth as a subject through her avid reading of Lewis Mumford. She also knew the architect and teacher Sir Charles Reilly, who not only had given Abercrombie his first academic job at Liverpool but also was simultaneously developing postwar planning ideas for the neighboring shipping center of Birkenhead.[20] Although not an official interpretation of the Plymouth Plan, *The Way We Live* is a valuable document for understanding the amount of emotion that reconstruction planning was able to generate.

In the film, an anonymous but well-spoken ex-serviceman, a journalist by trade, returns from abroad at the end of the war and decides that he wants to research a story on planning. He comes as a stranger, traveling from London to Plymouth and acting in the film as a neutral but sympathetic commentator.

He interviews James Paton Watson and, with the memorable cue line, "No-one knew what the professor was up to," introduces Abercrombie, who in his wide-striped suit and monocle wanders through the surviving Barbican visualizing the future Plymouth, which is illustrated by perspective renderings by J. D. M. Harvey, some taken directly from the Plymouth Plan, some specially drawn for the film. Abercrombie's voice takes over to advocate precinct planning and architectural harmony: "Plymouth needs pale colours to respond to the sunlight. Buildings in limestone and concrete. Flat and vertical masses to give balance to an interesting skyline. What is needed is a city to cheer people up."[21] Abercrombie appears again at a public meeting, confronting doubters and hecklers as he expounds on the plan and gradually convinces his audience, partly by explaining that his central vista is a memorial.

ABOVE CIVIC CENTER AS BUILT TO DESIGNS BY JELLICOE, BALLANTYNE AND COLERIDGE, 1960. PHOTO COURTESY JOHN HINDE INTERNATIONAL
BELOW CIVIC CENTER AS ORIGINALLY PROPOSED. FROM *A PLAN FOR PLYMOUTH*, 1943. COLLECTION OF ALAN POWERS

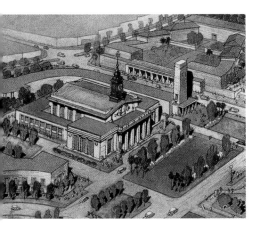

PROTEST MARCH FROM FINAL SEQUENCE OF *THE WAY WE LIVE* (1946). BRITISH FILM INSTITUTE, STILLS LIBRARY

The Plan is seen being further defended and debated at City Council meetings, but the film leaves a deliberate ambiguity about whether it will actually be realized. In a final fantasy sequence, a march of young people (whose viewpoint has been represented in a fictional subplot), carrying banners and appealing for new homes and amenities, appears to clinch the matter. The political and personal are merged in the film: the Labour candidate for Devonport Dockyard (one of the constituencies of central Plymouth) in the 1945 election was Michael Foot, future leader of the Labour Party, to whom Craigie was introduced by Paul Reilly, the son of Sir Charles. Foot is shown making a campaign speech in which he gives Labour support for the Plan, saying, "We really can have the most beautiful city in the world."[22] This proved a sound political move, for Foot defeated the sitting Tory M.P., Leslie Hore-Belisha. He and Craigie were married in 1949. The producer, J. Arthur Rank, found the film too left-wing and tried to suppress it, but a favorable review by C. A. Lejeune in the *London Observer* turned the tables and created public interest in it.

The Way We Live is remarkable for its attempt to create and sustain general interest in planning at a moment when disillusion was beginning to set in. The passage of the Town and Country Planning Act in 1947 appeared to mark the achievement of the broad planning aims of the previous twenty years, offering a framework for compulsory purchase of land, control of use, and preservation of buildings and open country, but its provisions were modified almost immediately and made less radical. As John Gold and Steven Ward write of the situation after 1947, "To officials and ministers the prospect of yet more government-sponsored films airily promising social benefits through planning was increasingly seen as tactless and politically dangerous."[23]

Physical progress on the Plymouth Plan was delayed by postwar shortages of building materials and by the economic changes resulting from the withdrawal of Marshall Plan aid by the United States in 1947. The actual buildings of the new city center only began to appear, slowly, starting in 1951 when Dingle's Department Store, designed by Burnet & Tait, opened on the corner of Royal Parade and Armada Way. With its late and rather sedate American Art Deco quality, the store was one of the few shop buildings constructed that was of individual interest. Uniformity was the desired intention of the Plan, strongly reflecting architectural thinking of the 1930s in Britain and elsewhere, which saw individualism as a threat to unity. According to Abercrombie and Paton Watson, "If we are to recapture the wonderful continuity of the street scene obtained by Nash and Wood the Younger, as in Old Regent Street and Bath, but in the modern idiom, then it is essential that the new streets shall be designed as a whole."[24] Sir Charles Reilly described the taste for individually distinctive buildings as "that vulgar old advertising way of doing things…which we hope has gone forever, and that once more we are all going to be gentlemen as we were when the terraces on the Hoe were built."[25]

The same attitude was taken by the critic Christopher Hussey in a discussion of the Plan in *Country Life*; he believed that the idea would work if "the architects of individual buildings also play their part and consider their designs in relation to the whole, not merely as personal solutions of isolated problems."[26] Writing well before the end of the war, when the case against Fascist architecture still needed to be argued, Hussey saw a political parable in the balance of control and freedom, as "that is how the structure of political democracy works, and it is the only way that town-planning in a democracy will produce characteristic townscapes, with the English quality of the picturesque in place of autocratic regimentation."[27]

These hopes for fine architecture under controlled conditions were exaggerated. As the adjoining sites began to be filled in, the quality declined. Abercrombie had proposed the architect William Crabtree—who with Reilly designed the Peter Jones store in London in 1936—as designer for a number of the main store buildings in the center.[28] The perspectives by J. D. M. Harvey, who also trained as an architect, suggest nothing of Peter Jones's elegance. Reilly commented, "town planners do not hold themselves responsible for the architecture shown by their perspective men. That is a mere detail."[29] As it transpired, Crabtree was given a purely advisory role, and the individual buildings of the commercial center were created by lesser names. The disappointing architectural realization of the plan contributed to lowering its status among designers and critics, although it should be stressed that some individual churches, banks, and other buildings rose well above the general level while remaining neotraditional in character.

PATRICK ABERCROMBIE (CENTER) WITH JILL CRAIGIE, DURING THE FILMING OF *THE WAY WE LIVE*, 1945. BRITISH FILM INSTITUTE, STILLS LIBRARY

The central vista of Abercrombie and Paton Watson's plan was the most controversial element and it is worth examining its motives more closely. The authors wrote, "We have permitted ourselves the one monumental feature of the whole of Plymouth rebuilding—a great view seen from the forecourt of the railway station across the Shopping and Civic Center, to the Naval War Memorial on the Hoe....The vista itself will be the visitor's guide and it will, literally, in itself cost nothing. ...It is to be no road or traffic approach, and its enrichment by stairs, terraces, *tapis verts* or other features of the landscape architect's and gardener's art can be left for gradual realisation."[30] The idea of "costing nothing" went beyond mere economy, for it showed the planner's skill at revealing something that was already there and giving it a new value. This was demonstrated again by the planners of the 1951 Festival of Britain South Bank exhibition who made the north bank of the Thames into the scenic background for their site and controlled a series of views of it.[31]

The description of Armada Way as primarily a landscape feature rather than a shopping street or traffic route indicates the extent to which concepts of landscape gardening underlay British planning practice. This was a reflection of the Edwardian period, when planning was seen in terms of vistas and *ronds points*, and several of the leading textbooks, by Thomas Mawson and Inigo Triggs, for example, were written by garden designers. There is a larger historical background to this affinity, of course, but it is one way of understanding why ideas represented by Patrick Geddes or Camillo Sitte celebrating the built fabric of the city were slow to penetrate a British mentality that was fundamentally anti-urban. *The Way We Live* has much more to say about housing and community, and about the regeneration of the Barbican, than about the central vista, indicating that it was not one of the most appealing aspects of the plan in the view of the general public.

As built, Armada Way was compromised in several respects. It was only partially pedestrianized—cross-routes intersected it—although the landscaping included some formal gardening. Its convenience as a walking route was only fully established in 1987–88 when underpasses were built. The building proposed to close the northern vista and serve as a railway hotel was never constructed, and to this day the north end of the vista is unresolved, leaving the railway station still awkwardly linked to the city center. In other respects, Armada Way has been rescued by the compromise of infilling its 150-foot width with abundant visual detail, which offers weather protection and visual incident, without a loss of drama.

ROYAL PARADE UNDER CONSTRUCTION, CIRCA 1947

Sir Charles Reilly commended the intention of Armada Way, but wished that the southern view centered on "something more worthy" than the Naval Monument, which had been designed by Sir Robert Lorimer in 1920–24. The most outspoken early critic, W. A. Eden (even though he, like Abercrombie and Reilly, was connected to the Liverpool School of Architecture), complained of Abercrombie and Paton Watson in 1943, stating that since they were "never quite certain what their city is, or whether its parts are functional or geographical or both, there is a small wonder that they have to deal violently with Plymouth in the interests of a unified plan, foreshadowing the transformation of an English seaport into something that might serve to house an international exhibition as these things were understood twenty years ago."[32]

The magazine Architects' Journal also found the concept outdated, and in an editorial discussing Plymouth in 1952 (the year the RIBA Annual Conference was held in the city), commented, "the three streets of offices and shops erected in the last few years will stand as a monument to the town planning ideals of the thirties and early forties," adding that it was time to move on.[33] An accompanying article by D. Rigby Childs and Colin Boyne reveals a stronger anti-monumental attitude, expressing the hope that Abercrombie's plan for a community center in the Barbican would never be implemented. Childs and Boyne condemned the uniformity of the commercial elevations as "facadism"—defined as "the evil of considering only the front of a building to the neglect of the rear, an error of taste which is the antithesis of good contemporary design."[34]

The new Civic Center by Jellicoe, Ballantyne and Coleridge was intended as a remedy for this mistake, although no revisions were made to the overall scheme for the commercial center. As Kenneth Browne in Architectural Review noted of the preliminary design for the civic center in 1959, "something was desperately needed to pin the whole thing down, something around which the city could revolve: a focal point."[35] These two comments demonstrate the alternative planning philosophy that succeeded Abercrombie's, that of "townscape," first introduced in 1949 with two Architectural Review articles, one by Ivor de Wolfe and the other by Gordon Cullen.[36] Townscape offered an alternative landscape analogy, that of the picturesque, involving intricacy and variety in place of axiality and uniformity. In truth, Abercrombie seemed to want both formality and variety, for his proposals for the Barbican came close to townscape philosophy. It is interesting that H. J. W. Stirling, the same city architect who promoted the Corbusian Civic Center, also commissioned small-scale infill in the Barbican that perfectly represents townscape principles.

Brian Chalkley and John Dalton, writing in 1991, expressed the same concern about the wasted effort of the central vista as W. A. Eden:

It has to be said that this layout is more striking and meaningful on the map than on the ground. The neat symmetry so evident from above is lost on the average pedestrian: indeed the grid-iron matrix can easily cause confusion. The city center lacks nodes, and the rectilinear grid has led to a situation in which no one intersection is significantly more strategic than any other. The similarity of the streets, the area's relative newness and the rather unmemorable quality of some of the post-war architecture all compound the problem of the townscape's lack of clarity.[37]

The same authors praise the landscaping carried out in the late 1980s, which introduced a much greater intricacy into Armada Way, helping it "to become a feature of resounding success, and one without which the city center grid, planned and so nearly bland, could have slumped into featureless banality."[38]

The crowning glory of the Abercrombie and Paton Watson plan inevitably appears today to be an aesthetic failure. It has also run close to being a commercial failure, as the central shops have been threatened by chain stores based elsewhere. The tasteful and reticent architectural background, so much approved in the 1930s, lacks a foreground to set it off. Admittedly, other postwar reconstruction schemes—in Coventry, Exeter, or Bristol—were architecturally no better.

The idea of neighborhood units, so strongly promoted by Abercrombie in London and Plymouth, was compromised by the failure to complete all the promised communal amenities. Furthermore, as the historian Junichi Hasegawa writes, "the inhabitants turned out to be indifferent to, or worse, loth to accept, the communal spirit which the planners expected it to induce."[39] Quoting the Anglophile Danish architect and urban historian Steen Eiler Rasmussen in 1948, Hasegawa asserts, "We should make no religion out of the neighborhood unit. The danger of bombs brought people together, the danger has gone, and so has the neighborhood spirit. Don't foster too much of local patriotism—it is just as bad as too much nationalism."[40]

113

PLYMOUTH. AERIAL VIEW OF ARMADA WAY, CIRCA 1962

The great success of Plymouth was the Barbican, and had Abercrombie's idea of a new city wall been implemented, it would have been a unique feature among postwar schemes, looking forward to the high-density planning ideals of Team X and based on a love of Italian hill towns, which the Barbican at moments resembles. Through no fault of Abercrombie's, the regeneration of the Barbican was slow to start and a number of important buildings were lost before the conservationist tide turned in the late 1950s.

The fact that Abercrombie and Paton Watson were making their plan well before the present concept of architectural preservation became current may itself remind us how much has changed. *The Way We Live* does not show "the way we live now." It is a distant piece of archaeology, representing the end of a wave of ideas that lasted less than fifty years from the beginning of the century, rather than the beginning of present thinking. Those who were skeptical of it at the time, such as W. A. Eden, were neither philistine nor commercially driven, and we probably agree with them.

On the other hand, some aspects of regionalist thinking in the Plymouth Plan seem increasingly relevant today. It is notable that the New York New Visions document "Principles for the Rebuilding of Lower Manhattan, February 2002" has as its fourth principle "A Renewed Relationship of Lower Manhattan and the Region," an idea that seems to derive from Mumford, and therefore connects back to Geddes and Abercrombie. In a Britain where agriculture has recently reached a point of near economic collapse, Abercrombie's desire to integrate rural land into a city region, something that was originally taken least seriously of all his proposals, might now seem the most radical and forward looking of all.

NOTES

1. Jeremy Paxman, *The English, A Portrait of a People* (London: Penguin, 1998), p. 171.

2. Christopher Sykes, *Nancy, The Life of Lady Astor* (London: Collins, 1972), pp. 434–35.

3. Ibid., pp. 436–37.

4. Frank Wintle, *The Plymouth Blitz* (Bodmin, U.K.: Bossiney Books, 1981), p. 56.

5. Ibid., p. 55.

6. Brian Chalkley and John Goodridge, "The 1943 Plan for Plymouth: War-Time Vision and Post-War Realities," in Brian Chalkley, David Dunkerley, and Peter Gripaios, eds., *Plymouth: Maritime City in Transition* (Newton Abbot, U.K.: David and Charles, 1991), pp. 62–63.

7. Maxwell Fry, "The New Britain Must be Planned," *Picture Post*, January 4, 1941, pp. 16–20.

8. Chalkley and Goodridge, "The 1943 Plan for Plymouth," pp. 65–66, fig. 4.1.

9. See ibid., p. 64. Also see Gerald Dix, "Patrick Abercrombie," in Gordon Cherry, ed., *Pioneers in British Planning* (London: The Architectural Press, 1981), pp. 103–30.

10. Chalkley and Goodridge, "The 1943 Plan for Plymouth," p. 69.

11. Ibid.

12. J. Paton Watson and Patrick Abercrombie, *A Plan for Plymouth, the report prepared for the City Council* (Plymouth, U.K.: Underhill, 1943). The main coverage was: "A Plan for Plymouth," *The Builder,* May 5, 1944, pp. 356–59; Christopher Hussey, "The New Plymouth," *Country Life,* May 12, 1944, pp. 812–13; and "Sir Charles Reilly Discusses the Plan for Plymouth," *Architects' Journal* 102, (September 13, 1945), pp. 187–89.

13. Paton Watson and Abercrombie, *A Plan for Plymouth*, p. iii.

14. The relationship between Geddes and Mumford cannot be adequately summarized here. See Donald l. Miller, *Lewis Mumford, A Life* (London: Weidenfeld & Nicolson, 1989).

15. Paton Watson and Abercrombie, *A Plan for Plymouth*, pp. 29, 38–40.

16. David Matless, "Appropriate Geography: Patrick Abercrombie and the Energy of the World," *Journal of Design History* 6, no. 3 (1993), p. 168.

17. Patrick Abercombie, *Town and Country Planning* (London: Thornton Butterworth, 1933), p. 230.

18. Ibid., p. 232.

19. Abercrombie and Paton Watson, *A Plan for Plymouth*, p. 70.

20. *The Way We Live* was filmed for Two Cities Films for the Rank Organisation in the course of 1945 and released in 1946. Craigie, born in 1914, had launched her career as a director with *Out of Chaos*, a film about war artists. See obituary of Jill Craigie by Tom Vallance, *The Independent*, December 15, 1999, sec. 2, p. 7. Also see commentary on

The Way We Live in John R. Gold and Stephen V. Ward, "Of Plans and Planners: Documentary Film and the Challenge of the Urban Future, 1935–52," in D. B. Clarke, ed., *The Cinematic City* (London: Routledge, 1997), pp. 59–82.

21. As transcribed in Gold and Ward, "Of Plans and Planners," p. 75. I am grateful to John Gold for the loan of a videotape of the film and other advice.

22. Foot as seen on film, quoted in Simon Hoggart and David Leigh, *Michael Foot, A Portrait* (London: Hodder & Stoughton, 1981), p. 91.

23. Gold and Ward, "Of Plans and Planners," p. 77.

24. Abercrombie and Paton Watson, *A Plan for Plymouth*, p. 77.

25. C. H. Reilly, "Sir Charles Discusses the Plan for Plymouth," p. 189.

26. Christopher Hussey, "The New Plymouth," *Country Life* 95 (May 12, 1944), p. 812.

27. Ibid.

28. Reilly, "Sir Charles Discusses the Plan for Plymouth," p. 188.

29. Ibid., p. 189.

30. Abercrombie and Paton Watson, *A Plan for Plymouth*, p. 67.

31. See Alan Powers, "The Expression of Levity," in Elain Harwood and Alan Powers, eds., *Festival of Britain* (London: Twentieth Century Society, 2001).

32. W. A. Eden, "The Art of Building Cities," *Town Planning Review* 19 (spring 1943), p. 95.

33. Editorial, *Architects' Journal* 115 (June 12, 1952), p. 715.

34. D. Rigby Childs and D. A. C. A. Boyne, "Plymouth: A Survey," *Architects' Journal* 115 (June 12, 1952), p. 718.

35. Kenneth Browne, "Plymouth Centered," *Architectural Review* 125 (May 1959), p. 327.

36. Ivor de Wolfe (pseudonym for H. de C. Hastings), "Townscape"; and Gordon Cullen, "A Townscape Textbook," *Architectural Review* 106 (December 1949), pp. 354–74.

37. Chalkley & Goodridge, "The 1943 Plan for Plymouth," p. 83.

38. Ibid., p. 85.

39. Junichi Hasegawa, "The Rise and Fall of Radical Reconstruction in 1940s Britain," *Twentieth Century British History* 10, no. 2 (1999), p. 156.

40. Steen Eiler Rasmussen, quoted in International Federation for Housing and Town Planning, *Summary Report of the 19th International Congress on Housing and Town Planning*, June 1948, p. 26.

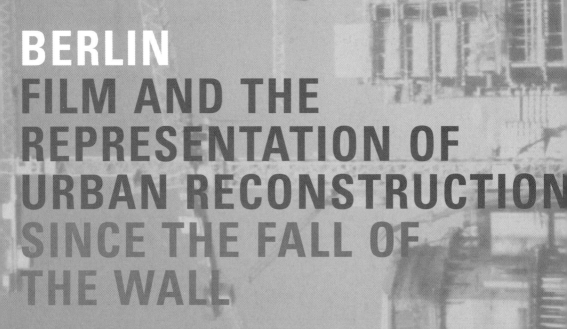

BERLIN

FILM AND THE REPRESENTATION OF URBAN RECONSTRUCTION SINCE THE FALL OF THE WALL

Hubertus Siegert and Ralph Stern

Images of the destruction of the World Trade Center were transmitted in real time throughout the world and these images, as well as the emotional impact associated with them, will remain with us long after lower Manhattan has been rebuilt. It is to be anticipated that documentaries will distill and condense both the horror of that clear September morning and the concerted efforts to clear the site of mountains of debris in the following months. Ultimately, as lower Manhattan rises "out of ground zero," it is certain that the reconstruction will also be documented. Hubertus Siegert's *Berlin Babylon* is, in many respects, just such a documentation of the reconstruction of Berlin after the fall of the Berlin Wall. Although it records many sites rather than a single, large one such as that of the World Trade Center, *Berlin Babylon* gives us an indication of the power of film to capture not only the tragedies of destruction, but also the complexities of reconstruction.

Before turning to the representation of Berlin's reconstruction, I wish to briefly put into context the manner and duration of its initial destruction. World War II brought massive devastation to cities throughout Europe. London, Rotterdam, and Warsaw were among the major cities outside of Germany suffering the effects of "total war." Inside Germany, it is the bombing of Dresden in the spring of 1945, a city famous as a *Kulturstadt* and overflowing with refugees fleeing the advancing Soviet troops, that most vividly brings to mind the horror of a military attack on a civilian population. Between 30,000 and 100,000 civilians perished as the city was engulfed in a firestorm. Other major German cities, particularly those crowded with late-medieval structures built largely of wood, suffered similar fates. Berlin, as capital of Germany's Third Reich, was also an obvious target of Allied bombardment and experienced air raids from the summer of 1940 on. In terms of civilian losses, the most devastating raids occurred toward the end of the war, as on February 8, 1945, when 22,000 civilians perished. Nonetheless, Berlin, unlike many older cities, did not suffer from the devastating effects of a firestorm. Largely a product of nineteenth-century industrialization, most of Berlin's buildings were constructed of fire-resistant masonry. Similarly, its wider streets, designed to accommodate the masses of a burgeoning metropolis, also slowed the spreading of fires.

117

Therefore, although Berlin did suffer terrible damage during the war, it is one of history's ironies that even more destruction of the older urban fabric was wrought in the years immediately following the war. Many damaged structures that might have been saved were demolished for reasons of safety and cost. Others fell prey to the experiments of architects and planners who believed that the destruction of inner cities offered a great opportunity to reintroduce "nature" into the "stony" heart of metropolitan Berlin. Further destruction, particularly in the city center, followed after the construction of the Wall in 1961. Thus Berlin became a city whose center turned into a periphery, a city filled with voids, a city haunted by a tumultuous past. It is this cumulative destruction and its psychological impact that must be taken into account in addressing Berlin's reconstruction.

In 1989, Berlin's reunification brought with it heady aspirations and a great building boom. As capital of a reunified Germany, Berlin was once again to become a thriving metropolis, a world city, a global city. Again, architects and planners saw Berlin as a great opportunity: this time to remedy not only the lingering effects of war, but also those of modernist planning and the politics of division. This, of course, meant further demolition—this time of modernist structures—but the overriding opinion was that the city was not only to be reconstructed, it was to be so "critically," with great attention being paid to the structure of what came to be termed the "traditional European city." Both local and internationally renowned architects participated in this frenzy of reconstruction—this building of a new, traditional city. The atmosphere of the period—its imagery, its optimism, its hubris, and its banality—is the subject of Hubertus Siegert's film.

Unlike so many who have recently moved to Berlin, Hubertus Siegert is no novice to the city. Born in (formerly West) Germany, Siegert moved to Berlin in 1980 and studied history, art history, and theater there before transferring to landscape architecture. In 1993, he founded a production company, S.U.M.O. Film. His filmography includes *Stravinsky in Berlin* (1993), *Das Sonnenjuwel* (1995), and *The Orange Kiss* (1996). In 1996, he began work on *Berlin Babylon*, which he completed in 2000 and released in 2001.

Documenting many of the most important sites associated with Berlin's post-reunification reconstruction, the film presents us with strikingly beautiful imagery and an evocative soundtrack. The German press has extolled Siegert's "fantastic, impressive images of unbelievable construction processes," shots of "steel mesh that looks like abstract painting," and portrayal of the "city as drama," beginning with "a low flight over Berlin" that recalls Ridley Scott's *Blade Runner*.

However, if the imagery is unquestionably impressive, its interpretation remains substantially more open. As one reviewer, Christine Franke, has suggested, *Berlin Babylon* "offers us a very individual and personal film experience" in which each observer develops an idea of the city for himself. Intriguingly, this film, only eighty-eight minutes long, intersects a myriad of discourses. Some of them are specifically connected to the history and politics of Berlin as well as the ideological inclinations of many of Berlin's contemporary architectural and political figures. Others more generally concern issues of the "city" and of memory and identity in an age of globalization. Still others have to do with the representation of the urban environment through images, particularly those of film.

FRONTISPIECE AND ALL IMAGES ACCOMPANYING THIS ARTICLE STILLS FROM *BERLIN BABYLON* (2001). COURTESY HUBERTUS SIEGERT AND S.U.M.O. FILM

First, we can view the film as a documentary about major construction sites that dominated Berlin's inner-city topography during the mid to late 1990s. As anyone familiar with the debates concerning the rebuilding of Berlin is aware, these sites and the buildings arising out of them were by no means neutral objects of economic speculation or artistic aspiration. Rather, they were frequently embroiled in heated ideological conflicts—concerning the relationship of the past to the present, traditionalism to modernism, globalism to regionalism, communism to democracy, the two of these political systems to fascism, and memory and identity to erasure and eradication. Ever since Weimar, if not before, Berlin's architecture and urbanism have served as a lightning rod for political debate and posturing. The period following reunification clearly continued in this tradition. One question that must certainly be asked is, how were the sites depicted in the film chosen, and why were others excluded?

Second, we can look at the film as an exploration of the "architect in film"—a topic that has a trajectory spanning from Michael Blackwood's documentaries on architectural luminaries; to fiction films by such noted directors as Michelangelo Antonioni (*L'Avventura*, 1961), Peter Greenaway (*The Belly of an Architect*, 1987), Woody Allen (*Hannah and her Sisters*, 1987), Spike Lee (*Jungle Fever*, 1991), and Peter Weir (*Fearless*, 1993); to spectacles emerging out of a more populist architectural "imaginary" like *Towering Inferno* and *Death Wish* (both 1974).

This is worth mentioning not least because while the distinction between a Pritzker Prize winner and a Paul Newman may be clear to those within the profession, it tends to be lost on the more general public, for whom the contemporary architect often appears as a "star," attracting a cult following not unlike that of famous actors. Therefore, another essential question to ask of this film is, for which "public" is *Berlin Babylon* intended: a public specific to the architectural profession, or one that is much broader?

119

Third, we can view *Berlin Babylon* as an extension of the more important exploration of the city in film, or of film in the city. Greater Berlin is of particular importance in this regard. Before World War II, it served as the center of Weimar film culture under, predominantly, the renowned UFA (Universum-Film Aktiengesellschaft) label. After the war, this tradition continued in the East under the remarkably prolific DEFA (Deutsche Film Aktiengesellschaft). More important still, Berlin has repeatedly been the subject of cinematic portrayal. Early films like Ernst Lubitsch's *Meyer aus Berlin* (1919), Karl Grune's *Die Strasse* (1923), and F. W. Murnau's *Der letzte Mann* (1924) depicted the city using a mix of real and imaginary images. But it was Walter Ruttmann's seminal film of 1927, *Berlin, Sinfonie der Grossstadt*, that set the standard of documentary depictions of the modern metropolis. Indeed, *Symphony of a Great City*, as it is known in English, has now been recreated in a contemporary, post-millennium version, and in Germany the original version has, on at least one occasion, been double-billed with *Berlin Babylon*, thus making the linkage explicit.

Nor did Berlin's relationship with film end in the silent era. It traverses the spectacle of Leni Riefenstahl's two *Olympia* films documenting the 1936 Berlin Olympics (*Fest der Völker* and *Fest der Schönheit*), and extends to the postwar "ruins" films by directors like Wolfgang Staudte (*Die Mörder sind unter uns*, 1946) and Roberto Rossellini (*Germania, anno zero*, 1947), which depict a Berlin devastated by war. Images of post–World War II Berlin reappear in *Berlin Babylon*.

The linking of Berlin's architecture and urbanism with a social vision and with political agendas continued through the late 1940s into the 1970s in the eastern half of the divided city with such DEFA productions as *Unser tägliche Brot* (Slatan Dudow, 1949), *Berlin, Ecke Schönhauser Allee* (Gerhard Klein, 1957), and *Die Legende von Paul und Paula* (Heiner Carow, 1973). Meanwhile, from the West came Billy Wilder's witty and biting film depictions of Americans in Berlin's immediate postwar turmoil of black markets—the "moral malaria" spread by the ever-sultry Marlene Dietrich (*A Foreign Affair*, 1948), and Cold War and Coca-Cola intrigue as played by an energetic James Cagney (*One, Two, Three*, 1961). In the 1980s and early 1990s, Wim Wenders developed another remarkably resonant and poetic vision of the city both before and after Berlin's (and Germany's) reunification, *Himmel über Berlin* (1987) and *In weiter Ferne, so nah* (1993).

Straddling this temporal divide was Peter Kahane's *Die Architekten* (1990). Begun just before reunification and completed immediately afterward, this film, a sort of "Big Chill goes east," specifically addresses the practice of architecture in East Germany. Today, where *Berlin Babylon* shows us a view of Berlin from above or below, Tom Tykwer's internationally successful *Run Lola Run* (1998) presents us with a punchy street-level take, offering three different stories all predicated on the element of urban chance. Most recently, Berlin has begun to explore the past few decades of division with what may be an unusual turn for many Germans: a great deal of humor. Leander Haussmann's *Sonnenallee* (1999) explores the East Berlin of the 1970s from a teenager's point of view. This film was provocatively advertised—for a country still divided by what is commonly known as the "Wall in the head"—with a trailer suggesting that, following the results of a popular referendum, the Wall would be rebuilt. Indeed, for many Berliners, life itself is a construction site, as Wolfgang Becker's film *Das Leben ist eine Baustelle* (1997) proudly proclaims.

Implicit in the title of *Berlin Babylon* is also another important discourse. In the film's opening sequence we read a text about the conflation between the Tower of Babel and the towers of Babylon. One can probe this at length, speculating on what a multiplicity of tongues implies in terms of the unity or fragmentation of today's Berlin, its various architectural idioms, its various cultures. We can ask what it means for the "construction site to remain empty"—as also appears in the opening text. This question is particularly important in Berlin, where much of the post-Wall reconstruction has involved further destruction, from the demolition of the Anhalter Bahnhof (prior to reunification) and the *Plattenbauten* of the former East to the well-known "Ku'Damm Eck" in the former West (post-reunification), all of which *Berlin Babylon* depicts.

The film's title also appears to be a deliberate reference to the titles of other films and film contexts, even if some are rather different in their concerns. There are the recent *Tokyo Babylon* and *Brooklyn Babylon* (in the latter "Babylon" assumes the connotations appropriate to Rastafarians) as well as a forthcoming *Barcelona Babylon*, currently scheduled for release in 2003. In the actual Berlin, the "Babylon" is a well-known, well-loved, and recently restored movie theater originally designed by Hans Poelzig.

The title also most certainly evokes D. W. Griffith's groundbreaking *Intolerance* (1916) and its depiction of the fall of Babylon, the abandoned stage sets of which dominated part of Los Angeles's Sunset Boulevard for a number of years. Might this lead us to understand Siegert's Berlin as a city of monumental stage sets? One where concrete and steel have as little permanence as the papier-mâché of film props? Here, one may well recall Berlin's tradition of Schinkel and his architectural and urban scenography.

Or does "Berlin Babylon" lead us down another road? While it does not quite approach Kenneth Anger's scandalous *Hollywood Babylon*, it might make us think about the exposing of secrets in a mode similar to film noir, whose manner has been adopted by urbanists like Mike Davis, but whose cinematic origins lie in German Expressionism and films like Fritz Lang's *M—Die Stadt sucht einen Mörder* (1931), depicting Berlin's multiple but overlapping social layers. It was the exodus of directors and writers like Lang, Robert Siodmak, and Billy Wilder, émigrés from Hitler's Berlin to Raymond Chandler's Los Angeles, that gave great impetus to the noir genre and its filmic representation of the city. Is Siegert, then, working as a neo-noir detective, uncovering the "true story" of Berlin's reconstruction in the nick of time or perhaps, as in the case of Jack Nicholson in Roman Polanski's *Chinatown* (1974), a moment too late, after the shot has been fired and a story of architectural incest has been silenced?

Or are we reminded of another, more successful detective, Peter Falk, the fallen angel in Wim Wenders's *Wings of Desire*? The German title of Wenders's film, *Himmel über Berlin*, is alternatively translatable as "sky" or "heaven" above Berlin. It is to this film, much more so than to *Blade Runner*, that we find remarkable parallels. Wenders opens with a view that circles the Radio Tower of West Berlin looking east; Siegert opens with a view that circles the Television Tower of East Berlin looking west. Other sites familiar to us from *Himmel über Berlin* appear as well, including the Victory Column and the Anhalter train station. Like Walter Benjamin's "angel of history" (who is quoted in *Berlin Babylon*), Wenders's angels appear not as detectives but as witnesses. They witness both the dramatic and the everyday, particularly the random and fragmentary thoughts that occupy our private lives. Although *Berlin Babylon* may remind us of cinéma vérité in that there is no narration and much emphasis is placed on the chance comment or detail, these details are not necessarily utilized in the interest of "realism."

Rather, Siegert depicts many of Berlin's most powerful architects and urbanists caught up in everyday—often minor—situations, expressing concern over the correct handrail detail or terrazzo finish. They are presented through neither the technique of interview nor narrative exposition. Instead, despite the magnitude of their projects (or hubris), they appear groping for words, even groping for ideas, in a manner that makes them less heroic, no longer larger-than-life, possibly more human. Curt Bois's poignant search for the old Potsdamer Platz in Wenders's film finds its rather second-rate terminus in the new Potsdamer Platz of Helmut Jahn and Hans Kollhoff. It is with this sensibility that the film, replete with Rem Koolhaas if not Howard Roark, escapes becoming yet another "big men building big buildings in a big city" drama.

Is the film then an apologia for Berlin's "critical reconstruction" of itself? Hans Stimmann, the city's powerful building director, himself trained as an architect, is depicted in the film in a number of guises: advocating the "densification" of the Karl-Marx-Allee against the protests of Thomas Flierl, the former East German building director who is now a senator; arguing for the demolition of the Palast der Republik with the architect Josef Paul Kleihues; presenting the virtuous reconstruction of Pariser Platz to a busload of acolytes. Stimmann, the Robert Moses of 1990s Berlin, was the official to whom architects brought sketches, either to approve or to "improve," and much of the polemic surrounding Berlin's architectural idioms resulted from the polarization he engendered.

Berlin Babylon thus presents us with a panoply of architects and architectural positions, but the often profound tensions between them remain obscure. We are uninformed about the difference in terms of politics, patronage, and funding of the truly "Berlin" projects, such as the reconstruction of the Friedrichstrasse (which is not shown) and the more "global" examples of corporate architecture, such as those of Potsdamer Platz. Nor does the film tell us of similar differences between municipal projects, those funded and controlled by the city of Berlin; national projects like the Chancellery and the Reichstag; and those extraterritorial creations, the embassies. We are uninformed that, after having completed a historically sensitive and intelligent IBA (Internationale Bauausstellung) project at Checkpoint Charlie in the 1980s, Rem Koolhaas was essentially banished from the city during the 1990s.

Nor are we made aware that Günther Behnisch, a renowned architect from southern Germany whose buildings feature large amounts of glass, was largely seen as an opponent by those architects who advocated an architecture predicated on the "solidity" of masonry construction. The film's juxtaposition of Helmut Jahn and his Sony Center tower with Hans Kollhoff and his tower directly across the street alludes to this glass versus masonry argument, but although the polarization dominated much of Berlin's architectural debate during the 1990s, the film does not allow us to discern the vehemence with which the parties fought for their respective positions. We may also note that in 1995, the year before the filming of *Berlin Babylon* began, Stimmann presented much of his position in a collection of essays entitled *Babylon, Berlin etc.: Das Vokabular der europäischen Stadt* (Babylon, Berlin, etc.: The vocabulary of a European city), which he edited.

Thus among the questions posed by *Berlin Babylon* are the following: Is it a construction film? A film about architects? A film about the city? Or a fable about the city in film? Is Hubertus Siegert an apologist, a witness, or a detective? The intention of the following discussion is to shed light on these questions.

HUBERTUS SIEGERT AND RALPH STERN
A DISCUSSION OF *BERLIN BABYLON*

SIEGERT

The construction of the film is such that it doesn't try to go in one
particular direction or convey a specific opinion. I didn't try to know
everything, but rather to document what was happening, and what
was happening was very confusing. What you get is an impression, a
montage, that is visually effective because it works with contrasts. It
is intended to fascinate, not necessarily to let you know more.

STERN

How did you select the various architects and politicians you portray
in the film? Was there a particular process of selection you used?

SIEGERT The basic idea for the film was conceptual. Starting in 1996 my film crew and I tried to contact everybody and anybody who was involved as a protagonist in Berlin's reconstruction—whether as a politician, an owner or investor, or an architect. We wanted a variety of perspectives and essentially we thought we would do a survey. Very few people refused; they let us follow them around for an hour or so whenever they were working. Our idea was to go beyond the prefabricated statements and opinions architects use to promote their careers (although this may be what they have to do to survive). This is not interesting to me and I did not want to go into the detail of each and every person and each and every place. My intent was to find out what happens when a huge area inside a city is rebuilt and what forces are involved in its reconstruction. Also I wanted to find out just how much people—that is, architects and politicians—are really aware of what they are doing. My basic impression was that they really did not know what they were doing although they all believed they did. This is not meant as a joke—it is very important and really the basic point of the film.

STERN You said that architects were relatively open in letting you accompany them. There is one building in the film—Daniel Libeskind's Jewish Museum—where you show the building but did not interview the architect. This seems to be an exception to the other projects that you filmed, all of which were accompanied by the architect.

SIEGERT This is just coincidence. We managed to obtain access to the construction site at the time that the building was first opened to the public and we started filming. What I found very interesting about this particular museum scene was the emptiness of the building before the exhibits were in place. The architecture is so strong and symbolic. By shooting inside, we wanted to capture the "pure" idea of the building. To me this emptiness particularly represents the issue of what Germany lost by destroying its Jewish population. The same thing is true of the Holocaust Memorial, which is depicted in this film as being simply an empty field. For me this is the stronger expression and something that's very real for Germans. For Jews, it's absolutely different, of course, but this emptiness was something I wanted to show.

STERN The sense of melancholy, of melancholia, the sense of emptiness—this is something that has often been remarked upon in relation to Berlin. It is possible to speak about this in several different ways. One is the literal "emptiness" of some of the spaces in the former East; an emptiness that has to do with the modernist planning principles now rejected by the critical reconstructions. The other is an emptiness concerned with the loss of culture, specifically the loss of Jewish culture in Germany, an emptiness that the Jewish Museum seeks to redress both in its form and in the content of its exhibits. You also, however, provide us with some strong contrasts to emptiness. For example, you show an image of the Reichstag with its inscription—*Dem deutschen Volke* ("to the German People"). This image is then juxtaposed with the wonderfully active shot of the Love Parade—the annual "techno" party that attracts more than half a million ravers. In doing so, you incorporate a flyover of the Victory column similar to that which Wenders uses in *Himmel über Berlin*.

But instead of showing us a Wenders-like emptiness, you show hundreds of thousands of young Germans, perhaps the "deutsche Volk" referenced in your shot of the Reichstag, gathering around the Victory Column in celebration. What significance does this filmic juxtaposition have for you?

SIEGERT It's really pure coincidence again. The last words of the dedication ceremony for the opening of the Reichstag were something to the effect of "Bring up a world of love." We therefore continued with the Love Parade, which, in fact, expresses my feelings. The Love Parade was the most unmelancholy event in Berlin in the 1990s. Almost all the rest of the city is troubled by the past. To build in Berlin at all, much less to build a new Berlin, is mixed with the sadness of a lost city. Only one-tenth of the city's buildings were left after World War II and its aftermath; ninety percent of the city was rebuilt. For a European city, which traditionally has been created much more slowly, this was a catastrophe. So, the question of what to do, how to rebuild, was always there and it became even more dramatic in the 1990s when a lot of money started coming into Berlin.

But what was possible to do with the city was always mixed with the question, how can we repair it? How can we handle the lost past? And I felt that there was no, or not enough, reflection on this question among architects and those who would rebuild Berlin. They just wanted to go ahead and build.

STERN One of the issues related to current discussions of trauma and traumatic urbanism that becomes an issue in Berlin—and I think your film addresses this issue—is that so much of the destruction that resulted in the 1940s did not necessarily result from the war itself. It resulted from further demolition in the postwar period, some of which you show in your film. Part of that demolition was done for architectural reasons, new understandings of urbanism, and partly it was undertaken for ideological reasons. One of the troubling issues today concerns the still present ideological split between the former East and West. Most of the German architects active in Berlin during the 1990s came from the former West, and many of them have been somewhat hostile to the architectural idioms of the former East. For example, you show this wonderfully biting discussion between Hans Stimmann and Thomas Flierl, in which Stimmann says, "Oh, you know that stuff won't work." He is referring to the Berlin created according to the modernist planning principles of the former East. Just as clearly, Flierl responds along the lines of, "This is how we live, this is how it was, this is how it will work. You know, we're talking about improving it and not destroying it." One of the issues confronting Berlin today is that it is repeating a form of destruction—urban erasure, if you will—that was prevalent from the late 1940s through 1970s. In the former West, but even more so in the former East, significant buildings that should have landmark status are being demolished because they are on the wrong side of the ideological fence. Given your interest in reconstruction, do you have any views on this sort of further destruction?

SIEGERT I think that the creation of ideological borders is always linked to money; this is the power behind the ideology that serves to create a city. The demolition after the war occurred because there was no money to rebuild. Reconstructing a building is very expensive. We would say today, "This train station was very beautiful and you should have kept it," but after the war, this was not affordable. Moreover, many of these damaged buildings were near collapse, a dangerous situation. So everything was demolished.

Then a new kind of architecture came along—the modern architecture of the 1960s and 1970s, which influenced city planning throughout Berlin, but especially in the eastern sector. And they built a lot. But today, architects and urban designers want to return to the nineteenth century or even to the medieval street plan because they think that these images will help to create a true, public urban life. This is very shortsighted, in my opinion. Thus they're thinking of destroying parts of the city again. On the other hand, some of the structures built as social housing are in really bad condition and much of the former East has not offered very good opportunities for development. So we must be fair and accept these economic realities. But the ideological component is strange and I don't agree with Mr. Stimmann and all the traditional architects of Berlin that it is necessary to rebuild everywhere in your own city. What is lost is lost. And returning to that point is always sad.

In Mitte, the central area of Berlin, there is a site owned by the state on which the former *Schloss*, the castle, stood. On this site the East German government built, in the 1970s, the Palace of the Republic. The building was full of asbestos, which needed to be removed. But this removal is being used as a pretext to destroy the building. And now, they don't know really know what to do with the site. Many want to rebuild the castle. This is a hopeless idea and urbanistically it was never a very good building. It didn't fit into the city well and the urban space around it was awkward. Also, there are no realistic plans for financing such a massive reconstruction; rebuilding the castle to its original state would be very expensive. It would also mean destroying the remainder of the Palace of the Republic, which some feel is tainted by Communism, but which many of the East German people still enjoy. In this instance, the ideological debate is pulling our tax money in the wrong direction.

STERN In terms of city marketing, there is a lot of attention being paid to the new Berlin, the new/old Berlin, the old/new Berlin. You have shown us demolition, new construction, and the insertion of new infrastructure—most particularly the remarkable images of the new traffic tunnel that was built under the Tiergarten. But with the exception of the Reichstag as seen from the outside, what you have not shown us is the reconstruction of old buildings. One of Berlin's most costly projects is the reconstruction of the museums on the Museum Island. Both in terms of Berlin's memory and its identity, this is a site that has a remarkable resonance. It is the site of Schinkel and the Altes Museum, and the Neues Museum behind it has been the site of recent architectural exhibits, its ruinous interiors frequently evoking, in very Romantic German terms, visions of the sublime. Although you have some flyovers of these structures, you never penetrate them, never explore their interiors. Did you have a reason to avoid them?

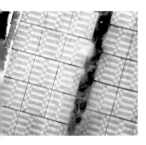

SIEGERT Once again, it is just coincidence. At the time when we were shooting the film, the construction of the museums had not started, so there was no reason to go there. But this is only an issue of restoring old museums, which is not a problem. The problem is the *Schloss,* which is also on the Museum Island.

STERN To conclude this discussion, let me ask you if you see any parallel between the reconstruction of Berlin and lower Manhattan, between the reconstruction of the *Schloss* and the World Trade Center towers. Do you have any recommendations to make?

SIEGERT I would like to offer a story that makes a larger point, within the framework of which you might find an answer to your question. In Warsaw, the Polish people also had a *Schloss*. During World War II, the Germans destroyed it completely. I'm not aware of all the details, but this structure was completely eradicated. Thereafter, it took some thirty years to rebuild this castle. The Poles, even under the Communist regime, wanted to do so, and in they end, they did. They're very good masons, so it also looks perfect.

In my view, this was absolutely natural because the only chance the Polish people had to do regain their identity was to retrieve their castle, one that others had destroyed for absolutely no reason—the Poles hadn't done anything to the Germans. With the Berlin castle, it's quite different. The Germans started the war and they lost the war—and they lost a castle. After the war, it was in ruins and the East German government decided to tear it down completely. It could have been rebuilt, but it would have been expensive and the East Germans didn't want to rebuild a Prussian castle. They had a new idea, a new hope, a utopian ideal of a socialist state—although it's true that under Stalin perhaps they had no choice. Therefore, to rebuild the *Schloss* would be very strange today because it's so implicated with the wrong stories. So I would say, just leave it as it is.

So, what about the World Trade Center? People in New York have to decide what stories are involved with this building. Do you really need to build it back? For what reason? You have the chance to build something new. It's the continuity of invention that is important. For the Polish people, rebuilding was really a continuity of invention because they had lost everything. For the Germans, the castle is not a continuity of invention; it's just stupid traditionalism. So it's up to New Yorkers to decide which stories of the World Trade Center are to be told and which are not.

URBICIDE
AND CHANCES FOR
THE RECONSTRUCTION
OF **BALKAN CITIES**

Milan Prodanovic

Any hope today for a meaningful reconstruction of cities and for their "reinvention," including that of New York in the wake of September 11, 2001, must take into account the global forces that have led to their destruction. The much wider significance of what developmental economist Michael Safier has described, in relation to the attacks on the World Trade Center, as "deliberately planned death and destruction in the heart of a great 'world city' perpetrated by groups intent on maximizing the terror and trauma of citizens without a specifically related cause and in the absence of any warning"[1] leads us to consider a variety of issues for cities throughout the world. Although local circumstances differ among cities, their similarities attest to the new cultural paradigm imposed by globalization. This worldwide reshaping of social, institutional, and security arrangements necessitates, among other things, a new concept of the city and a related transformation of traditional political and urban design paradigms.

PATTERNS OF DESTRUCTION IN THE RECENT BALKAN WAR

The painful readjustment of local and global imperatives within the so-called new world order is exemplified by the bloody regional war in the Balkans and the collapse of the former Yugoslavia. Among the destructive actions that took place in the context of the local conflicts of the last decade are those that may be termed *urbicide*. Bogdan Bogdanovic, mayor of Belgrade during the early 1980s and again in the 1990s, has used this word to describe the intentional, planned destruction and disintegration of an entire way of life in the city through the killing of its citizens as well as its culture of civility and diversity.[2]

This deliberate campaign in the Balkans resulted in devastation not only to the economy, landscape, and urban culture but also to the very idea of urbanity. Along with the hundreds of thousands of dead and several million more people displaced by "ethnic cleansing," deep scars were inflicted on cultural life, educational institutions, and public debate.

Various theories have blamed the atrocious events on the *nomenclatura*—the dominant class of post-Communist state bureaucrats—attempting to maintain their own hegemony through the systematic misuse of instruments of power inherited from the previous era, as well as through the acquisition of new information and media technology (primarily television), which gave them a monopoly on knowledge. This control of information enabled what were initially informal groups of apparatchiks, faced with the prospect of democratic political reforms and a free-market economy, to instigate first regional conflicts and later the larger Balkan war as a principal means of retaining power. Their activities brought into being a new form of regime that can be termed a "postmodern dictatorship." The overwhelming popular support that made this form of regime possible may be explained in terms of the deliberate fostering of attitudes best described as fundamentalist. These attitudes, relating to cultural heritage, drew sustenance from the long-standing anti-urbanism that has existed historically in the Balkans (and elsewhere). Without an understanding of these deep-seated ideas and their entanglement with what Manuel Castells has called the "rise of the network society," one cannot understand the concomitant rise of the "power of identity" and its easy manipulation into pernicious forms of fundamentalism.[3]

The attempt to reconstruct a "normal" post-conflict life in the Balkans today and to achieve a more socially acceptable transition to democracy must go hand in hand with a profound interrogation of the void created by the ingrained notion of ethnic identity as the exclusive source of cultural affiliation and "meaning." There also needs to be a serious reevaluation of currently existing models of urban life, of urban-industrial processes, of the urban-rural dichotomy, and of relations between regions. All these models are in process of economic and political transformation today, destabilizing old patterns of social, cultural, and personal identity.

FRONTISPIECE STREET CELEBRATIONS IN BELGRADE FOLLOWING THE TOPPLING OF SLOBODAN MILOSEVIC, OCTOBER 5, 2000

RIGHT SARAJEVO. FORMER PARLIAMENT BUILDING. PHOTO BY CURT HOLTZ

THE STRATEGY OF URBICIDE

The widely used strategy of urbicide carried out in the Balkan war has been further described by Bogdanovic as

the deliberate targeting of cities, seeking to destroy the security, public order, civility and quality of life of all their citizens, and damage or destroy the viability and livability of the city itself. This is a common element of acts of campaigns of terror of all kinds.[4]

The former Belgrade mayor used this term in condemning the destruction of Vukovar (Croatia) in 1991–92 by military and paramilitary forces under the formal and informal command of Slobodan Milosevic and his junta-like collaborators. The urbicidal acts included the attempted "murder" of the city virtually and symbolically; its physical destruction by random bombing, shelling, grenading, and the like; its strangling through denial of food, water, and energy; its terrorizing through sniper fire from surrounding hills and bombing of public places; and its ethnic cleansing, displacing populations from their homes by force. The motivation for these deviant acts—related, again, to a fundamentalist way of thinking—is linked to the cultural origins of hatred for the city, traceable to biblical times, and to archetypal feelings of hostility on the part of rural society toward the rise of cities.

But the recent events and their related symptoms also appear as a new kind of urban-rural confrontation, one in which a non-urban (anti-civic) element—specifically a mutant strain of former Soviet "sub-urban" culture—has found an existence within the transitional circumstances of the emergent new geography of world economy and global mobility. It has been facilitated by the popular support lent to the misuse of state power by xenophobic elements using legalized and organized oppressive force.

In the most recent Balkan war, the attacks on the city of Sarajevo, for instance, illustrate a strategy designed to humiliate and destroy not only citizens but also an entire city, along with the humanity, civility, and cultural diversity it symbolizes. The aggression against Sarajevo by superior armed forces was animated by a determination to "cleanse" the city of its very qualities of civilized life, using national, religious, ethnic, or political traditions as an ideological cover for what were crimes against humanity. The cities of Mostar, Dubrovnik, and Vukovar—each with a particularly rich, multicultural urban heritage—also endured this kind of assault, although the type and extent of the suffering and damage varied in each case.

Belgrade too experienced a particular form of urbicide, one in which a different configuration of internal as well as external forces was at play, including military action by the international community. NATO's intervention not only caused physical damage to military targets but also political detriment to internally struggling civic-minded movements. Belgrade's inhabitants became victims of a campaign waged against their city by national regimes indifferent or hostile to their plight, and the "collateral damage" they suffered—the literal as well as figurative fallout from the bombardments—was undertaken with full foreknowledge of the results.[5]

VUKOVAR. EXPULSION OF ETHNIC CROATS, 1991

As a consequence of these actions, many irreplaceable architectural landmarks were destroyed, including the Yugoslav National Army Headquarters, built in the 1960s, the major work of the noted architect and educator Nikola Dobrovic. After studying in Prague in the 1920s, Dobrovic established a career in Belgrade, becoming the first urban planner under Tito. In the late 1940s, he drew up the initial urban plan for the "New Belgrade," projecting an entire new town across the Sava River. But in 1960, disenchanted with the country's dictatorship, Dubrovic lamented, "What would have happened to Frank Lloyd Wright and Mies van der Rohe if instead of America they had come to Yugoslavia?" He continued, "The regression is evident; architecture [would have been] reduced to pure building."[6] Today one simply feels sad at the absence of Dobrovic's headquarters building from the urban scenery.

EXAMPLES OF URBICIDE

The experience of several cities can serve as representative of urbicide in the Balkans. In the case of the attack and siege of the city of Sarajevo, capital of the former Yugoslav republic of Bosnia and Herzegovina, the city was targeted for destruction precisely, as already suggested, because it symbolized the coexistence of a variety of interrelated ethnic and cultural groups. The local warlords insisted that they could not (or should not) live side by side. The city's geographic location, in a deep valley surrounded by steep hillside mountains, allowed the attacking forces under the command of the Serbian junta to dominate militarily from points above the city, thereby controlling its vital services—the supply of electricity, water, food and other necessities, and even humanitarian aid. What amounted to a modern-day medieval siege lasted almost 1,000 days, during which time the city was heavily shelled by grenades and pounded by mortar attacks. Sniper fire served as a pressure tactic for political negotiations. In fact, the war was a smokescreen for very complex machinations including social and geostrategic restructurings that were occurring behind the scenes. But this power struggle was made possible by the local warlords, who, with the backing of the government in Belgrade, garnered public support for an urbicide rooted in the anti-civic attitudes just described.

YUGOSLAV NATIONAL ARMY HEADQUARTERS, BELGRADE. DESIGNED BY NIKOLA DOBROVIC. BUILT 1963, DESTROYED 1999

With respect to the ancient port of Dubrovnik, now in Croatia, the city was a landmark reflecting the spread of the European Renaissance to the Balkans and a symbol of civility and tolerance since the fifteenth century, the era of the City Republic. As such, it engendered considerable mistrust, jealousy, and hatred among the socially isolated tribal groups living in the surrounding mountains. These groups, manipulated by the media, and armed not just with a distorted sense of history and mythical lore but also modern weaponry, shelled the city from both the hillsides and the sea. They then looted the houses and villages they had destroyed, at the same time brazenly claiming their right to the very same city. Their sweeping disregard for life, and the fact that the old walled city had been on the UNESCO World Heritage List since 1979, raised the possibility in 2001 of expanding the description of crimes against humanity to include attacks on and destruction of world monuments as crimes against culture or cultural property.[7]

DUBROVNIK, 1991. STREET UNDER SIEGE

The city of Mostar, chief city and former capital of Herzegovina, located on the Neretva River, suffered a much more severe destruction at the hands of Croatian forces between 1992 and 1995. It too was on UNESCO's list of monuments by virtue of its urban morphology and its symbolic and historic Old Stone Bridge. With the destruction of the bridge in 1993, it became clear that urbicide and hatred of the city was not just a Serbian predisposition. Here too post-Communist apparatchiks stirred up an entrenched hostility to the city that is typical of ethnic groups living in the belt of mountains extending from Greece and Albania to Kosovo, Montenegro, and Herzegovina, and to Krajina in Croatia. Ironically, these anti-urban, anti-civic sentiments, easily mobilized in periods of upheaval and change, know no boundaries even as they also serve to maintain territoriality and cultural differences.

OLD STONE BRIDGE, MOSTAR. BUILT 1566   OLD STONE BRIDGE, MOSTAR. DESTROYED 1993 BY CROAT FORCES

Another city, Vukovar in Croatia, which has a historical significance and cultural heritage equal to that of Dubrovnik and Mostar, was the first urban area to be attacked during the Balkan war—as early as 1991–92—by the still dominant Yugoslav National Army. These first attacks, while maniacal, were extremely inefficient (however cynical it may sound to say so). Jet planes were used to bombard a city of 30,000. They were met with a strong civilian resistance, which defended itself from inside the besieged city until the assault was reinforced by paramilitary forces, including large numbers of ex-convicts and criminals. The latter committed numerous atrocities, murdering civilians and wounding people in hospitals, many of whom were young people from ethnically mixed backgrounds. The commanders of these operations were officers of the Yugoslav Army, who often came from the same ethnic backgrounds, but were linked in some way to the archaic, anti-civic traditions of tribal affiliation. Vukovar still stands as one of the most dramatic cases of genocide committed during the war.

The loss of urbanity such as occurred in Belgrade and in other military command centers under the sway of governing warlords belongs to yet another category of urbicide.[8] A more subtle and sustained version of city-killing, it involves a general state of lawlessness, war-crisis economy, and Mafia-type control of most civic functions, from public utilities, banking (bringing about inflation and unregulated printing of national currency), and retailing (inducing artificial scarcities of goods), to the built environment. Characteristically, massive illegal construction, in which there is no control of development or enforcement of building regulations, further weakens an already eroded infrastructure (including the whole network of public health and educational institutions, parks and recreation facilities, and so on), and leads to a general implosion of urban life.[9]

Finally, the international community has also perpetrated a form of urbicide through its attempts to stop the war by using sanctions and, later, long-distance bombing. These actions only reinforced the ethnic fundamentalists in their vendetta against local civic- and democratic-minded forces.[10]

THE ORIGINS AND PERSISTENCE OF ETHNIC FUNDAMENTALISM

The long and vested tradition of anti-urbanism in the Balkans can be traced as far back as the formation of the early medieval state of Serbia, which emerged onto the historic scene in the eleventh and twelfth centuries with the destruction of Byzantine cities and urban culture by feudal lords.[11] In the absence of urbanity, hostility toward cities flourished in the Balkan mountains and became part of the local collective memory. Today's efforts to redefine identities must deal with these vestiges of archaic civilization, which means with cultures possessing only an orally transmitted tradition of history and continued illiteracy, and which have coexisted but not interacted with the major civilizations that have shaped much of the world as we know it today. The remains of Pericles's Athens, Diocletian's villas, and many Roman cities in the Balkans are reminders of this history of coexistence. Nonetheless, a self-perpetuating subculture with a latent hostility toward "alien" forms of civilization has persisted and prevailed. The geography of remote, almost inaccessible mountains, semi-nomadic existence, tribal culture, and difficult communications has facilitated the lasting avoidance of major civilizing influences. Yet such influences more than two millennia ago reshaped the polis of ancient Greece and brought about the transition from Homer's rhythmic narrative poetry and Platonic philosophy to Aristotle's prose. They inaugurated the shift to a society based on rational norms and the founding forms of civic life—the democratic city-state, *civitas*, civility, the culture of the free citizen; as well as tolerance for different sensibilities and different communication modes.[12]

The Slavic tribes whose indigenous culture has survived to the present day arrived in the Balkans in the sixth century A.D. The medieval division of the Christian Church into western and eastern Orthodoxy (a division without clear differences) further exacerbated their isolation. The history of settlement patterns and of rural-urban relations testifies to a continuing complex dynamic between internal and external factors. Selective aspects of this history have been manipulated by recent and contemporary political ideologies and by ethno-nationalist movements as part of their mobilization of violently adversarial sentiments toward other national cultural traditions and toward civility itself.

Combating these distorted "interpretations" of history is undoubtedly crucial to efforts to move toward a more integrated and peaceful future society. This is especially so as the recent revival of interest in indigenous cultural traditions on the part of dominant ethno-nationalist regimes in these regions has been animated by the "production of culture" as a mode of legitimation. In the eighteenth and nineteenth centuries, European cartographic techniques were adopted in the Balkans. While these conceptual and representational devices came out of an Enlightenment tradition of rationalism, they were used within the Balkan context to demonstrate the nature and value of "ethnic territoriality." They thereby served to justify the idea of the homogeneity of cultural communities within a nation-state paradigm.

145

JAHORINA, BOSNIA. CONTEMPORARY VIEW

In addition to such misleading and misguided interpretations, the nineteenth century witnessed the emergence of the concept of "balkanization." This term has become a colloquialism signifying small, isolated, self-interested groups defending their territories against one another. Again, the cultural roots of the concept go back to the closed tribal societies without a tradition of written communication. Combined with notions of intense attachment to place, this defensive posture has reinforced the perception of the inevitability of ethnic territories. In the recent conflicts, one frequently heard the expression "driven from one's own hearth"—an echo of an almost Neolithic sentiment of deep racial kinship and ties to the soil.

In the twentieth century, the succession of capitalism and socialism in the Balkans—still only marginally involved with the European trajectory of Renaissance, Enlightenment, and modern society and the corresponding market or redistributive economic systems—further fragmented the region's culture and subculture. Meanwhile, under communism, the concept of ethnic nationality came to be translated by the socialist-realist slogan "socialist in content, national in form"—a form of nationalism almost equally antithetical to civic life.

All this has contributed to the disastrous consequences that followed upon the disintegration of the region into antagonistic regimes, with what we have called postmodern dictatorships being shored up by fundamentalist attitudes.

HOW TO REDRESS THE PRESENT SITUATION?

The need for a new discourse and a new disciplinary framework for the reinvention of the city and of historic spaces within the post-Communist Balkans is self-evident. Spurred by a local desire for stability and inclusion in the global processes, such a project must address issues of both design and communications. It must retheorize the relationship between the artificial and the natural—in line with Herbert Simon's seminal distinctions between the normative and the descriptive, and the inner and outer environment[13]—and come up with new ideas about how to link the past with the future. But the fact that fresh memories and remnants of urbicidal tendencies are still present, together with a general hostility toward a robust civic life, means that any "reinvention" must begin by persuading citizens of the benefits of civility and its related qualities of life.

The contexts for reinventing civil society fall within a wide spectrum, ranging from projects focused on the coexistence of diverse groups, to ones relating to the conduct of "normal" life within a common urban space, to emphasis on the meanings of unity and the collective whole as foundations of common identity. The Cosmopolitan Charter proposed by Michael Safier as early as 1994, in the midst of urban warfare, for Sarajevo and other Bosnian cities in zones under the protection of the United Nations, advanced the rubric of "cosmopolitan identity" as a basis for conflict resolution. The intent was to initiate a social movement that would bring about a gradual sense of belonging on the part of all urban citizens—a kind of abstract "patriotism" in relation to the multicultural city, based on solidarity with other citizens and a sense of place rather than on ethnic affiliations. The possibility of developing this type of identity, however, although optimistic and well-intentioned, seems remote in present-day Bosnia, a country in the grip of ethnic groups with a tenacious attachment to clan, kinship, place, and territory. The transformation of consciousness obviously requires a much deeper strategy and longer-term actions.

Likewise, the concept of "open city" tried out in Bosnia and Herzegovina, on the model of Rome during World War II, has failed to bring peace and the return of normalcy to social groups in those cities. Still, it remains a good starting point. The open city concept recalls Karl Popper's idea of the "open society,"[14] which is particularly relevant to the reinvention of a new urban design paradigm. (The notion has even been used successfully as a "brand" by the Open Society Foundation, a non-governmental organization that has been actively involved in supporting long-term efforts to develop political, social, and environmental awareness in post-Communist countries.)

Also of paramount importance for the concept of civicism or civility being put forward here are ideas found in the writings of Lewis Mumford, especially his historical account (in *The Culture of Cities*) of the city as a transmitter of organizational principles in cultural form—meaning as a translator of social patterns into symbolic forms. The idea of a culture's built representations as embodying its traditions of both civil society and multicultural coexistence—also elaborated by many of Mumford's followers—is something underdeveloped to date in Balkan architecture but not negligible.

In addition, Manuel Castells's insights may contribute to the construction of a new urban paradigm—specifically, as already suggested, with respect to the rise of the network society in its relationship to the opposing trend, the power of identity, including the rise of fundamentalism as a form of resistance to the pressures of globalization. From a somewhat different standpoint, Paul Virilio's considerations on the "information bomb"—the impact of information and communications technology and the new media—may round out a meaningful conceptual framework.[15]

All of these offer a valuable basis for countering the influential, but for the Balkans counterproductive—even disastrous—concepts of Francis Fukuyama and Samuel Huntington, exemplified in their notions of "the last man" and "the clash of civilizations."[16] They can help us to confront the problem of cultural pluralism in a globalizing world—which is, it seems, our "postmodern heritage," with its implicit correlates of interconnectedness, tolerance, and the acceptance of all trends and ideas.

To return to the late 1960s and 1970s, one saw the emergence—at the same time as the revival of Beaux-Arts traditionalism and the "post-" styles promoted by authors like Charles Jencks—of the more significant and relevant ideas of Bernard Rudofsky, articulated in his concept of "architecture without architects,"[17] and by his followers, who saw architecture as being in a state of crisis owing to its lack of grounding in meaningful sociocultural contexts. The subsequent revival of regionalism in relation to modern architecture, especially the versions of "critical regionalism" defined and promoted by David Harvey and Kenneth Frampton, aided in the formulation of a new model with which to approach issues of the built environment.[18] Inasmuch as such concepts directly address the interplay and tensions between the global and the local, the network and individual identity, high culture and vernacular, they hold significant promise for a region like the Balkans, and may serve as an antidote to the distortions, "humps,"[19] maladies, and regressions that have brought about cultural destruction and finally urbicide.

CONCRETE RECOMMENDATIONS

What I am proposing here, then, is a strategic reorganization of knowledge and information. This is admittedly a grand undertaking. But it opens a vista onto a much broader movement for change than is now occurring. Indeed, at the present rate, it appears that it will take generations for a genuine change in attitudes toward urban culture to evolve in the Balkans. In the short run, however, and in the current transitional state of things, initial steps may be taken, above all with respect to educational reforms. Some of these reforms have already begun in the lower schools. At the university level, curriculum revision is key to modifying the traditional production and dissemination of knowledge and information. In particular, a multidisciplinary approach to the urban environment, with urban design as its component of action, is needed. The new program must integrate design with research and teaching, and find a way of placing the new concerns with globalization into the perspective of local context. It is within this conceptual framework that some colleagues and I at the University of Novi Sad and the University of Belgrade have launched a project entitled "Reinventing the Balkan City within a Sustainable European Paradigm."[20]

The belief that urbanity must play an integrative role in the post-Communist Balkans and counter the false oppositions between "open city" and ethnic territory, cultural pluralism and the idea of a single culture, is the starting point for change. Also among our basic objectives is to direct attention to the interactions among the forces of globalization, multinational organizations (the European Union, in this case), and local identity formation.

Any strategy for producing forms of knowledge relevant to sustaining urbanism must accord a prominent role to the study of urban processes. The "reinventing" of individual Balkan cities has to take place as part of a broader regional reconstruction plan, one that takes into consideration indigenous Balkan traditions. If adequately integrated, these can contribute real richness. At the same time, engagement with the innovative and modernizing influences offered by an advanced European framework and body of knowledge can ensure that Balkan cities become centers of open communication, overcoming their current provincialism and rudimentary traditions of civicism. In short, by emphasizing the understanding of local context, the concept of redefined identities, and the integrative role of urbanity, the project has the potential to initiate urban processes with far-reaching consequences for the stability of the region.

With respect to actual physical manifestations, the discipline of urban design as taught at most universities in the Balkan region (as well as elsewhere) has traditionally been linked to a conventional curriculum of architecture, dominated by a focus on high design. A basic result of such physical determinism has been to impose "authoritarian" methods on urban design. Especially within today's pluralistic framework, however, architecture has more than ever to be viewed as an essentially collective creative undertaking. It must enter into dialogue with the local government, non-governmental organizations, and commercial enterprises. Above all, the process of decision-making must be transparent and inclusive.

This reorganization of the processes of information and research at the university level, and of teaching practices, should also involve cross-cultural cooperation with partner universities in neighboring countries in the region as well as representatives from institutions like the European Union.

Undergraduate, graduate, and postgraduate programs in urban studies and architecture should incorporate meetings, courses and seminars, and public lectures that are widely publicized in the media, involve academic exchanges with institutions in both the Balkans and other European countries, and are available on the Internet. Such an integrated dissemination of knowledge can potentially overcome the fragmentation of cultural space, and in the long run, encourage peaceful cooperation.

The practices of urbicide we have examined in the Balkan context shed light on the grave dangers that arise from the lack of a real civic model. But with new information and technology, and most especially a new approach to the overall development of the region predicated on the reinvention of historic space, the kind of educational program proposed here may be expected to lead to a reinvention of urban life. Ultimately, education based on a democratic, participatory, and open transfer of knowledge remains the pillar of civil society-building.

NOTES

1. Michael Safier, "Confronting 'Urbicide': Commentaries on September 11," CITY 5, no. 3 (November 2001), p. 416.

2. Safier, ibid., quoting Bogdan Bogdanovic.

3. See volumes 1 and 2, respectively, of the trilogy The Information Age: Economy, Society, and Culture by Manuel Castells: The Rise of the Network Society (Oxford, U.K.: Blackwell, 1996; rev. ed., 2000); and The Power of Identity (Oxford, U.K.: Blackwell, 1997).

4. Safier, "Confronting 'Urbicide.'"

5. On March 27, 1999, the author sent the following e-mail message to friends: "We are witnessing at this very moment the military action of NATO over Yugoslavia (rockets and bombs are bursting around us in Belgrade every minute while we sit in our basement studio with e-mail). As we have already stated on many occasions, such an action of bombing will only strengthen the present disastrous regime. Human suffering and disaster will continue and even worsen." Quoted in CITY 4, no. 2 (July 2000), p. 286.

6. Nikola Dobrovic, quoted in Milan Prodanovic, "Belgrade at the End of an Era: In Search of a Vision," Journal of the Association of Free Cities of Serbia 19 (October 1998).

7. Prompted by the demolition of the Bamiyan Buddhas in Afghanistan, a recent board meeting of the World Monuments Fund (attended by the author) reconsidered the case of Dubrovnik. See New York Times, April 6, 2002.

8. In 1997, during the Serbian struggle against the Slobodan Milosevic dictatorship, a local democratic opposition formed the Association of Free Cities of Serbia, with an initiative coordinated by Milan Prodanovic called "City and Citizen in Serbia" and sponsored by the dissident paper Republika and the Belgrade Media Center, and supported by the Open Society Foundation.

9. Milan Prodanovic, "Wandel und Krieg—Urbanes Chaos—Urbane Mafia—Zukunft," in City Mapping—Mapping Europe (Vienna: Europaforum Wien—Centrum für Städtedialog, 1996).

10. March 27, 1999, e-mail sent by the author during the bombing of Belgrade.

11. Bogdan Bogdanovic, "Srpska Utopija" (Serbian utopia), Republika 17 (Belgrade, April 1996), special issue titled City and Citizen.

12. As put forward in the works of Harold Innis and later elaborated in Marshall McLuhan's work on mass media. See Harold Innis, Empire and Communication (Toronto: University of Toronto Press, 1972; first published 1950); and Marshall McLuhan, The Gutenberg Galaxy: The Making of Typographic Man (New York: New American Library, 1969; first published 1962).

13. See Herbert Simon, The Sciences of the Artificial (Cambridge, Mass.: MIT Press, 1969).

14. See Karl Popper, The Open Society and Its Enemies (London: Routledge, first published 1945).

15. See Castells, The Rise of the Network Society and The Power of Identity; and Paul Virilio, The Information Bomb (London: Verso, 2001)

16. See Francis Fukuyama, The End of History and the Last Man (New York: The Free Press, 1992); and Samuel P. Huntington, The Clash of Civilizations and the Remaking of World Order (New York: Simon & Schuster, 1996).

17. See Bernard Rudofsky, Architecture without Architects (New York: Museum of Modern Art, 1964).

18. "Context and Modernity" was the title of an international seminar held in Delft, the Netherlands, in 1990, out of which the concept of "critical regionalism" (already elaborated by Kenneth Frampton) emerged as a working principle.

19. The term "hump" is borrowed from Roger Connah, How Architecture Got Its Hump (Cambridge, Mass.: MIT Press, 2001).

20. The project is currently awaiting support and funding by the special "TEMPUS" curriculum development program sponsored by the European Union. Also being explored is the launching of the Alternative Academic Educational Network Belgrade.

JERUSALEM
THE SYMBOLISM OF THE DOME OF THE ROCK FROM THE SEVENTH CENTURY TO THE PRESENT

Kanan Makiya

In 1982, a thirty-eight-year-old Jewish American, Alan Goodman, shot his way into the first and oldest monument of Islam, the Dome of the Rock, with an M-16 automatic rifle. Once inside, he climbed over a railing and onto the Stone of Foundation, the *Even Shetiyah*, as it is known in Hebrew, or the *Sakhrah*, as it is known in Arabic. Waving his M-16 above his head, perhaps in a desire to emulate Moses standing on Mount Sinai flourishing the Tablets of the Law, Goodman announced his aim was one of liberating the Temple Mount from Muslim control. He then quietly surrendered to the Israeli police, who, in leading him out of the Dome, had to contend with the serious rioting that ensued.

Since this incident, a few dozen people have been apprehended by the Israeli police for planning an apocalyptic act of violence on the great platform known as Haram al-Sharif, or Temple Mount. Some were convicted; others were charged but released for lack of evidence. Nothing, for instance, could be proved against Meir Kahane of the Jewish Defense League who, before his own assassination at the hands of a Palestinian, was twice placed under arrest to prevent his preparing a spectacular attack related to the site at whose heart sits an ordinary piece of calcium carbonate—no different or more remarkable than any other piece of limestone, the most ubiquitous type of stone in the whole greater Jerusalem area.

In 1984, a strange sect of Kabbalists was caught hoarding explosives with which it intended to blow up the Dome. This incident was followed by one involving twenty-eight yeshiva students who were caught carrying guns, ropes, and ladders with which to scale the western wall of the Temple Mount, otherwise known as the Wailing Wall. Perhaps the most important incident occurred in 1985, when a more professional underground organization, numbering twenty-two people, was caught red-handed as it was plotting to blow up the Dome of the Rock along with a fleet of Arab buses.

In all these cases the perpetrators were working with the idea that they could set off a chain reaction leading to a version of Armageddon, which in Islam, no less than in Christianity and some interpretations of Judaism, is always associated with the Temple Mount area. So seriously was this chain reaction scenario entertained that during the 1980s several American universities held simulation games in which World War III breaks out because of a dramatic act of violence at the Haram or Temple Mount area. Even Noam Chomsky made the argument that a global war could be ignited by an incident on the Temple Mount; and Henry Kissinger, although he thought it unlikely, also considered the idea.

All of this underscores the point that if one wanted to think of a lightning rod for complete and total disaster in the Middle East, it would be the Dome of the Rock. Ariel Sharon's visit to the Temple Mount in the summer of 2000 may not have been the cause of the second Palestinian intifada (which has, as of this writing, cost at least 400 Israeli and more than 1,000 Palestinian lives), but it was the spark that lit the fuse that set off the conflagration that raged throughout the Palestinian cities of the West Bank in the spring of 2002. Here, in other words, is a building that is to Jerusalem and Israel/Palestine what the World Trade Center towers proved to be to New York and to America on September 11, 2001.

By saying the World Trade towers, it is understood that the symbolism is American. An attack on the World Trade Center is a broad-brush attack on American values and civilization, not just an attack on American policies in the Middle East. That is what makes September 11 so new and diabolically imaginative as an event. The same point is much harder to make about Jerusalem's Dome of the Rock, the image of which has been used by Jews and Muslims throughout the Middle Ages, and is used today both by the Israeli government for tourism-promoting purposes and by the Palestinian National Authority on its first stamp.

Whose Jerusalem is symbolized by the Dome of the Rock? The Jewish extremists who have attacked it since 1967 believe they are attacking a Muslim usurpation of a Jewish holy site, upon which they intend to build the Third Temple. The story Muslims give today for why the Dome of the Rock was built relates to an event in the Prophet's life in which he allegedly stepped up to heaven and returned from the surface of the Sakhra. It is, in other words, a story wholly internal to the Muslim faith, with no reference to any Jewish antecedents.

It is instructive to look at the real history of why this remarkable building was built, a history that has been erased from both Muslim and Jewish memory to live on only in very technical and barely read scholarly articles. This history tells a different tale, one that does not serve the nationalist and exclusionary purposes of either Muslim or Jew. It is that story to which I wish to turn.

FRONTISPIECE DETAIL OF ILLUSTRATION ON FACING PAGE

DESTRUCTION BY FIRE OF THE TEMPLE OF JERUSALEM AS DEPICTED IN AL-BIRUNI'S *AL-ATHAR AL-BAQIYA*. ILLUSTRATION FROM AN EARLY FOURTEENTH-CENTURY EDITION OF THE MANUSCRIPT PRODUCED IN TABRIZ. EDINBURGH UNIVERSITY LIBRARY, MS. 161, FOL. 134V

The destruction of the First Jewish Temple built by Solomon is depicted in an illustration that appears in a fourteenth-century edition of the Muslim historian al-Biruni's eleventh-century masterpiece, *Al-Athar al-Baqiya an al-Qurun al-Khaliya*, or *Surviving Traces of Past Centuries*, in the section that deals with Jewish religious holidays. Under the month of Ab (August), al-Biruni discusses various aspects of the Temple's destruction, including a great fire.

An accompanying illustration depicts the Temple in flames. A white inscription at the base of the burning structure reads, "Bayt al-Maqdis." The phrase *Bayt al-Maqdis* comes from the Hebrew *Bet ha-miqdash*, which means Holy House or Temple. It is significant that the earliest Arabic name for Jerusalem is *Madinat Bayt al-Maqdis*, or "the City of the Holy House." Today's Arabic name for Jerusalem, *al-Quds*, is a later derivation of *Bayt al-Maqdis*.

The Temple is shown as a large domed structure supported by a circular colonnade and enclosed by a wall—in other words, it has the main elements of the design of the Dome of the Rock as we know it. The artist imagines the First Jewish Temple as a tentlike structure, an allusion, however indirect, to the origins of both the Temple and the Dome of the Rock in tent construction. The predecessor of the First Temple was the Tabernacle, the mobile, tentlike dwelling place of the Ark of the Covenant during the years of wandering in the wilderness. The Arabic word *qubbah*, as in *Qubbat al-Sakhra*, or Dome of the Rock, a word that today means dome or cupola, meant something else entirely in the first century of Islam. It meant tent, or a temporary covering of some kind. The use of the word *qubbah* in the inscription on the outer face of the octagon of the Dome of the Rock, a building completed in 692, "is the first [known] example of a new usage for a traditional Arabic word,"[1] according to scholars. The memory of that original meaning also seems to have been preserved in the custom of covering the Rock with a tent, a custom that lasted through the nineteenth century.

There are other parallels between the Temple of Solomon and the Dome of the Rock as well. The Dome of the Rock was the first monumental edifice to be built by the newly emerging religion of Islam, just as the Temple of Solomon was the first monument to be built by the people of ancient Israel. Like that temple in the history of Western architecture, the Dome of the Rock occupies a special place in the history of Islamic art and architecture. It is the starting point of an entire aesthetic revolution that went on to produce such architectural marvels as the Taj Mahal in India, the Friday Mosque of Isfahan in Iran, and all the extraordinary works associated with Islamic art and architecture.

A second point is that there were no precursors in the Arabian peninsula for the sophisticated aesthetic statement represented by the Dome of the Rock in Jerusalem, just as there were no precursors for Solomon's temple among the ancient Israelites. Both buildings have in common the remarkable quality of appearing as if they have come out of nowhere, all of a sudden. For these reasons, perhaps, neither the temple nor the Dome of the Rock were built by the people who commissioned them. The Temple of Solomon was for all practical purposes a Canaanite-Baal temple, built, according to the biblical account, with the help of the king of Tyre. The Dome of the Rock is a typical Byzantine martyrium housing a relic, one that relied on local Christian craftsmen and ideas, and that borrowed forms already in use in Jerusalem at the time, in buildings like the Church of the Holy Sepulchre and the Church of the Ascension.

Finally, both Solomon's Temple and the Dome of the Rock were very costly, pioneering, and highly contested projects at the time of their construction. There is evidence in the Bible that during Solomon's time a strong current of opinion existed against the centralization of power in Jerusalem—a centralization whose architectural counterpart was the building of a temple associated with the house of David, the conqueror of the city.

Similarly, the building of the Dome of the Rock represented the resolution of a number of conflicts within Islam. For one thing, it symbolized the triumph of Syria (where the Dome was then located) over central Arabia. The governing center of Muslim affairs shifted from the city of Medina to Damascus. Crucial to this northward shift was the crowning of the Umayyad Caliph Mu'awiya as king in Jerusalem. This ended the principle of nomination for the succession and elevated the dynastic principle of succession through the bloodline of the reigning caliph, who was now a king in all but name. In other words, the same issue of kingship that existed for the Jews was at work in the rise of Jerusalem's importance for Muslims at the end of the seventh century—an importance that reached its climax with the building of the Dome of the Rock, at which point Jerusalem might very well have been, for a while at least, the holiest city in the Muslim worldview.

What makes the parallels between the Dome of the Rock and the First Temple so interesting, and more than just coincidence, is that we know from Muslim sources that Caliph Abd al-Malik, who commissioned the Dome of the Rock and whose name was inscribed on the building, was enamored with the person of Solomon, to the point of naming one of his sons after him. We know that at the time of the opening of the Dome he issued a coin in Jerusalem bearing a menorah. Moreover, according to Sibt al-Jawzi's thirteenth-century manuscript, *Mir'aat al-Zaman*, the caliph appointed Jewish Guardians of the Sanctuary to act as caretakers of the Haram precinct.

TWO SIDES OF A COPPER COIN WITH A MENORAH-STYLE CANDLESTICK AND THE INSCRIPTION "MUHAMMED MESSENGER OF GOD" ON THE REVERSE. ISSUED IN JERUSALEM AS THE DOME OF THE ROCK WAS NEARING COMPLETION. NUMISMATIC COLLECTION, YALE UNIVERSITY

I bring up all these parallels between early Muslim and Jewish history by way of introduction to the themes that I have attempted to tackle in fictional form in my book *The Rock: A Tale of Seventh-Century Jerusalem*. I am not a historian, having neither the training nor the temperament of one. Nor is my purpose, in this discussion or in the book on which it is based, the writing of the actual history of Muslims and Jews in Jerusalem in the seventh century, a history that scholars agree reached an important climax in the making of the Dome of the Rock. On the other hand, I like to think that I have abided by the principle that the human significance of a work of historical fiction is greatly enhanced by a close adherence to that history, at least as far as modern scholarship makes it available to us.

The problem that everyone faces in thinking about Jerusalem and the Dome of the Rock in the seventh century is that there are not many hard facts about the first century of Islam, the time of the Dome's construction. We know so little; so many sources have been lost. Most of what we do know only began to be written down at least a century after the events they describe. So, the question is, how can anyone, writer or scholar, go about providing an account of the way this apparently universal marker of such a deeply contested city was imagined into existence?

Fiction, it seems to me, is a way of stepping into the breach that scholarship will never be able to fill. Not any kind of fiction, but a fiction of assembly. In *The Rock* I saw myself as piecing together a variety of stories culled from the literature of three religious traditions, as though I were making a mosaic. You find the piece, smooth and perhaps trim the edges, and then try to fit it into a shape that in all likelihood originates in your own most private fears and desires. The outcome is new, unmistakably so, but new in a way that mimics the assembly of a building according to a new plan, using the detritus of greatly esteemed predecessors as its raw material—predecessors that in the case of the Dome, as it so happens, were all designed to celebrate the same much revered site.

This way of telling a tale happens, not coincidentally, to correspond to that of the chief protagonist of my book, a learned former Jew from the Yemen, Ka'b al-Ahbar, who may even have been an ex-rabbi, and who is said to have accompanied the Muslim Caliph Umar ibn al-Khattab during his conquest of Jerusalem in 638. Jewish and Christian sources tell us nothing about Ka'b. The little that we know comes from Islamic literature, in which he occupies a rather shadowy place. As far as anyone can judge, Ka'b is the oldest authority among Muslims on Jewish scripture and the source of many, if not most, of the Muslim traditions on the merits of the Holy City. It is reasonable to think that he, or someone like him, was the source of much of the "rock lore" around which Islam's first and oldest monument was built.

Ka'b arrived in Medina around the time of the Prophet's death. According to one version of events, he is said to have accepted the prophecy of Muhammad during the Caliphate of Abu Bakr (632–34). Mu'awiyya, the founder of the Umayyad Caliphate and a contemporary of Ka'b, is cited by the highly respected compiler of traditions Bukhari as saying that Ka'b "possessed knowledge like fruit, but we were remiss in relating it from him."[2]

What exactly did a man like Ka'b al-Ahbar do? Ka'b dealt in a genre of stories known as *Isra'iliyat* (Judaica). These eventually fell into disrepute and were frowned upon by Muslim scholars. But Ka'b had been dead for at least a century by the time such distrust became widespread. Thus, the *Isra'iliyat* are a historian's logical first line of inquiry into the question of what the building celebrating the Rock meant to the people who built it.

I imagine Ka'b as a *qassas*, or popular storyteller and preacher, a forerunner of the genre of storytelling that later produced works such as the *Thousand and One Nights*. The fortunes of Ka'b's vocation fluctuated over the centuries, combining interpretation of sacred texts, soaring flights of the imagination, and outright charlatanism. That is not to say that Ka'b would not have taken his storytelling as seriously as his listeners, for whom it was a way of dealing with the great metaphysical questions of existence. Ka'b, after all, had the reputation of being a very wise man—but so have many scoundrels in the past.

I further imagine this storyteller cobbling together the Bible, the Koran, rabbinical literature, southern Arabian folklore, his personal likes and dislikes, and, perhaps, what he felt his audience wanted to hear. I think of the historical Ka'b as an entertaining rogue, a man with an agenda but also one who liked playing to the gallery. His modus operandi, not his truthfulness, is what makes his contribution to the raucous world of early Islam so invaluable. In its early years, Islam needed men like him to flesh out its appeal and ground the Prophet's message in a larger cultural framework than that of bedouin Arabia.

What kind of a Muslim was Ka'b? We don't really know. He had after all converted on the very eve of Umar's departure to Jerusalem, and may even have been pressured into doing so by his puritanical and ascetic protector, Umar. Ka'b was a very old man when he converted, perhaps in his seventies or eighties—another unencouraging sign of a genuine conversion.

We also know, however, that allegiance to Muhammad as God's messenger was all that conversion entailed during those years in which Ka'b became a kind of Muslim. One could be a Muslim and continue praying toward Jerusalem, as all Muslims did in the first years of Muhammad's mission. Muhammad's followers also are said to have fasted on the Jewish Day of Atonement in the early years. In fact, one probably could be a Muslim and a Jew at the same time as long as one accepted that the revelation that had descended upon Muhammad actually came from God. Historians tell us that during the time of the Prophet, Jews used to read the Torah in Hebrew and interpret it to his followers in Arabic. A very early Christian church historian, Sozomen, had already observed these deep affinities between the beliefs of the Arabs and the Jews. So, the question arises, what was Ka'b? Was he a Believer in Allah, with all that later generations of Muslims read into that statement? Or was he a dissembling Jew, a fraud and an opportunist, as has also been claimed by some Western scholars and modern Islamists alike?

The larger point is that being a Muslim or a Jew in the seventh century was worlds apart from being one today. Sibling rivalries, which took two hundred years to jell into completely distinct and antagonistic religious identities in the case of Christianity and Judaism, were in a state of flux at the time of the Muslim conquest of Jerusalem. It is not even clear that they were really rivalries at all in relation to Jerusalem. This was another world, in other words, one with all the roles reversed, almost perfectly so, from what we would expect them to be from looking at the abysmal state of Arab-Israeli relations, and Muslim-Jewish relations, today.

I noted earlier that Ka'b went to Jerusalem in the company of Caliph Umar. The circumstances of that extraordinary visit are worth looking at more closely. Umar went to Jerusalem at the invitation of the patriarch of the city, Sophronius, a stubborn old Greek born in Damascus. Sophronius was about to do the hardest thing he had ever been called upon to do in his life—sign a treaty surrendering the seat of his patriarchate and the crown jewel of his entire belief system. And he was surrendering it to a man that he must have viewed as an upstart conqueror, a desert chieftain, and a barbarian. It is unlikely that Sophronius knew much of anything about Umar or his religion—the Koran had not yet even been put together into a book at this time.

To make matters worse, Umar came with a counselor and adviser on the holy sites of Jerusalem who was, in the eyes of his host, Sophronius, a Jew. And no matter how genuine his conversion to Islam was, or wasn't, in Sophronius's eyes, Ka'b would always be simply a Jew. Let us not forget that Ka'b's reason for being there, his role as Umar's counselor, and the enormous esteem he clearly commanded among the first generations of Muslims all must have derived from his Jewish learning, irrespective of what his religion might or might not have been. I surmise such a statement. I do not claim to know it for a fact. That is something a writer of historical fiction can do, which his historian counterpart cannot. In point of fact, the sources tell us nothing about an encounter between Sophronius and Ka'b.

They talk about Umar and Sophronius's tour of the Holy City, and in a separate fragment from the great Muslim historian of the Classical period, al-Tabari, they tell us what happened when Ka'b and Umar uncovered the Rock on the Temple Mount. As for Ka'b and Sophronius actually meeting, I made that up, on the grounds of its plausibility, assuming that everything else I have described so far is plausible.

At the time of this historic encounter between the two leaders of Christendom and Islam—Jewish resonances being very much a part of the person of Ka'b—Palestinian Jewry was in full decline, having experienced forced conversions and massive persecution in the previous two centuries. These had culminated in a Jewish massacre of Christians and a Christian massacre of Jews during the interlude of Persian rule (615–30). The last Persian emperor, Heraclius, instigated a massive pogrom of Jerusalem's Jews on the very eve of his own defeat by Umar's bedouin army, approximately in the year 638. So it is fair to assume, as I do in my novel, that a man like Sophronius was steeped in the kind of hatred of Jews that was so typical of the times. Moreover, we happen to know, from Sophronius's own words, that he blamed the Jews for the Persian conquest of the city in 615. Sophronius, in short, would not have taken kindly to the presence of Ka'b al-Ahbar at the moment of his greatest humiliation and capitulation.

HOLY ROCK, SUMMIT OF MOUNT MORIAH, JERUSALEM, 1891. WATERCOLOR BY CARL HAAG.
CHRISTIE'S IMAGES, LONDON

Why, one might legitimately ask, was Sophronius even there, presiding over a meeting in which a thoroughly Christianized Jerusalem—from which every Jewish trace had been rubbed out—was about to be handed over to a new Abrahamic faith, one that in those days ardently sought after Jewish lore and scriptural interpretations? Sources tell us that the Byzantine army had been routed on the banks of the Yarmuk River a year or two earlier and the garrison of defenders left in Jerusalem had long since fled. Sophronius's cowardly commander was hiding in Alexandria. Jerusalem, the holiest city of Christendom, was an island in a sea of enemies, the last city in the Fertile Crescent to fall to the Muslim armies. So what on earth was Sophronius doing there, dressed as the Muslim sources claim, in long silken robes with golden chains trailing after him?

He was there, I surmise, because the places of Jesus's life, suffering, death, burial, and resurrection were more important to him than life itself. We can tell that much about the man from his writings. At the heart of the Christian story, since Constantine and until the end of the Crusades, there was a place, and that place was Jerusalem. On the strength of his feelings for that place Sophronius had the gall to write to Umar in Medina and offer him a peaceful transfer of sovereignty in Jerusalem, but on the condition that he come all the way from Medina to receive the keys of the city from him personally. Sophronius did this knowing that the battle had already been lost from a strictly military standpoint. Still, he hoped to use the force of his personality, and all the pomp and circumstance of Byzantine art and architecture, to wrest from his adversary some measure of protection for those churches and places that meant so much to him as a Christian. To an extent, the strategy worked. Caliph Umar of course was not won over to Christianity, but he did end up granting the wily Sophronius pretty much everything he asked for.

Yet there is a twist to the way this story ends, a twist arising from Sophronius's ignorance of a man like Umar, and one that would have the greatest implication for the physical transformation of Jerusalem, a transformation that began with the building of the Dome of the Rock. Muslim and Christian sources agree on two things that came out of this historic encounter between Umar and Sophronius. The first is that Sophronius took Umar—I surmise in the company of Ka'b—on a tour of the Holy City. Both sets of sources are also agreed that Umar, who visited many fine churches, including the center of gravity of Christian Jerusalem, the Church of the Holy Sepulchre, really was interested in only one site some seventy-five to eighty-five yards away. That site was the Temple Mount.

At the time of the Muslim conquest, the Temple Mount area, which had been the focal point of Jerusalem at the time of Christ, was, literally, the city garbage dump. The Christian Holy City that the Empress Helena had forged into existence in the fourth century daily emptied its bowels onto the holiest site of Judaism. Whether this was deliberate is a matter of debate, but there is no disputing the fact that all Muslim historians during the Classical period believed that it was deliberate. It was to this city dump that Umar insisted on going, in spite of Sophronius's attempts to dissuade him.

The story of what happened on the Temple Mount is the stuff of myth and legend, which I will not go into here. But one fact I would like to point out is the first Muslim decision concerning the city Muslims now ruled, and toward which only thirteen years earlier they prayed: the cleaning of the holy precinct and the exposure of the Rock that today lies graced by the Dome. That decision, coupled as it was by a removal of the ban on Jews settling in Jerusalem—a ban that had been in place since the emperor Hadrian leveled the Temple Mount area and rebuilt the city in the second century—laid the foundations for the modern city we know today.

Why then was the Dome of the Rock, the first and oldest Muslim monument (which looks today almost exactly as it did in the seventh century) and the first great work of art and architecture of Muslim civilization, constructed? The evidence suggests that it was not built for the reason Muslims today believe it was built. The evidence suggests that it was built to celebrate and revere a Jewish rock, the last remaining vestige of the long-gone temple of the Jews and a relic that Jewish sages since the second century had vested with such importance that they called it *Even Shetiyah*, the Stone of Foundation, the navel of the universe, the place of Adam's fall and burial, the site of Abraham's sacrifice and Jacob's dream, and many other names. There is good reason to think that because of men like Ka'b, the voice of the Rock in my book, many or some of these associations had to have been on Muslim minds when the Dome of the Rock was built. But it is also true to say we do not know which of the many Jewish associations that the Rock had in the seventh century most appealed to the Muslims of that time.

Whatever those Jewish associations were in the seventh century—and scholars have debated the likelihood of this one versus that—there is no doubt whatsoever that none of them are on Muslim minds today. Both Muslims and Jews have forgotten, or deliberately erased from their traditions, all memory of these first beginnings. You will not find Ka'b mentioned in a Jewish source. He was, after all, an apostate, a renegade from the faith.

On the Muslim side the contribution of marginal figures like Ka'b, and others, has gone unappreciated, especially in the twentieth century. In 1946, an article was published entitled "Ka'b al-Ahbar, the First Zionist." The author, a disciple of the Islamo-Arabist leader Rashid Rida, set out to prove that Ka'b, the oldest authority among Muslims on Jewish scripture, had been involved in a conspiracy to murder his friend and patron, Caliph Umar. The article was criticized by Muslim religious scholars in Egypt at the time, but it is suggestive of the new wounded and defensive mindset that has surfaced with a vengeance on both sides since the creation of the state of Israel and the escalation of the Arab-Israeli conflict. A historical character like Ka'b goes unappreciated by Muslims today in part out of a fear that acknowledging his contribution might undermine the authenticity of the Muslim claim to Jerusalem. I believe the precise opposite is the case. The most recent consequence of this fear has been Palestinian denial that there ever was a Jewish temple on the Haram platform. In the summer of 2000, during the latest phase of the Clinton-led negotiations, a senior Palestinian negotiator was led to ask his Israeli counterpart: "How do you know that your Holy Temple was located there [on the Haram]?" Not only are such fears belied by the whole pre-modern corpus of Muslim tradition, I submit they make total nonsense of it.

In point of fact, the history of the site, of the building erected upon it, and of the rock it was built to celebrate, is a tale of deep complicity and connectedness between early Islam and Judaism; it is a tale of how much these two religions had in common when what was at stake was wresting the city away from Christian power and restoring the sanctity of Judaism's holiest site. Yet Palestinians today do not want to remember the fact that their great Dome was built as a continuation of the first Temple of Solomon, just as Israelis do not want to remember that their forefathers owed their resettlement in Jerusalem to the Muslim conquest.

I am going to "escape" into a different "ending" by way of citing an extract from *The Rock*. I do so not as a way of suggesting that history can be used to "imagine" or "foresee" a happy resolution of the abysmal state of Arab-Israeli relations today. Optimism is unimaginable in the context of what is going on at this moment. But it is one of the ironies of Jerusalem—a city richly endowed with them—that the very trip wire for complete and total catastrophe may well be the Dome of the Rock, a Muslim monument built by Christian craftsmen to celebrate a rock imbued with Jewish significance.

The passages that follow are by the narrator of my story, Ishaq, the son of Ka'b, whom I imagine to be the architect of the Dome. Ka'b may have been responsible for the lore surrounding the Rock, but he had been dead for thirty years when Abd al-Malik conceived the idea of his Dome. Fortunately, for me, there is nothing in the sources about Ishaq and so I had a more or less free hand in creating this character. The passages come from a chapter entitled "The Importance of Eight" and describe Ishaq's moment of epiphany when he comes up with the right shape for the design of the building that Abd al-Malik wants constructed:

I consulted Nicholas, a Greek master builder responsible for many of the finest churches in Syria. Knowing that the secrets of his trade were handed down from father to son, and could only be imparted under the strictest of vows and never to a man of alien faith, he refused to talk to me about his craft at first, fearing both the admonition of his Church and the ire of his family. By appealing to our years of friendship…and the pride he took in his considerable skills, I eventually won Nicholas over, and enticed him into a conversation on the setting out of domes.

"Give me a point, and a square," he said after crossing himself repeatedly to ward off the possibility that he might be committing a grave sin, "and I can erect any dome you want."

The point sat at the center of the square, where its two diagonals intersected. From the same intersection, another square could be drawn at right angles to the first. Thus were created eight equidistant points.

"Now think of these as describing the circumference of a circle. That is the drum of your Dome, and that is how I would mark it out with pegs on the ground."

I took to playing with this geometry, using a stick in the sand—as I often did when deciding upon a frame for chapters of the Holy Book… [Ishaq is a bookbinder by profession.]

In so tracing lines on a prepared patch of fine sand, I stumbled upon a remarkable consequence of Nicholas's rules. By taking the original superimposed set of squares, and extending all eight of their sides, a new set of intersections was harmoniously generated. I had made a new octagon, bigger than the first, but as perfectly derived from its archetype as the ripples made by a stone thrown into the stillness of a pond.

Extending the sides of the octagon…generated yet another pair of superimposed squares, larger than their predecessors. One could go on and on I realized. The pattern emerging was like a living crystal, infinitely extendable around a point of origin and always with perfect symmetry in every direction. Connecting the outer eight points gave me…closure, a boundary wall enveloping two interior ambulatories, which, in turn, enclosed a circle out of which was going to rise the highest and most splendid Dome imaginable. There before my eyes in the sand was what I had been looking for—a graded passage from this world to the next by way of the Rock.

Eight is the number of Paradise just as surely as Arabic is its language. God provided His creatures with eight paradises and only seven hells, Ka'b used to say.

"Why the difference?" I asked.

"Because His mercy is greater than His wrath. Is not the covenant between a newborn and his Maker made on the eighth day, the day his foreskin is cut? And did not the Prophet say that the Garden of Refuge for the Companions of the Right, virtue's ultimate reward, is the eighth level of Paradise?"

Four rivers—of water unstaling, of milk uncurdling, of honey purified, and of wine delightful—irrigate this highest level. The Garden is near the Lote-Tree of the Boundary under the Throne of God, itself carried by eight angels, all hovering in the heavens directly above the Rock. Fountains gush everywhere. Shade trees, date palms, pomegranate trees, and other fruit trees abound. The air is redolent of musk, camphor, and ginger. In such a place the God-fearing shall dwell in the presence of their King Omnipotent, and find out that all that their Lord had promised them was true.

Believers know these things because they are written. But not all of them know about the importance of eight. A bare handful realize that all the Peoples of the Book are folded under that number's divine wings.

Christians say that Jesus rose to heaven on the eighth day of the Passion. The pool in which they circumcise the hearts of their children is shaped like an octagon. Baptism, as they call it, makes the newborn a companion of Jesus on the Day of Resurrection. My Dome was in the shape of this number of the afterlife. The thought of it brought tears to my eyes.

In the course of a lifetime, a man is lucky to be granted two, three at most, insights into what is unmistakably right. Normally, the brain contents itself with shuffling around the dead facts of experience, trying this and then that, invariably settling on a compromise of sorts. But in the rare event of such an insight, the veils are stripped off life's clutter to reveal the bright forehead of exactitude. The soul has grasped a living truth! The Beautiful, a deeply overpowering sensation that fills the soul with the warmth of Rightness, is revealed.

What is Rightness if not also Truth and Justice? My commission was one of immortalizing in stone the Truth and the Justice of my father's Rock. Nothing about it was contingent. Like a harmonious chord, the building had materialized in my mind as an emanation of cosmic laws. The architecture was rhythmical and sequenced as it should be; it rejected the confusion of the superficial. Even the circumference of the Dome fell into place by itself, as it were, according to a definite proportion and in perfect harmony with every other dimension. As did the locations of the piers and columns that fell naturally on the points of intersection of my lines. I did not choose those points; they made themselves known to me. Nor did they conceal one another in the plan, but rather permitted, from any point in the interior, a view all the way across to the other side. Transparency, as all men know, is the rule in Paradise.

Can rotating a square around a point accomplish all this? Can it determine the appropriate correlation between His ineffable nature and Architecture? To find forms properly grounded in scripture and the stories of the Prophets from so few rules is more reminiscent of Him than months, even years, of knowing Him through words alone. And all of it happened while I was playing like a child in the sand. When His Design was traced out with my stick, I was blessed with a glimpse into the dawn of what was to come. I knew then that finally I had awakened from the dream of this life to the reality of the next.

NOTES

1. Cited in G.H.A. Juynboll, *The Authenticity of the Tradition Literature: Discussions in Modern Egypt* (Leiden: E. J. Brill, 1969), p. 123.

2. Ibid.

VIEW OF THE ROCK FROM THE APEX OF THE DOME

CREATIVELY DESTROYING
NEW YORK
FANTASIES, PREMONITIONS, AND REALITIES IN THE PROVISIONAL CITY

Max Page

Since September 11, 2001, virtually everyone in this country has been telling stories—about where you were, about what happened, about what is going to happen. My story is simple and was personally chilling: late on September 10, 2001, I completed a proposal for an exhibition at the New-York Historical Society with the title "Destroying New York." It was to explore all the ways New Yorkers and Americans more generally have imagined the destruction of the city.

Thinking about that exhibition, which I imagined initially would have an almost "fun" and campy tone to it, now brings a wave of humility to this historian. What was once primarily an imagining of fantasies and nightmares became a reality on September 11 and it stunned many historians into temporary silence. That exhibition will have to be transformed, take on a new gravity, and become something of a memorial to the events and the victims.

Talking and writing about the background to and the meaning of September 11 has been humbling not only because of the enormity of the event but also because of the many sinkholes that have opened beneath my feet, as I walked where maybe I shouldn't have—into the future. I am reminded of the continuing problem of those of us who are historians: we feel we have a special knowledge of the present (since we think we know where it came from) and yet we also know how rapidly the present changes, and how wrong our predictions usually are. We would do well continually to remind ourselves of what the historian E. H. Carr once wrote about the precariousness of the historian's vantage point:

The historian, then, is an individual human being. Like other individuals, he is also a social phenomenon, both the product and the conscious or unconscious spokesman of the society to which he belongs; it is in this capacity that he approaches the facts of the historical past. We sometimes speak of the course of history as a "moving procession." The metaphor is fair enough, provided it does not tempt the historian to think of himself as an eagle surveying the scene from a lonely crag or as a V.I.P. at the saluting base. Nothing of the kind! The historian is just another dim figure trudging along in another part of the procession. And as the procession winds along, swerving now to the right and now to the left, and sometimes doubling back on itself, the relative positions of different parts of the procession are constantly changing, so that it may make perfectly good sense to say, for example, that we are nearer today to the Middle Ages than were our great-grandfathers a century ago, or that the age of Caesar is nearer to us than the age of Dante. New vistas, new angles of vision, constantly appear as the procession—and the historian with it—moves along. The historian is part of history. The point in the procession at which he finds himself determines his angle of vision over the past.[1]

Suddenly history seems more important than it has in a long while. Scholars and the general public alike are craving—perhaps only for a short time—for a longer vision on New York's history, on the history of Islam, on the history of our relations with the Middle East. Historians should leap at the chance to provide the insights afforded by decades of research, but we should do so with great caution.

My goal in this essay is threefold. First, I would like to offer a reminder that while what happened on September 11, 2001, was a horrible act of destruction, it follows two centuries of real and imagined destruction of New York City. Second, I want to urge that we understand the three general ways in which New York has been demolished. First are the fantasies, nightmares, and premonitions of New York's destruction that have pervaded New York and American culture for more than a century.

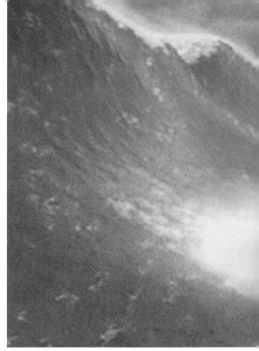

STILL FROM *DEEP IMPACT* (DREAMWORKS, 1998)

Second is the "regular" destruction and rebuilding endemic to a capitalist city of such intense development. Finally, there are the extraordinary moments of destruction, by natural and unnatural causes, such as the fire of 1835 and the blizzard of 1888, as well as the 1920 bombing of Wall Street, and, of course, September 11. By the end of this discussion, I will—not without some trepidation—suggest at least a few lessons we might take from these previous bouts of destruction and rebuilding. I will argue that if we seek to honor New York history and gain some redemption from this horrific event, then out of ground zero must come more than simply some striking new skyscrapers or a blazing memorial. We must find a new commitment to the public life that has been at the heart of New York's greatness.

Unimaginable. That is the word people screamed, aloud and in their heads, throughout much of September and October of 2001, and perhaps still do. It is the word survivors and witnesses repeated over and over: It was simply unimaginable that the World Trade Center towers were attacked like this, and that they collapsed into oblivion. But in fact people have been imagining this for years, and for decades.

In the summer before September 11, New York and its World Trade Center were repeatedly destroyed. The Japanese animation movie *Final Fantasy* portrayed a devastated Lower Manhattan beneath a dome, erected to protect the city from the assaults of viruslike aliens. In *A.I.*, a child robot finds himself drawn to a forbidden zone, called "Man-Hattan," overflowing with water. He makes his way, a child searching for home, past the almost submerged Statue of Liberty, past the lonely World Trade Center towers peeking out above the water, and back to the laboratory where he was "born."

Long before 2001, American culture had returned repeatedly to the theme of New York's destruction almost as a leitmotif—a tic we couldn't stop. In movies and literature, painting and photography, software and advertising, New York has been destroyed, by fire, by bomb, by flood, by riot, by earthquake, by wrecking ball, and by monsters. The range of ways America's writers and image makers have visualized New York's demise is stunning:

In Joaquin Miller's 1886 novel *The Destruction of Gotham*, a great fire engulfs the city as lower-class mobs violently attack the homes and stores of the wealthy. Only when Manhattan has "burned and burned and burned to the very bed-rock" is the apocalypse complete.[2]

On a visit to one of New York's beaches, the housing reformer Jacob Riis worried about the "resistless flood" of immigrants he feared would overwhelm New York. At Coney Island, a few years later, he would have found a different type of fantasy or nightmare of New York's destruction—the hourly tenement fires shown at Coney Island's amusement parks.[3]

STILL FROM *PLANET OF THE APES* (TWENTIETH CENTURY FOX, 1968)

In his essay "Here is New York" from 1949, the city's greatest celebrant, E. B. White, imagined the nightmare of an atom bomb dropping on New York: "If it were to go, all would go—this city, this mischievous and marvelous monument which not to look upon would be like death."[4]

In the paintings of Chesley Bonestell from the 1950s, the city is repeatedly devastated by atom bombs, with smoke and fire enveloping all of lower Manhattan, not unlike the visions many people in New York experienced on September 11 and countless others witnessed on television.[5]

In James Merrill's 1960 poem "Urban Convalescence," the poet laments, "As usual in New York, everything is torn down/before you have had time to care for it."[6]

The cover of the hip-hop group Busta Rhyme's 1998 album *E.L.E.*, which stands for "Extinction Level Event," is an image of a massive ball of fire engulfing all of lower Manhattan. Apparently another hip-hop group planned an album cover showing the destruction of the World Trade Center towers.

With SimCity software, computer users have been able to choose what disaster will strike New York, or just watch as programmed disasters play out before their eyes. With Microsoft's Flight Simulator software it was possible to fly between the World Trade towers, or, if one wasn't skilled enough, to crash into them.

Then there is the endless list of movies that portray the destruction of New York and its aftermath. In the original *Planet of the Apes*, it is the last image—of a buried Statue of Liberty—that we remember. In the recent movie *Godzilla*, the Chrysler Building crashes to the ground, hit by a stray missile seeking to stop the monster on its march through the city. Just a few years ago, in the movie *Deep Impact*, huge waves rose over the World Trade Center, obliterating all in its path.

The yearly summer blockbuster action movies to come will undoubtedly feature creative new ways of destroying the city, despite the pious claims in the early months after September 11 that our culture would never deign to make light of New York's tragedy by making it an object of enjoyment on the silver screen. In the millions, we have watched these movies, and played these games, all to get a charge from watching the skyscrapers of Manhattan toppling over.

What, then, do these fantasies tell us, other than that they have been unavoidable to generations of writers and filmmakers and software designers? On one level, the answer is very clear: New York has been the preeminent city of the United States for over a century. Despite its economic travails in the 1970s and the rise of Los Angeles (which has, not surprisingly, seen a growth in its own brand of destruction movies and novels), New York remains the city to beat in all arenas. To destroy New York is to strike symbolically at the heart of the United States.

Beyond New York's preeminence lies New York's form and the aesthetics of destruction. We have seen, especially in recent years, a genre of film and television that we might term "disaster porn"—a salacious obsession with graphically portraying death, mayhem, and destruction, whether at the mouths of alligators, by "extreme cops," or by alien spaceships.[7] With this cultural ferment, no place looks better destroyed than does New York. Godzilla pounding through Phoenix instead of the canyons of Manhattan would not have the same visual impact. Those who watched the disaster on television from afar found the sight of the World Trade Centers falling horrifying and—if they will admit it—also frighteningly beautiful on an aesthetic level. It was a remarkable "site," in all senses of that word.

We have continued to destroy New York in books, on canvas, and on movie screens and computer monitors for many reasons. But we should not ignore the psychological and the sociological—the more abstract—benefits this society has gained from watching New York being destroyed repeatedly. New York has always embodied the most troubling and longstanding tensions in American history and life: the ambivalence toward cities, the troubled reaction to immigrants and racial diversity, the fear of technology's impact, and the tensions between natural and human-made disaster. For this history and these reasons, New York remains a place apart, to many an island thankfully on the edge of the continent. To Americans beyond the city's boundaries, New York City has been and remains a touchstone, the symbol of the best and worst of everything, the barometer of the nation's health and sickness, poverty and wealth. Americans are married, not always happily but always intensely and profoundly, to New York.

In a nation as religious as the United States—and the United States is the most religious of Western industrialized nations—with a strong apocalyptic strain in its popular culture, it is perhaps not surprising to find so many examples of violent catastrophes. But the focus of so many of these imaginings on New York City is an important aspect of this history that has been little explored. We will have missed a central element of New York City history and American popular culture if we ignore the fantasies of this city's demise.

I would argue, finally, that we destroy New York in our culture because it is so unimaginable for us in reality not to have this city. It is, in a Freudian way, a healthy displacement of our fears onto the screen. As E. B. White wrote, "New York is to the nation what the white church spire is to the village—the visible symbol of aspiration and faith, the white plume saying the way is up!"[8] The white plume we saw on Tuesday, September 11, 2001, was the billowing debris of two massive towers falling down, taking with them thousands of lives. This was shrewdly done by those who knew well the spate of films and programs depicting New York's destruction—they succeeded in making our fantasies and our nightmares horrible reality, turning gleaming symbols of the city into burning signs of terror.

Cultural forms also express, and often reproduce, social experience and relations. This leitmotif of New York's destruction in our culture stems, at least in part, from the real, lived experience of New Yorkers—that their lives and the life of the city have been powerfully and permanently shaped by very real destruction and rebuilding. It is to the "regular" acts of destruction and rebuilding that I now turn.

WALL STREET, SOUTH, AND DE PEYSTER STREETS, NOVEMBER 26, 1935.
PHOTO BY BERENICE ABBOTT. MUSEUM OF THE CITY OF NEW YORK

During his brief return in 1904 from self-imposed exile in Europe, Henry James played an eloquent variation on a powerful theme about New York. The city is "crowned not only with no history, but with no credible possibility of time for history." New York is, always has been, and always will be, wrote James, a "provisional city," defined by a "dreadful chill of change."[9] Thirty years later, in 1935, a long-awaited visitor came from Europe to inspect Manhattan. Like Henry James, who had journeyed back to his hometown, the Swiss architect Le Corbusier came to see how well the most modern of cities measured up. In Manhattan he found a perfect soapbox for pontificating about his vision of the modern city, a "radiant city" of mile-high towers, submerged highways, and wide-open park space. Accompanied by reporters and architects, Le Corbusier toured New York, walking the narrow streets of lower Manhattan and gliding to the top of the Empire State Building.[10] Summarizing the essence of the island, he echoed James, declaring ephemerality to be the city's most defining feature. "New York," wrote Le Corbusier, "is nothing more than a provisional city. A city which will be replaced by another city."[11]

Though they used the same words, there was little similarity between these two men. For Henry James the "restless renewals" of Manhattan were a nightmare. The city's mad, money-hungry speculation had brought down his boyhood home and replaced it with a loft factory, and his genteel Fifth Avenue was filled with garish mansions of the nouveau riche. But what Henry James had put forward as an indictment, Le Corbusier now offered as high praise. New York was "a city in the process of becoming." He celebrated the city for being "overwhelming, amazing, exciting, violently alive—a wilderness of stupendous experiment toward the new order that is to replace the current tumult."[12]

Those two almost identical comments, made thirty years apart, remind us that this is perhaps the central tension in New York life: between celebrating and lamenting the city's propensity to destroy and rebuild constantly and its desire to hold onto parts of the past. It is also transposed into the cultural life of the city: the constant transformation of the physical landscape is mimicked in its social and cultural life. Conversely, the city's cultural vitality has been reinforced by the city's physical reinvention.

James and Le Corbusier followed and perpetuated a long tradition of seeing New York's essence. From the time of nineteenth-century New York's great diarist Philip Hone, who first declared New York's favorite maxim to be "overturn, overturn, overturn!" to Luc Sante and his biting critique that in New York the "past has no truck," the city has lived up to its cliché.[13] It is a city where the physical remnants of early generations are repeatedly, and apparently inevitably, visited by the wrecking ball.

The economist Joseph Schumpeter captured the essential process of capitalism—the never-ending cycle of destroying and inventing new products and methods of production—with his phrase "creative destruction." "Capitalism," wrote Schumpeter in 1942, "is by nature a form or method of economic change and not only never is but never can be stationary. This process of Creative Destruction is the essential fact about capitalism....To ignore this central fact is like Hamlet without the Danish prince."[14]

SLUM CLEARANCE ON THE LOWER EAST SIDE TO MAKE WAY FOR PUBLIC HOUSING, 1931. FORSYTH STREET, VIEW NORTH FROM GRAND STREET. COLLECTIONS OF THE MUNICIPAL ARCHIVES OF THE CITY OF NEW YORK

TOP MULBERRY BEND IN LOWER MANHATTAN, CIRCA 1890. PHOTO BY JACOB RIIS. MUSEUM OF THE CITY OF NEW YORK, THE JACOB A. RIIS COLLECTION

BOTTOM MULBERRY BEND TODAY. PHOTO BY MAX PAGE

By applying Schumpeter's concept of economic creative destruction to the literal physical destruction and creation of buildings and natural landscapes in Manhattan, I want to suggest how capitalism inscribed its economic and social processes onto the physical landscape of the city, and then into the minds of city people. Marx's pungent phrase "all that is solid melts into air" applies to both the transitory physical landscape of New York and the social and cultural dynamism that came to characterize the city. Schumpeter's phrase, apart from his celebration of capitalist innovation, suggests how the creative destruction of the physical landscape posed for New Yorkers the fundamental tension between the creative possibilities and the destructive effects of the modern city.

If one looks to New York's past, it is easy to see how one could view "creative destruction" as a natural, inevitable part of New York life, lodged in the very DNA or the bedrock of the city. In the early decades of the twentieth century, for example, the range of ways the city was destroyed and rebuilt in the course of a few decades is stunning. Along Fifth Avenue, the "spine of Gotham," the mansions of America's wealthiest citizens gave way rapidly to the apartment towers of the 1910s and 1920s. On the Lower East Side, century-old tenements, which could, if asked, remember the visit of Charles Dickens in 1832 to the most notorious of American slums, were demolished by federally financed bulldozers in the 1930s. Jacob Riis started the wrecking ball swinging with his campaign against Mulberry Bend in New York's legendary Five Points area in the 1890s. After decades of resistance by property owners who found these tenements profitable, and the development of new attitudes toward public takings, many of the slums of the Lower East Side and elsewhere across the city disappeared. The era of Robert Moses had arrived.

The extraordinary transformation of the city applied not only to private mansions and lowly slums but also to nature within the city. Residents who well remembered how lush and dense Manhattan's natural wealth was in the nineteenth century were appalled by the rapidity with which trees were removed from the city's streets and imprisoned within the city's new parks.

Certainly, the eloquent Henry James, along with his predecessor Philip Hone and his successor Le Corbusier, among many others, was not wrong about this characteristic of the city. Where he was wrong was in his rhetoric of inevitability, and his rhetoric of the naturalness of New York's "creative destruction." Rather than look at New York's history and see a steady, unending series of destruction and rebuilding waves, one should see instead an urban capitalism that produced and continues to produce an urban development process that is both vibrant and often chaotic. The upheavals of New York City were neither the result of dramatic, isolated natural disasters nor the "natural" result of government-sponsored urban renewal projects but, rather, necessary episodes in the process of capitalist urbanization. The city of creative destruction, which so many commentators witnessed, produced a remarkably uneven landscape of development, with excessive destruction by private capital in one area and too little in another. Along Fifth Avenue, the engine of destruction and rebuilding was revved to a dangerous level, to the point that the wealthiest of Americans— who owned homes and businesses along the avenue—fought to slow the engine down. On the Lower East Side, the problem was precisely the opposite: the engine was not working hard or quickly enough, with little private investment to fuel the tearing down and the building of new housing.

In the city that is so often called the "capital of capitalism," the crucial agents employed to regulate this engine were the municipal and federal governments. In New York history, one usually finds that at the heart of places deemed exemplars of the free market are governmental interventions and investments. This accounts, for example, for the peculiar paradox of Fifth Avenue: even as it displayed the "pure" market forces that drove the creative destruction of New York, Fifth Avenue became, in the early years of the twentieth century, the center of intense efforts to resist that market's destructive dynamic and to preserve a particular, tangible sense of place. Indeed, Fifth Avenue, the ultimate market in private property, was also one of the most regulated pieces of land in the nation. The modern methods of controlling urban land values, uses, and aesthetics all found some of their first trials on Fifth Avenue. It was the site of one of the earliest business districts and business district associations; it was influential in the passing of America's first comprehensive zoning law (the 1916 Zoning Resolution); and it was subject to informal as well as legal restrictions on architectural form. Simply put, even as it was seen as a symbol of nothing less than America's wealth generated by "free" capitalistic entrepreneurship, Fifth Avenue was the birthplace of modern city planning and some of the most far-reaching efforts at controlling the capitalist market in space.

Finally, history—or the invented past, at least—has been a powerful tool in the development of the city. New York's landscape, a place swept by change, rarely offered the opportunity to look forward and backward. This did not mean, however, that New Yorkers abandoned the past. But contrary to the popular sense of New York as an ahistorical city, the past—as recalled, invented, and manipulated by powerful New Yorkers—was, in fact, at the heart of defining how the city would henceforth be built. Indeed, all of the diverse city-building efforts New Yorkers took part in and witnessed were shaped by the use and invention of collective memories. Collective memories were fashioned and used with abandon by the city's builders, in complex and sometimes contradictory ways: by real-estate developers hoping to enhance the prestige of Fifth Avenue; by historic preservation advocates seeking moral inspiration and assimilationist lessons through the safeguarding of historic landmarks; by tenement reformers eager to expunge deplorable memories of slums; and by street-tree advocates who saw in nature a link to a more stable pace of change that would serve as a palliative for the ills of the modern city. In the ultimate capitalist city, where a square foot of earth in 1900 could command upward of a thousand dollars, and where time itself no longer seemed a dependable substance, collective memories anchored in substances more tangible than words were a rare and powerful commodity. For those who had the capital to impose their economic and political programs on a wider public, collective memories became valuable tools in the development of space.

In most ways, New York has been seen as the city of extremes. But, ironically, the city has not had the single destructive event that other cities can claim. Chicago had its fire, San Francisco its earthquake, Galveston and Johnstown their floods. But New York has never had the defining natural disaster that would divide its history in two.

This fact should not blind historians to the many bouts with catastrophe in the city's history. The list is long. In 1776, the city was burned and a full third of the urban fabric destroyed during the Battle of New York, which almost saw the end of George Washington and his army. Indeed, when Washington returned in 1789 to be inaugurated as the first president of the new nation, he walked by the charred embers of the British burning that had occurred over a decade earlier. The 1835 fire was even more devastating, with 674 buildings in lower Manhattan destroyed in a blaze begun in a warehouse. In 1863, riots erupted over the Civil War draft, which had claimed the lives of more than one hundred people. On June 15, 1904, in an event all but forgotten by New Yorkers, the *General Slocum* disaster, 1,021 people were killed aboard a steamboat that had caught fire in the East River. The milestones continued into the twentieth century: the Triangle Shirtwaist factory fire of March 25, 1911, when 146 workers died; the anarchist bombing on Wall Street in 1920; the plane that struck the Empire State Building in 1945. New York has had its share of disasters.

ADVERTISEMENT FOR THE FIFTH AVENUE COACH COMPANY. FROM COLLINS BROWN, *FIFTH AVENUE OLD AND NEW, 1824–1924* (1924)

It would be historically faulty, however, to see the attacks of September 11, 2001, as simply the latest in a string of calamities that have afflicted the city. The character of this disaster differed markedly from earlier, and especially nineteenth-century, disasters. Despite the powerful sense of shared catastrophe—which has left emotional scars on New Yorkers that will last for years—this was not a disaster whose tragedy was shared by all in physical terms. The attacks happened "down there"— downtown, in the financial district.

This was not the case in the disasters of earlier centuries. The city's early history is littered with events in which the distinctions of wealth and race were swept aside. In a city where rich and poor coexisted, with pigs and prostitutes living alongside Astors and Lenoxes, natural and human disasters were more likely to encompass everyone. The seven-year occupation and eventual burning of the city by the British in the Revolutionary War, already mentioned, was one such moment. The fires of 1835 and then the cholera epidemics of the early nineteenth century swept through much of the city.

In the twentieth century, disasters have not directly affected the whole city. The catastrophes of the past century physically and psychologically decimated individual communities. But the modern city has been defined if anything by the localization of disaster, even one as dramatic and vast as the World Trade Center attacks. Once the dust was scrubbed from downtown in an astute psychological strategy to contain the crisis, the site largely receded from most New Yorkers' everyday view, leaving only the vacant sky.

The notion that New York is somehow immune to natural and human catastrophes—and hence the shock of September 11—is a relatively new idea. To New Yorkers of the nineteenth century, who may have been told stories of the burning of the city during the British occupation, or lost family members to the series of cholera epidemics in the 1830s and perhaps watched the burning of much of lower Manhattan in 1835, or who later saw rioting mobs rage through the city in 1863, the notion that the city was "forever" was simply ludicrous. September 11 did not create a new city, but rather has brought us back to an older New York, where it was understood that the city is extremely fragile.

Thus there are commonalities between disasters past and present in New York. The painter Wassily Kandinsky once spoke of "a great city built in accordance with all the rules of architecture and suddenly shaken by an unpredictable and incalculable force." But we may more soberly ask, how "shaken" have New York and other cities been by disasters? How fundamentally shaken have the economic and political structures been that shape our physical environment after September 11?

New York has been, like other cities, remarkably resilient in the wake of disasters. Past disasters—"natural" or human-made—have not thrown it off its course. Indeed, far "smaller" events and longer-term shifts have ultimately had much greater impact than catastrophes. The completion of the Erie Canal in 1825, the rise of the automobile, the revitalizing impact of waves of immigrants during the past thirty years, for example, all have had a much greater impact on New York's economic and physical trajectory than individual moments of calamity.

In fact, city builders throughout American history have recognized that disasters tend to spur economic growth. There are countless examples of disasters that inspired economic booms, and commentators who baldly said so.[15] Indeed, while today it would be highly impolitic to talk about the "benefits" of September 11, for much of America's history a widely held belief among elites has been that disasters were in fact good for a particular city and the country as a whole. Editors and investors, philosophers and economists welcomed catastrophes such as the San Francisco earthquake and the Chicago fire as valuable opportunities for urban design and economic development.

Yet this seemingly callous response to calamities on the part of planners and developers also cannot displace what is another common experience of cities responding to sudden disaster. New York, like other cities, has been characterized in the wake of September 11 by a powerful psychological bonding and sense of common experience among its citizens. If the rhetoric of the city of creative destruction—the "regular" destruction of New York City life—is more about the inevitability of contestation, open and raw, the rhetoric of disaster is more of personal despair sublimated beneath community despair, of group cohesion in the rebuilding effort. José Martí, the Cuban revolutionary who lived in New York at the end of the nineteenth century, spoke admiringly of the city's resilience in the wake of the crippling blizzard of 1888. New York, "like the victim of an outrage, goes about freeing itself of its shroud." The democracy of snowfall, covering Fifth Avenue as heavily as it did Mulberry Bend on the Lower East Side, had brought out a "sense of great humility and a sudden rush of kindness, as though the dread hand had touched the shoulders of all men."[16]

During the month or two following September 11—and to a lesser degree ever since—the nation witnessed and participated in a similarly remarkable outpouring of generosity and humility. New Yorkers revealed a depth of empathy and kindness that not even the most optimistic expected. The heroism of the city government and the unions of firefighters, police, construction workers, ironworkers, transit workers, and boilermakers (the list could go on and on) who died trying to save others, and who worked unflaggingly to locate the remains of the dead, stunned a city that seemed to have forgotten the working people who built it. On September 11, blue-collar New York headed up the burning towers to save white-collar New York. Both came down together, in a deadly collapse. No doubt at the very moment of the collapse, somewhere in the World Trade Center a New York firefighter was carrying an injured bond trader. The efforts of those workers, and the sympathy for the dead and living victims, elicited a vast outpouring of love—it was nothing less—offered in innumerable ways by New Yorkers of every type.

Without undermining the true wellspring of generosity, it is worth noting a parallel experience in the wake of other catastrophes. There is often among witnesses to disaster almost a glee in having been a part of such epoch-making events. There is a sense of having lived in history, of having experienced an "authentic," potentially life-transforming experience. The philosopher William James spoke of the "pure delight" he felt at having witnessed the 1906 earthquake, and admired the universal "cheerfulness" of the San Franciscans he spoke with.[17]

Disasters also open the door to new development possibilities. American planners long ago recognized both the weakness of planning powers in the United States and the opportunities offered to their European counterparts by the Continent's many wars. They salivated over the examples of the radical remaking of European cities in the nineteenth and early twentieth centuries. Lewis Mumford commented in 1942, for example, that "there is a sense in which the demolition that is taking place through the war has not yet gone far enough" to allow for complete reconstruction along healthier lines after the war.[18]

In the aftermath of September 11, new models, new approaches to social services and to rebuilding, have been posed and debated—the sort of visionary ideas only rarely seen. The city has been the beneficiary of a remarkable outpouring of public monies and services for the victims of September 11, from the social services offered at Chelsea Piers for months after the disaster, to the paying of rents for victims' families and those living downtown, to grants and loans for businesses in the area. All these were offered with relatively little suspicion or skepticism about whether the recipients were "deserving." (It is ironic that just as New York has freely dispensed millions to residents and businesses, the city is in the midst of reauthorizing the 1996 welfare reform law and making many of its work requirements more stringent and its penalties more draconian.) New Yorkers and others have given without demanding "proof" of need, without the kind of distrust of citizens—especially of the poor—that Americans have come to attach to public benefits. In this way, September 11 has brought a rare weakening, perhaps momentary, in the attack on public functions and services that has swept the country over the past two decades.

The flip side of this opening of new possibilities is that disasters and the process of rebuilding rarely, if ever, radically transform economic divisions and power structures, as already suggested. Indeed, previous structures of inequality—economic and political—reassert themselves in the rebuilding process. This too has happened since September 11; virtually all public policies have remained in place, with indications being that elites in New York will become even more powerful than they were before the disaster.

The Victims' Compensation Fund is but one example of inequitable approaches to dividing public investments in the wake of September 11. What might have been a first step toward national, no-fault insurance, or at least a fair and equitable disaster-relief policy, turned into yet another iteration of market tyranny. In choosing a method of disbursing money, Ken Feinberg, the "Special Master," chose a market model: basing compensation on the victims' earnings and potential earnings "in the market" had they lived. Recognizing that September 11 was a political attack that victimized citizens, he might have based compensation on a political model. The victims were not only wage earners, but also members of the community. Compensation might be provided equally because those three thousand people were unwitting soldiers in the struggle against terrorism equally. Unlike the market system, a democratic political system declares that all citizens have the same rights. Relying on a democratic model—the ideal represented by the flags flying everywhere—one could easily have imagined a solution as radical as democracy itself: all lives are precious; all victims deserve the same compensation.[19]

181

One might also take a hard look at the renewal of public and governmental action, which seemed to have a resurgence in the wake of September 11. Now it seems more doubtful, despite a few gleaming examples. It should not be surprising that it appears that the greatest citizen input will be around the design of the memorial; the larger development decisions will be narrowly decided by a limited group of city and state power brokers. Indeed, previous power structures—the ones of the 1990s—will in many cases be reinforced. Those structures may be strengthened through the economic investment of the federal government in rebuilding the World Trade Center site and through a master plan that emphasizes private development in accord with now well-established models. The fundamentals of the redevelopment approach already in place by the six-month anniversary of September 11 were virtually indistinguishable from plans of the 1980s and 1990s: an emphasis on sleek and undistinguished office towers, complemented by high-end apartments and condominiums, with a generous helping of other uses to encourage a lively, walking neighborhood.

These designs are the architectural forms of the pragmatism called for by city and state leaders in the immediate aftermath of the disaster. Rebuild quickly, officials have urged. Rebuild along development lines we now know well. What lies behind this "pragmatic" approach is a belief that the 1990s truly represented one of the greatest eras of economic growth in American history. This is certainly true if one looks only at the total wealth generated and not at how it was distributed. For a large proportion of New Yorkers, however, the 1990s was an economic wash and not the great age of prosperity they have been told it was.

The 1990s did not see wealth "trickle down," nor did it bring the tilling of the fertile ground of prosperity, rooted in real opportunities, for working-class citizens. Rather, New York became something more akin to a profit-extraction city, strip-mined by financial and investment firms. This is hardly a model for rebuilding New York on more equitable terms.

Indeed, we have already witnessed the cessation of the larger initial discussions about ground zero despite multiple public hearings and neighborhood meetings sponsored by the Lower Manhattan Development Commission and other groups. Already we have to make an effort to remember these early discussions and writings about broadening "the site" to include rebuilding New York along new economic lines. Michael Sorkin, writing for the *New York Times Magazine*, for example, suggested that the city seize the moment to reconfigure itself into multiple centers—at the heart of Brooklyn, in the Bronx hub, and in Flushing.[20] This idea has largely disappeared from post-September 11 public discourse.

Witold Rybczynski, on the editorial page of the *New York Times*, neatly encapsulated the stunted thinking that prevailed by spring of 2002 in many minds: the whole rebuilding of New York comes down, in his opinion, to reconnecting the old street lines of lower Manhattan.[21] If this is all the rebuilding of ground zero comes to—some reconnected streets, a public memorial park, and a lot of financial office towers—then truly we will have vacated our dreams. Not long after September 11, on the other hand, the architect Rafael Viñoly called for "filling the void with beauty."[22] Perhaps it is not too late to ask: how are we going to define "beauty" in the urban context? Architecture critic Herbert Muschamp urged New Yorkers to look around the city at works of "progressive" architecture and use them as inspiration for the rebuilding of the World Trade Center site.

Beyond architecture, however, one of the things that makes New York beautiful, and great, is the expansive public sphere that has enriched so many lives and uplifted so many people. New York has represented, in its finest hours, something better than the pursuit of "social capital" or just "capital": the pursuit of social justice with the tools of the community, which is another name for government.[23] The World Trade Center was the symbol of capitalism and the free market. But it would be well to remember that it was built with state dollars and unionized workers, was owned by the Port Authority, a governmental agency, and on a daily basis was made possible by the remarkable New York City subway system and all the other services the city provides. When the buildings horribly and devastatingly came down, it was New York's workers and New York's municipal government that picked up the pieces.

As we decide what to rebuild at the World Trade Center site, and aim to reaffirm that New York is, as E. B. White wrote, "the greatest human concentrate on earth, the poem whose magic is comprehensible to millions," perhaps we will refrain from selling off a large piece of lower Manhattan for the proverbial trinkets, and rather make it the foundation stone of a new faith in public life and in our governments.

NOTES

1. Edward Hallett Carr, What Is History? (New York: St. Martin's Press, 1961), pp. 42–43.

2. Joaquin Miller, The Destruction of Gotham (New York: Funk & Wagnalls, 1886), p. 232.

3. Jacob Riis, How the Other Half Lives (New York: Charles Scribner's Sons, 1890), p. 229.

4. E. B. White, "Here is New York," in Essays of E. B. White (New York: Harper & Row, 1977), p. 132.

5. See Ron Miller and Frederick C. Durant III, The Art of Chesley Bonestell (New York: Sterling Publishing Company, 2001).

6. In James Merrill, Water Street (New York: Athenaeum, 1980), p. 3.

7. Historians have explored this recent tendency and its roots. See, for example, Mike Davis, The Ecology of Fear: Los Angeles and the Imagination of Disaster (New York: Metropolitan Books, 1998); and Paul Boyer, When Time Shall Be No More: Prophecy Belief in Modern American Culture (Cambridge, Mass.: Harvard University Press, 1992).

8. White, "Here is New York," p. 123.

9. Henry James, New York Revisited (New York: Franklin Square Press, 1994; originally published 1906 in Harper's Monthly Magazine), p. 34. This section is derived from my book, The Creative Destruction of Manhattan, 1900–1940 (Chicago: University of Chicago Press, 1999).

10. See H. I. Brock, "Le Corbusier Scans Gotham's Towers," New York Times Magazine, November 3, 1935.

11. Le Corbusier, When the Cathedrals Were White (New York: Reynal & Hitchcock, 1947), p. 45. Also see Nathan Silver, Lost New York, expanded ed. (Boston: Houghton Mifflin, 2000), p. 11.

12. Le Corbusier, p. 45.

13. Diary of Philip Hone (1845), quoted in William Cole, ed., Quotable New York: A Literary Companion (New York: Penguin, 1992), p. 50; Luc Sante, Low Life: Lures and Snares of Old New York (New York: Random House, 1991), p. x.

14. See Joseph A. Schumpeter, "The Process of Creative Destruction," chap. 7 in Capitalism, Socialism and Democracy (New York: Harper & Row, 1976; originally published 1942).

15. See Kevin Rozario, "What Comes Down Must Go Up: Why Disasters Have Been Good for American Capitalism," in Steven Biel, ed., American Disasters (New York: New York University Press, 2001).

16. José Martí, "New York under the Snow," in Phillip Lopate, ed., Writing New York: A Literary Anthology (New York: Library of America, 1998), p. 277.

17. William James quoted in Rozario, "What Comes Down Must Go Up," manuscript version of essay (cited note 15) in possession of the author.

18. Lewis Mumford, City Development: Studies in Renewal and Development (New York: Harcourt, Brace, 1946), p. 157, quoted in Rozario, p. 74.

19. See Eve Weinbaum and Max Page, "Measuring the Value of Lives," Christian Science Monitor, January 4, 2002.

20. Michael Sorkin, "Manifestoes for the Next New York: Michael Sorkin on the Boroughs," New York Times Magazine, November 11, 2001.

21. Witold Rybzyinski, "How Quickly a City Can Grow," New York Times, March 25, 2002, sec. A, p. 21.

22. Rafael Viñoly, "Fill the Void with Beauty," New York Times, September 23, 2001.

23. For a discussion of "social capital," see Robert Putnam, Bowling Alone: The Collapse and Revival of American Community (New York: Simon and Schuster, 2000). For an outstanding look at the golden age of New York's social democratic policies, see Joshua Freeman, Working-Class New York: Life and Labor since World War II (New York: New Press, 2000).

EPILOGUE
AN ARCHITECTURE OF LIBERTY?
THE CITY AS DEMOCRACY'S FORGE

Benjamin R. Barber

The issue of the city and democracy can be explored only in a historical and conceptual context: is there an architecture of liberty defined by the construction of the city (with its roots in the polis and the town) that has consequences for democracy in an era of suburbanization and globalization? To answer so broad a question is necessarily to take certain rather egregious liberties with both history and political and social theory as well as with the architecture of democratic space. Yet only in this way can the connections between social form and physical space, between civic culture and architecture, be illuminated—the kind of thing I suspect architects with a social conscience think about (or ought to think about) quite a lot. These will make it possible to envision linkages to the governing norms of societies and to the nature of human beings in society—to the human genus, the social genus, and the economic genus.

	SOCIAL FORM	SOCIAL SPACE	SOCIAL BUILDING	GOVERNING NORM	HUMAN TYPE	SOCIAL TYPE	ECONOMIC TYPE
	POLIS	AGORA (PUBLIC MARKET)	OUTDOOR ASSEMBLY	JUSTICE	CITIZEN	*GEMEINSCHAFT*	ARTISAN (PASTORAL)
	CITY	CROSSROADS	CITY HALL (MARKET/UNIVERSITY/ CATHEDRAL)	EQUALITY	INDIVIDUAL (LONER)	CIVIL SOCIETY	TRADE
	NATION-STATE (CAPITAL CITY)	BOULEVARD	CAPITOL	LIBERTY / LAW	LEGAL PERSON	*GESELLSCHAFT*	INDUSTRIAL (MANUFACTURING)
	SUBURBIA	MALL	MULTIPLEX	PROFIT	CONSUMER	MARKET	CONSUMPTION
	COSMO-POLIS (GLOBAL "CITY")	PORT/PORTAL	WEB	INFORMATION	VIRTUAL- INTERACTOR	NETWORK	INFOTAINMENT

INTERDEPENDENCE ←——→ INDEPENDENCE

THE EVOLVING ARCHITECTURE OF DEMOCRATIC SPACE

The conceptual chart above offers a visual shorthand of my argument. It represents an evolutionary graph linking types of democracy to forms of social organization and styles of architecture. The three traditional ideal types (polis, town, and city) speak to the past and present. Our future situation is given by the last two rows, identified on the chart as suburbia and the virtual portal, the latter a coming global form—part virtual, part real—whose architecture is not yet specified. This projected future goes to the heart of the issues facing us today. The three historical forms I have posited (with apologies to historical reality) act as a backdrop.

Obviously, in making such broad connections, I am generalizing in ways about which those who take responsibility for any one of the relevant domains—economists, sociologists, anthropologists, political and ethical philosophers, architects, and anthropologists—will be appropriately appalled. But since my goal is to develop a framework within which we can ask some larger normative and prescriptive questions about the issue of what globalization and the virtualization of space are likely to mean for democracy, and what a global physical space might look like architecturally if its purpose is to generate and sustain democracy, I feel vindicated in the grossness of these generalizations.

1.

I begin with the well-worn but justifiable assumption that democracy was born in the world of the polis—a very peculiar, particular, and limited world of the tribe on the way to becoming self-governing in small tribal communities like ancient Athens, Sparta, and Thebes. The spatial architecture of the polis is dominated by the agora or open marketplace, a marketplace of ideas as well as goods. The primary spaces of the Athenian polis are constituted not so much by buildings but by open-air plazas and hillside venues. These spaces include the Pnyx (the meeting place for the assembly) and the Acropolis, whose temples were the seat of the city's defining religious cults and historically embedded deities—and in time the seat of Athenian justice as well (as tribal earth gods yielded to cosmopolitan air gods).

For the Athenians, Aristotle reminds us, man is a *zoon politikon*, a political animal whose essence (unlike either gods or beasts) is social and interactive, making him a natural denizen of towns and cities. The citizen is understood not as one particular kind of human being but as the crux of what it means to be human. What makes the tribe human is its civic quality.

To certain participatory democratic purists, this polis form of democracy alone is truly democratic. For them, there can be no real democracy outside the polis, so (they argue) there has been none for several thousand years. To be consistently purist, however, requires that one deny the possibility of a genuine democracy altogether. After all, the democracy of Athens was a democracy in which only about one person in five or six was actually a citizen. Most of us prefer to think that democracy is always a process rather than an end state, and hence always an experiment in process—imperfect and human, but better than the alternatives. In any case, the polis is the source for the idea of the *Gemeinde* (community), and the archetype that Ferdinand Tönnies calls the *Gemeinschaft*, that small and intimate form of human association based on kinship relations and natural affinity where people know one another "face to face," a form of association closely connected to an artisan pastoral economy rooted in labor.

The town or *Gemeinde* then becomes the ideal space associated with the birth of democracy, understood as a simple tribal form of self-government among a narrow group of men who share culture, history, values, religion, and a common past. It is a form of governance derived from the polis for a homogeneous limited society, and in its physical spaces and its economy it is stringently delimited and rooted in autarky (economic self-sufficiency). An economic isolation that yields economic independence from the rest of the world is its virtue and its defect.

With the modern nation-state, the intimacy of the polis and *Gemeinde* is superseded by a larger, more pluralistic entity rooted in power, sovereignty, and contract. It is this premise that undergirds the thought of modern political theorists from Machiavelli, Rousseau, Locke, and Madison down to Dewey and Arendt, all of whom accept a compromised form of democracy in building their contract theories. In modern social thought, democracy is most often associated not with the insular tribal polis or the small town (*Gemeinde*), but with the principality, what in time becomes the city (although, as Rousseau suggests, capital cities have features inimical to democracy). Hence there arises the defining modern idea of democracy in the city or of the city as the forge of democracy. Where the polis is small and parochial, often based on exclusionary forms of identity, the city embodies a far more encompassing set of associations that are more anonymous in character and more open to the outside (centered in trade rather than in autarky). The city is the polis expanded, the polis opened up, the polis pushed to interaction. It is no longer a closed agora, but an open crossroads where the "outside" mixes with the agora's provincial "inside," and where the econom y is penetrated by the political (a city hall), the religious (a cathedral), the arts (a theater), and the civic (schools, guilds, civic associations). The tightly wound identities that defined the inner spaces of the polis are replaced by more diversified social and public spaces.

In the modern construction that is the city, the citizen defined by his common religion and historical values, whose commonality with others rests on a common past, is displaced by the tradesman, the traveler, the vagabond, and the loner—women and men no longer defined by a common past but by aspiring individual futures, by displacement rather than by place, by movement rather than by stasis. Where the architecture of the polis privileges the public (common market and religious and assembly places where the *res publica*, literally "things of the public," are manifest), the architecture of the city privileges the private and the personal (distinctive neighborhoods, broad thoroughfares leading to the outside, innumerable private and civic spaces where individuals and groups can pursue different goals). Where common identity makes for an understanding of the person as a public citizen, difference defines the city dweller as a private being with social characteristics that differentiate one from the next.

From this is born a more individualized form of democracy oriented toward private liberty and personal property rather than toward civic duties and public justice (compare Aristotle and Locke). Civic intimacy is lost, but the freedom of a liberating anonymity is gained (the example of small-town gays and rebels who have fled their birthright to find a place for themselves in big cities comes to mind). Scale makes common identity more difficult but facilitates individual freedom. As Sheldon Wolin notes in his *Politics and Vision* (1960), the publicness of polis life (in which the private and the economic were relegated to a homebound private family life overseen by uncivic women) is displaced in the city by the privateness of city life. The outside moves inside, public space is privatized, and the personal comes to trump the political. Where in the polis public justice is the highest good, in the city, and in the new liberal forms of democracy associated with it, private liberty (and the property by which it is defined) is the highest good, a move that effectively privatizes the public good. In time, this privatization of the public leads people to understand the idea of the public as inimical to liberty—a way of thinking wholly foreign to the polis and the town.

With the new social genus produced by the city's diversity of habitations and identities comes a new democratic equality. In the ancient world of the polis, citizens were equal but most men and women were not citizens. In the modern world of the city, whether citizens or not, all residents achieve a kind of base identity rooted in their anonymous economic status as producers and consumers, which puts them on an equal footing. It is the equality of anonymity, of individuals whose wants and needs are roughly commensurable, who are encouraged to pursue their liberty through a politics of contractualism and bilateral treaties. Even the social bond is contractual—a surrender of natural liberty in the name of communal security (this is equality and social contract as portrayed by Thomas Hobbes, in which the weakest can in concert kill the strongest, and in which even the best men are plagued by the needs and wants of the worst). This is the equality of opportunity that comes with a life in the city, an equality favored by urban architecture and encompassing spaces that deny the aristocracy of special souls (one thinks of Plato and Aristotle). To be sure, the city still reflects economic inequalities, but these (unlike the inequalities of "natural aristocracy") are a matter of ambition and the willingness to work, not some preternatural human nature. For men, in the new city, are "born equal."

How different is the democracy that emerges from this urban architecture. The change is, of course, hardly sudden. The Athenian polis is succeeded by the town republic, which in time becomes feudal empire and then after hundreds of years breaks again into discrete habitats marked by trading towns that rise up along rivers, seaways, and trading routes. Only after centuries do such cities conquer the lands around them and constitute themselves as nation-states, centered by great capital cities whose cultures define the cultures of the new nations to which they help give birth. Lisbon is Portugal, Paris is France, London is England: the city grows around its new urban core in expanding territorial circles until a whole nation is united.

Ironically, in acquiring territory and boundaries, the nation-state loses some of the flexibility and openness of the trading city. It looks inward not outward, aware again of its vulnerabilities and surrounded by frontiers that serve the same purposes as the fallen walls of medieval towns. Its economy becomes more parochial and mercantile—discomfiting the very free-trading cities that lie at its heart. The governing norm of this new, more expansive polity is law, and its citizens are now legal persons or rights-bearing individuals whose liberty is defined less by their participation in politics than by the birthright that comes with their territorially defined nationhood. Their possession of liberty and (especially) property is now predicated on their membership in the nation.

This brief history is roughly the one traced by Ferdinand Tönnies (in his nineteenth-century classic *Gemeinschaft und Gesellschaft*), as he describes the evolution of the small Germanic tribal *Gemeinschaft* into the large associational *Gesellschaft*—an expansive legal and contractual entity in which citizens are united not by kinship and community but by reciprocal self-interest and the law that serves it. The limited economy of the agora and the mercantile economy of young nation-states give way to an industrial, manufacturing economy that is at once protectionist and bent on global trade. Thus can we summarize several thousand years in a few clichéd historical archetypes.

2.

In reality, of course, these historical "stages" overlap and intersect; there are few modern nations in which elements of the agora, the provincial town, the cosmopolitan city, and the burgeoning nation-state cannot be found, and in which the several elements of democratic citizenship (the responsible citizen, the contract-prone property owner, the expansive trader, the rights-bearing individual) cannot be identified. Americans are exactly such historical amalgams. Spend a day in Stockbridge, Massachusetts (a polis-like small town); Macon, Georgia (a small Southern city once rooted in agriculture); St. Louis, Missouri (a trading city whose river geography has determined its identity); and New York (a global, multicultural city that bursts the bonds of the nation-state), and you traverse thousands of years of history within a single nation and time period, watching evolving city-spaces and changing economies alter how people live, what they understand as citizenship, and how they interact. Still, the denizens of these varied venues are all modern Americans.

What this history of the city fails to capture, however, is the emergence of a new form of social geography in the United States before and after World War II. Spurred by the automobile and its mobility (an immanent architecture in its own right) as well as a growing fear of the diversity, anonymity, and risk associated with urban life, America dispersed its population to new suburbs. There, forms of social existence and geographical space unlike any known to villages, towns, or cities appeared, deeply imprinting modern American life with a suburban culture that was neither rural nor urban, neither town nor city—a culture that was anything but civic and only problematically democratic. Whether or not it can be seen as hegemonic for all of America, the new suburban culture encompasses more than half the American population, and has impressed itself on urban life as well (through the branding, malling, multiplexing, and decentralization of city life as represented, for example, in the new Times Square). Fifty-five to sixty percent of the American population live neither in what we would call rural areas, nor in towns, nor in cities, but in burgeoning zones encircling the cities and swallowing up the towns and villages that once dotted the landscape between cities.

As a powerful and novel defining social form of life in America, suburbia is quickly being replicated elsewhere. Europe, linked by rail rather than by automobiles, remains more city-centered than America, and suburbs there have first often been the home of poor, de-urbanized minorities rather than of well-off majorities trying to escape them. But the private home with a yard and a garage for the car that makes the home possible is a dream of global reach, and it seems to seduce people around the world before they can consider its impact on democracy and on citizenship. (Of course, where people see themselves as private individuals first rather than as citizens, this may not seem of much importance.)

Yet the physical and architectural constraints of suburbia bring with them a whole new set of political ideas radically different from those that preceded them. In the polis, the city, and the urbanized, industrial nation-state, one can see family resemblances between what I have called the governing norms, the human genus, the social genus, and the economic genus. With suburbia comes a radical rupture—a transformation occasioned by what is an eclipse of the city in any of its historical forms, from village to capital city. Anyone who has traveled on New Jersey Transit, or down the Jersey turnpike from New York to Philadelphia, or from Washington, D.C., up to Baltimore, knows what it means to be in a place where cities mean little and townships, though historically significant, still less, and where center-less, sidewalk-less tracts of small-lot homes interspersed with car-littered strip malls constitute the geography of everyday life.

Come with me and visit Piscataway, New Jersey, where I spent a dozen years of my life. Come and ask me to go "downtown" or "into town" to pick up the mail and do a little shopping. Where would I take you? There is no agora, there is no busy traders' crossroads with teeming markets, no historical township, no boulevards, no mixed work/residential neighborhoods, no local shops, no park square where the rising sun casts shadows of a town hall next to a village restaurant up against a Methodist church sitting beside a town middle school adjoining a community theater and the town grocery store. There are instead interstate highways and county roads linking them; strip malls abound and the occasional upscale covered mall is to be found between them. There is an industrial park and a "municipal government" area where a police headquarters and town dump surrounds the mayor's administrative office; but schools are lonely islands among the corporate headquarters and churches sit like older multiplexes, solitary edifices on a concrete tarmac of parked cars.

What does this decentered architecture of civic space mean for citizenship? How might one conceive of public goods (the *res publica*) in these relentlessly private spaces? What does it do to chance "civic" encounters when they can occur only in malls where shopping is the common activity and consumerism is a surrogate for citizenship? Can kids in neighborhoods without sidewalks have bicycle friends or local baseball acquaintances? Is "soccer mom"-driven organized sport a surrogate for the neighborhood sandlot and the local swimming hole? Disjointed, disconnected, disjunctive—how can citizens forge common ideas and common values in the absence of common spaces? These are the vital questions posed by a suburban architecture that have yet even to be properly asked, let alone answered.

The older political theory surely would argue that the multiplex cannot substitute for the church, the school set in an industrial park cannot anchor a neighborhood, the subdivision without sidewalks cannot sponsor a block party. To be unable to "go to town" seems the same thing as being unable to exercise your citizenship. And though they find themselves in "common" spaces, consumers are not citizens. But are these inferences, drawn from the old political theory of the city, appropriate to these new spaces? I will offer a radical critique here, but its intent is not to make an argument but to raise important questions that need to be addressed by citizens and architects alike.

It is my contention (and this is the argument of my book *Jihad vs. McWorld*, 1995) that suburbia has been built on premises that, if not strictly antidemocratic, are at best a-democratic. Take the ubiquity of shopping in the mall-littered suburbs. Shopping to fulfill human needs and wants is as old as human civilization (and one of its defining aspects). The agora was first of all a marketplace. But shopping as one of many activities and shopping as the only activity of a human habitation are two entirely distinctive notions. Moreover, the shopping afforded in the suburban mall (in my view the defining space of suburbia) is itself a new kind of shopping. It is not shopping as part of a civic and social experience where you exchange views with the pastor outside the church, and stop to visit neighbors on a park square bench before going into the five-and-dime, and sit for a soda and a chat with a new resident at the café next to the grocery store, or hear the latest gossip about the town council while getting a haircut.

Shopping in the mall is about consuming pure and simple, and often for socially constructed and well-merchandised wants rather than anything resembling human needs. Many of its stores are devoted to discretionary shopping (the Nature Store, the Disney Store, Brookstone's, Victoria's Secret, The Sharper Image) and the essentials of life are notable by their absence. Try to wash some clothes or pick up some nails and screws or get a quart of milk or drop off the dry-cleaning or select some fresh vegetables for dinner or get a haircut or rent a video at the mall: you are out of luck in almost all of these otherwise well-stocked suburban marketplaces, which feature dozens (sometimes hundreds) of retail outlets that sell things you don't really need (however much you "want" them once you get inside the door). Mall life is less about shopping than about consuming in an era where the production of goods has outstripped the satisfaction of needs, so that new wants must be manufactured (via brand marketing and merchandising) along with the goods that will putatively satisfy them.

This is postmodern capitalism, in which consumption trumps production, in which it is not the production of goods to meet real human needs but the manufacture of wants that makes possible consumption of the endless goods produced that is crucial. Unlike the town-based stores that merge with the civic life of schools and theaters and churches and city halls, the suburban mall is an exclusive venue for radical and unending consumption of the goods that (thanks to relentless merchandising) we have come to want, however little we actually need them.

No wonder this postmodern economy demands a different form of space than the city—where consumption is but one vital part of our nature and but one aspect of our social interactivity. No wonder that suburban work is isolated from living, and shopping segregated from both. No wonder malls are cut off from the public by the intentional exclusion of public transportation—which keeps out the minorities and the many dangerous "others" who inhabit the cities and from whom suburbanites are trying to escape when they leave the cities in the first place. No wonder that state courts have listened sympathetically to developers and vendors who insist that malls are private not public spaces, and that political demonstrators and religious witnesses who try to use such spaces to air their civic and moral views are seen as behaving not as good citizens might but as violators of private property do, and hence as bad citizens. No wonder restless teens trying to pretend the local mall is a downtown sidewalk where they can strut and flirt and hang out and show off are barred from seeking their independence in the sacred spaces of consumerism where those unwilling to spend dollars have no place. No wonder there are neither clocks (to remind you it's time to go home) nor restaurants (which might take up two or three hours of shopping time in a pleasant social exchange) nor anything to divert you from shopping (the food courts are energy pit stops intended to provide quick fuel for another round of shopping).

The consequence of suburbanization for a new generation of Americans is the vanishing of what for twenty-five hundred years has been the civic world of towns and cities, and with it of the different and evolving but always public behaviors of men, women, and children whose identities have been defined by the polis and the town, the city, and the metropolis. A public existence is not possible in an architecture designed exclusively for private consumption. It is not the commercialization of space but the privatization of space that plays havoc with citizenship. Education privatized, art and culture privatized, recreation privatized, religion privatized, means the death of community and the eclipse of citizenship, the eclipse of the idea of public and political creatures who share a social existence.

The wan efforts to bring a little of the city to the suburbs does more to mock the city than transfer its meaning to suburbia. The so-called New Urbanism mimics the urban in order to give to suburbia some artificial sense of city life, minus its diversity, its risks, its openness, its excitement, and its dangers. It synthesizes an ersatz citizenship and phony neighborliness. It thinks, Hollywood style, an urban facade can create (or substitute for) an inner civic life. Ironically, as the New Urbanism tries to bring the form but not the substance of city life to the suburbs, the theme-parking and mallification of cities try to bring the substance but not the form of the suburbs to the cities. If only Times Square can be as safe as the enclosed mall. If only we can get a whiff of urban disorder into the orderly and managed environment of the suburban theme park ("city world," like "Westworld" and "Jungleworld," offers the aesthetic of adventure inside the safety of home).

WOODBURY, NEW YORK. "VILLAGE STYLE" MALL. PHOTO BY ALEX S. MACLEAN/LANDSLIDES

Mall architects have been careful to leave no accidental and random spaces for leisure, people-watching, sitting, daydreaming, socializing, or encountering strangers in their carefully designed venues for consumption. Christmas caroling in the suburbs is impossible, and even a Christmas concert is reduced to a shopper's come-on in the sole "common space" of a mall around an elevator bank or some central shopping crossroads where "empty space" is accidentally created. Malls are about consumption, and consuming is about spending, and anything averse to spending is commercial loitering and not to be brooked. "Hanging out" (a healthy concomitant of citizenship) is taboo, which is why teens and the elderly (who prefer hanging out to shopping) are so unwelcome in malls, unless they are wearing their wallets on their sleeves. From the agora to the arcade, from Aristotle to Walter Benjamin, the marketplace traditionally has been a place for citizenship as well as for buying and selling, for the exchange of feelings and ideas as well as of goods—until the mall.

Our world today is then one whose architecture is increasingly defined not so much by justice, equality, and law (orderly public buildings) as by personal interest and private profit (entertainment palaces and shopping malls). Identity in this world is refashioned, a product not of church, family, and nation but of brand and logo. In the consumer zone of branded identities, who one is may be mediated by what one buys—or more accurately, the lifestyle embodied in the branded products one buys. In the tribal world, and into the world of *Gemeinschaft*, identity arose from birth and blood. In the legal world of contractual nation-states, identity was voluntary, a product of citizenship and civic values. In the new globalizing world of commerce, identity is neither an attribute of birth nor a product of will, but an accoutrement of shopping and a reflection of the places where we acquire goods—Calvin Klein (sexy babes) or Gap Kids (innocent babes), Old Navy (retro nostalgia) or Koolhaas's Prada (postmodern chic).

193

The key is that you self-identify by what you drink, eat, and wear rather than by where you go to church or temple or mosque. You think Ralph Lauren rather than Protestant, DKNY rather than Jewish, Nike rather than Muslim. Being a woman isn't the issue: being a Prada kind of woman (or man) is, as Koolhaas seems to understand.

If we are what we consume, what we consume pervades our being. The young Jewish teens in New York who go to *shul* still wear yarmulkes, but their skull caps today are often emblazoned with the Nike swoosh, problematizing their identity not just for others but for themselves. The meanings of logos need not even be clear for them to be pervasive: Indian young people have been seen wearing a Mets cap and a Yankees shirt in a contradiction that would be impossible in New York.

It may be that the postmodern consumer economy sells us products we don't need, but it offers us identities that we apparently do need—which is why the logo is more significant than the product, the brand more consuming than the item it happens to appropriate. As Naomi Klein points out in *No Logo* (2000), some of the most important brands, like Oprah and Martha Stewart, are real people who are associated with various goods but who contribute nothing in particular to the brand. The Pepsi Generation is not about cola at all, any more than Ralph Lauren is about clothes or Nike is about shoes. The brand literally brands us as belonging to an environment, a lifestyle, a way of living.

Our historical urban environments yielded several kinds of citizen and hence several kinds of democracy: the polis produced the engaged, participatory activist; the early city produced the legal person and rights-bearing individual; the nation-state produced the nationalist member and representative democracy. The mall produces a whole new genus of "citizen": the branded consumer. What sort of democracy does the branded consumer produce? The Republic of Goods? The Democracy of Dollars? The equality of green? The freedom to choose among a hundred toothpastes? As a political genus, the branded consumer has in fact produced the politics of secession (see Robert Reich's 1996 article "Secession of the Successful"), in which privately spent dollars create surrogate public/private services for people who no longer regard themselves as belonging to the polity. Gated communities, private schools, private sanitation and guard services, and a refusal to pay much in the way of taxes define the new suburban citizen. Whether or not such a privatized politics can work even for consumers (I believe it cannot and does not), it is disastrous for the polity in general and for democracy in particular. It skimps on taxes, leaving government with no revenue for genuine public services. It compels public schools and public culture and public prisons to privatize and throw themselves on the mercy of private capital—which offers its meager support at a high price (make it pay off for shareholders, privatize its public character, commercialize its ends). In sum, decentered suburban consumers turn out to be terrible citizens who no longer even understand the meaning of public goods or public values.

Is this all an egregious exaggeration? Of course it is. Are there suburban dwellers who really are nothing but branded consumers? Hardly. In fact suburbanites vote more than city dwellers (for reasons associated with economic status, race, and age). Yet the tendencies to which I point, widely explored by critics and sociologists on the right and the left for more than fifty years (including Walter Benjamin, Daniel Bell, William Leach, Herbert Marcuse, and Naomi Klein, to name only a few), are undeniably present in our suburbanizing, privatizing, commercializing culture, and they are being promoted rather than inhibited by economic globalization, which tends to privilege economic changes and curtail the growth of democratic responses to them. Moreover, for those who regard themselves as architects of physical and civic space—who attempt to design environments for human beings that can nurture certain forms of identity associated with civic freedom, with artistic creativity, with political dissidence, or with participatory citizenship—the challenge is clear. Whether we look at urban renewal, suburban expansion, or the architecture of virtual space (the Internet), we see a move toward the private and the commercial and away from the public and the democratic. It may be that architecture can only follow social change, but historically it has claimed (aspired?) to lead as well. To lead, it must understand its relationship to the new social and economic environments that are replacing cities and that, willy-nilly, it is complicit in designing.

The challenge faced is painfully evident in the way in which architects of suburbia have both recognized traditional urban landscapes and then, on the way to trying to assimilate them, eviscerated them of their essence. The New Urbanism to which I have already alluded, for example, has tried to expropriate certain anodyne features of urban identity, of the life of the city, without running any of its risks, without taking chances, without being soiled by the city's tawdry anonymity and noisy rambunctiousness. Parasitic of its messy cosmetic look, the New Urbanism studiously avoids its productively disordered essence (see Richard Sennett's classic *The Uses of Disorder*, 1970). They take no chances with the chance-taking that is the secret of urban life: grittiness without drug dealers or prostitutes, color without people of color, winding alleys where you always know where you are, feeling like you're a loner on a Harley when you park the family Camry in the well-patrolled lot and haul the kids to an animated feature film, pornography without sex (a neon flashiness but no "GIRLS!" in the words the neon spells out)—in other words, the chaste promise of the newer and better urbanism that lets you visit the city while staying safely in the gussied-up mall next to your subdivision and that assures you the real get-down-and-dirty-and-equal of the city will never disturb your pleasant suburban dreams.

The architect here is the small god of the safe city: a mall built to look urban in a zone inaccessible to public transportation so that real urban dwellers can't get to it, the hot songs of the city piped over a muted mall P.A. system calculated to leave you feeling cool, a mishmash of urban styles minus the actual human diversity that gives the real city mishmash its multicultural funkiness and bracing sense of otherness that sometimes feels, ever so seductively, like peril. Which of course is not the city at all, but merely its pale and sanitized reflection. The imitation city: urbanism as a theme-park ride.

What is perhaps most ironic in this architectural culture of mimicry is that at the very moment when the suburbs are trying to reproduce and replicate the feel of urbanism with artificial and superficial design components, the city—actual cities like New York and Baltimore and Las Vegas—are busy trying to reproduce and replicate the feel of suburbia through a process of mallification that turns gritty inner-city squares into branded and safe mall-spaces. Those yearning for the very sanitized predictability that drove earlier generations of city dwellers to the suburbs are placated, while suburbanites are drawn back to town as city tourists who can have it all: urban otherness and suburban sameness by just stepping off the charter bus taking them to a show. As the suburbs busy themselves trying to feel like cities without actually becoming cities, cities busy themselves trying to become suburban malls—"cleaning up" without moving out. Then there are those truly weird hybrids like Las Vegas, which already are cities but which in their confusion about who and what they want to be insist on disguising their small-time parochialism with miniature urbanscapes of "real" cities like New York and Paris, while living off the mall culture of the suburban mentality that defines their soul.

America's "new towns," which began as municipal experiments in innovative design for living, gradually got mixed up in this suburban/urban confusion as well, one in which, though the grass always looked greener out there across the river in the city dweller's or the suburbanite's backyard, no one was actually anxious to leave home. Disney's Celebration, not far from Orlando, Florida, tells a dizzying (Disneying) tale of trying to clone the theme park as a residential neighborhood: the polis recreated as a gated community where consumers are surrogates for citizens; but the company of which they are clients actually runs their lives for them. In the early brochures handed out to prospective buyers, Celebration promised a kind of instant *Gemeinschaft*: "We give you community, which you will experience on the very first day you arrive in Celebration because there will be a cocktail party just for you!" This is *Gemeinschaft* without a past, without a "people," without tradition (other than Disney ready-to-wear traditions and Celebration's incessant celebration of itself). The anguished (and time-consuming) history through which authentic communities are forged and won can be bypassed, or synthesized in the "imagineering" factory of Disney's "creative" departments. The real ethnic and economic diversity of the city (and the globe) can be reduced to a safe choice between Mediterranean or Tudor facades on otherwise identical housing units.

Celebration was first and last a Disney experiment in city-building, however. The problems of public safety, education, signage, lifestyles—the essence of politics in the real politics of real people who had come in order to live their lives in real towns rather than to spend a weekend in a theme park—proved rather too daunting, and Disney prudently decided to get out of the town-making business. Orlando was a little too close by, and like many recent mall developers, Disney may have figured out it could not ultimately insulate its new town from the all too real urban America just down the interstate, not at least without drawing unfavorable criticism. So, although suburbia continues to want to escape its own ineluctable sterility by importing the cosmopolitan diversity of the city into its cultural wasteland, it isn't really willing to pay the price of the city. The cosmetics can't engineer a serious face-lift, and in any case a changed face is not an altered soul. Soulscapes are the product of history and sociology and cannot be reproduced in exclusively architectural ways. A neo-Greek style no more reproduces the polis than an Italianate facade gives you lower Manhattan's Little Italy. Disney's imagineering techniques work well enough for make-believe theme parks, but are less successful with not quite so pliable human lives.

Still, like Celebration, suburbia has always been an attempt to have it all. People who live in the suburbs will say happily: we want the excitement of being near cities with their cultural diversity and urban edginess (otherwise known as danger), but at the same time the peace and the stability of living in a rural subdivision (otherwise known as difference-free). In trying to have both, the suburbanite often ends up with neither, at a considerable cost to democracy and citizenship.

3.

This review of historical urban archetypes and the new suburbanism of postwar America brings us to today's threshold question: what will the human townscape look like in the coming age of global interdependence? What will define its physical and its ever more virtual habitats? For, if globalization's economics are the economics of the information age, and are rooted in the technologies of media and telecommunications, the new architecture of public (or private) space will have to refer to the Web as well as the mall. The time horizon here for significant change is not a decade but a century. We are, however, already in the era of experimentation and planning, in which today's decisions will dictate tomorrow's possibilities—not just tomorrow's habitats but tomorrow's political and cultural forms, the very meaning of democracy.

In an age of interactivity and global horizons, it is apparent that global habitats are going to have to have the qualities of ports, and their virtual extensions, portals. They will demand an interactivity that is instantaneous. They will have to encompass global differences in a technology of particularized sameness. They are likely to connect localities that will be linked together not as states and nations but as global regions like Europe or NAFTA, or into truly global entities yet to be constructed. Certainly states are no longer likely to be the primary players, the principal actors. Certainly territory is no longer likely to be the first marker of our identities or of the kinds of social behaviors and political affiliations in which we engage. Already, the portals that bring us into the virtual world of cyberspace are, at least for young people, increasingly becoming theme parks of identity, ways of moving beyond the kinds of parochial identity once afforded by polis, city, and nationality. Perhaps the young (in the developed world) are attuned to the mall and the Web, to suburbia and cyberspace, because they have grown up in a world of branded identities that puts lifestyle and consumer choices first and birthright and heritage second.

The young have a hard time looking back, while the polis, the city, and the nation-state all are rooted in history and its time-wrapped traditions, ethnicities, languages, and cultures. Suburbia offers a world without roots and hence seems suited to a people without a past, kids who find in video games and MTV more meaning than in the history books and Bibles of their parents' fading civilization.

Some commentators might even assert that suburbia in a certain sense is the ideal expression of America, because America has always represented an uprooting, a necessary deracination for immigrants from around the world who came to the new world to escape the old, who came to make their own history anew because the histories they carried on their backs had become too onerous. America—its frontier, its mobility—was precisely what made it possible to forget roots. The point was not to reproduce but to suppress the memory of the habitats that had once oppressed them.

In earlier times, immigrants passed through cities first, and tended there to reproduce the cultures they had emigrated from to escape; but more recently they have migrated directly to the suburbs from overseas, forgoing the stage of cultural reproduction and plunging directly into those bleak mallscapes in which identity is given by what you buy rather than where you come from. The gateway port cities represented islands of memory as well as of forgetfulness: in the suburbs, memory evaporates. What it took the public schools two generations to accomplish in the inner cities of America is now achieved almost overnight by a branded commercial culture that subsumes all historical identities to the magic of the multiplex and the ministrations of the mall.

The Indian and Pakistani children with whom my daughter went to school in Piscataway were already as American as she was— perhaps more so because they were more attached to the fast-food chains and video games and big-box mall outlets that circumscribed their young lives than she was. The Vietnamese quickly learned they could inhabit the coastal towns and suburbs along the Gulf of Mexico without stopping for a generation in Houston, just as Asians now skip San Francisco on their way to Sacramento and points east. For those who come here as an act of forgetting, suburbia makes for a more radical amnesia than the city.

But the true new ports are the portals of the Web. It is the encompassing anonymity of these portals leading to cyberspace that constitute the new suburbs of a globalizing, ever more virtual world. Not surprisingly, they share quite a few of suburbia's leading characteristics. The coming global world is governed not by equality, or law, or profit, but by information (hence, the "information economy"). The modus operandi for the individual is neither the citizen nor the private individual, neither the legal person nor the consumer, but the virtual inter-actor, a participatory spectator who is proactive by virtue of watching. The denizen of tomorrow's cyberworld is a body interacting with a computer screen via a keyboard—but just for the time being. Soon the body will touch the screen or speak directly to it in an orgy of passive energy. The screen literally becomes a portal to a world in which immediate surrounding physical spaces are no longer necessary to a sense of community. In many American college towns, cafés and restaurants and bowling alleys and other student hangouts have shut down, deferring to the virtual hangout of the World Wide Web. The community young people find there, if it is a community, is a *Gemeinde* with a difference—no longer defined by the geography of the town in which the college exists, but rather by the world of cyberspace. Exactly what kind of "citizens" this will make them remains to be seen. Better? Worse? In any case, different.

The precise form of this new community is likely to depend on exactly how virtuality is shaped and formed. It too has an architecture no less important to sociability's character than the width of a boulevard or the design of a crossroads. What will be the virtual equivalent of the English-style "circus"? The stop-lighted intersection? The park plaza pedestrian mall? The civic power of the agora was derived from its initial presence as a shopping space designed to give immediate access to cultural, political, and social interactions that went far beyond shopping—from family gossip to high-minded debate. Athenians discovered their ultimate being as public citizens in what started out as a private experience of shopping—by design.

Today, we can see how the anonymous encounter on the city crossroads, on the subway, on the bus, or in the lunchtime plaza where street vendors sell pretzels and chili dogs forges from a multicultural conglomeration of strangers some genuine sense of place and community. The city allows us to meet people different from us—the classical "other"—in ways that manifest how we share our city. This gives integrity and unity to megalopolises of diversity and perhaps signals the birth of global cities, an alternative to suburbanized virtual communities. What will the configuration of the new cyber-portals with their virtual community do to our children's sense of who they are, and of who their virtual kinfolk are supposed to be? Will the new virtual community be a self-selected specialty segment of the population—cloned communities of the like-minded where we need never encounter strangers? (Think of Web sites for Scottish Protestant fly-fishermen who enjoy California white wines, for gay truck drivers who refuse to join unions, for single Jewish mothers who have children interested in sports.) This is the question Cass Sunstein asks in his new (2001) book called *Republic.com* (he is not sanguine).

Or will the Internet live up to its early pioneering potential as a new electronic frontier for participatory democracy? Will there be any such thing as a "public" in virtual space? Manuel Castells writes pointedly in *The Rise of the Network Society* (1996), the first volume of his trilogy *The Information Age*, about the new globalization inherent in a world of networks that weave societies together even as they divide individuals. Terrorists and merchandisers alike use the Internet to communicate to their "clients." The cells and the individuals who populate them are no longer the crucial thing: the network, the system, is crucial—not the neurons but the synapses linking them. But what do such metaphors mean for our political and civic relations? If town centers and city neighborhoods no longer are the key to social and civic interaction, around which centers are they to revolve? If the politics of suburbia has become the apolitics of suburbia, involving a radical privatization of public space, what will be the politics of cyberspace? Will there be one?

The answer is likely to be dialectical: as with the polis and the city, cyberspace can lend itself to new productive forms of democratic interaction as well as to new and destructive forms of hegemonic interaction. The vices are already apparent: a speed that is the enemy of deliberateness and quiet reflection (necessities of democracy); a penchant for segmentation that can keep us from the chance encounters with "others" that are so crucial to democratic pluralism and tolerance (another Sunstein theme); an antipathy to hierarchy that, while it may spur horizontal equality and interactivity, makes tutelage, education, and the development of mature civic judgment problematic. Which cyber-architecture will enhance our capacity to enjoy liberty? Certainly the current enthusiasm for privatization and commercialization does little for civic and public liberty—although it does embellish consumer choice.

Historically, evolving forms of municipality have enhanced liberty. De Tocqueville could say with conviction in the 1830s that the very essence of the new democratic liberty forged in America was local and municipal in character. What sort of freedom, if any, is facilitated by the architecture of the Web? Magazines like *Wired*, which are dedicated to the premise that wired means free, do little to ground that premise. And if the evolution of the polis into the capital city has been an exercise in balancing freedom and democracy, there is little to suggest that either principle elicits much interest from the programmers and platform builders of the new global software.

In the ancient polis and the New England town, participation and democracy, for those who were citizens, were purchased at the price of exclusion of others; community, fraternity, and kinship meant that many stayed on the outside. The modern city finally opened the way for individual liberty, personal expression, and political dissent in a framework defined by tolerance, inclusion, and justice. The city allowed outsiders and vagabonds and immigrants and adventurers to share the liberty of anonymous cityscapes and participate in a thin but equal citizenship. The modern nation-state effects a balance between liberty and equality, individualism and justice, the legal person and the responsible community. Its habitations, incarnate in the capital city, reinforce its values.

Yet it has been my argument here that in the last fifty years with the move from city to suburb, although motivated by a will to freedom no less than an escape from diversity, there has been a loss of both liberty and democracy—a loss of public space because the habitat of suburbia is private, commercial, and anti-civic. Aristotle's *zoon politikon* has become *homo privatus*—the kids of Columbine and the adults of Celebration.

To me, this promises a particularly dismal manifestation of human social being in a world that seems unlikely to be very democratic. At least if it is left to its own devices, and these devices are the products of today's suburban, neo-liberal ideology of privatization. Compare the mall to the boulevard, the Internet to the public square, cyberspace to the agora: where are we to find citizens at the multiplex or in the food courts? Revisit the monuments of capital city crossroads in Vienna or Paris or the markets around the cathedrals of Rheims or Augsburg and ask yourself whether the "citoyens" and "burghers" of these towns are likely to resemble those who reappear at McDonald's or at the Nike Superstore.

I feel a deep and natural sympathy for both the engaged citizen climbing toward the summit of the Pnyx to attend the assembly and for the angry dissident artist living an alienated but active life among a coterie of rebels in an anonymous urban environment: I am not sure if either will find a place in today's suburb or tomorrow's cyber-community. Or, to put it more bluntly, I am not sure that those who command these new spaces have even thought about what it might mean to design them to accommodate either of these democratic types. The consumer turns out to be a pretty paltry citizen and a pretty wan rebel, passive rather than engaged, reactive rather than proactive, avoiding conflict rather than confronting and adjudicating it, averse to otherness and hence to growth and renewal (though not to manufactured "newness").

As passivity is a denial of that active essence that makes us human, privatization takes us from our public selves and secretes us in islands of isolation. If the polis was the most public of all the collective habitations we have had, the city made room for the private and the personal without surrendering its essentially civic character. But the private suburban marketplace—whether physical or virtual—seems particularly ill-suited to civility, nurturing a particularly unproductive, a particularly shrunken and narrow conception of human association.

I do not mean to suggest that the architecture of the new technologies will be overdetermining in shaping the political and civic character of our future lives. Technology tends not to condition and determine the world, but rather, at least in its initial impact, to reflect and mirror it. Hence, while the new virtual technologies suggested to many thoughtful and imaginative people at the time of their inception new forms of interactivity, of civic and cultural expression, they have in fact fairly quickly been reduced to tired instruments of the same old commerce, the same suburbanization of value that has been shrinking citizenship in recent decades. Perhaps that is because there never was anywhere "to go" in suburbia, and so the young stepped into cyberspace rather than out into the malls. The technologies allowed them to stay home and discover the world—or at least *a* world, even if it resembled the commercial world of the mall rather more closely than they might have hoped.

For the Net looks more like a consumer mall than anything else at this point. Over ninety-five percent of its content is commercial, and one-third of the hits registered are on pornographic sites. There is more discussion about whether it is appropriate to regulate Web porn than about whether the Net might be used for cultural, educational, or civic purposes. In the spring of 2002, the Supreme Court ruled that vendors who use adults pretending to be children on the way to selling pornography on the Net could not be censored so long as they were not using actual children. This was a provocative stand in favor of free expression, in its most commercial and debased form (which is not to say it does not as such still merit protection). But where is the debate about engendering and protecting political and democratic expression on a World Wide Web that has been just about wholly privatized? This is the extraordinary new virtual technology that was supposed to transform our political and social lives, which instead has become one more tired vehicle for the world's oldest vocation.

Surely young architects today can see in virtual space a new frontier. Yet just as surely there is no more closed and private space, no space more resistant to innovation, than the Web, where those who think at all about its shape seem to rehearse the old forms and imitate the hyped, brightly lit signage of an urban advertising approach that is already more than a hundred years old. Actually, the interest of the courts in the protection of commercial rather than democratic space is now a cliché. The 1934 Federal Communications Act gave to radio broadcasting special public responsibilities, but more recently television and the Internet have demanded none and only commercial speech has been subjected to debate. Since the new technologies putatively offer a "spectrum abundance" in which wavelength scarcity is no longer an issue, the government has removed itself from the debate about what the architecture of the new technologies ought to look like: this was the precise effect of the 1996 Federal Communications Act, which undid the public good legislated by its 1934 forebear. The state has spoken and said there is no public interest in the virtual public architecture that will define our common future. This is shortsightedness on a colossal scale, one that appalled even Republican presidential candidate Bob Dole in 1996.

The result is an Internet that serves the pornographers, the advertisers, the merchandisers, the virtual mall developers, and is effectively closed to artists and politicians, to civic groups and NGOs, to statesmen and citizens alike; not legally closed, of course, since anyone can put up a Web site, but effectively closed because the Web has become a primarily private, commercial (and pornographic) medium owned by private corporations and used primarily to the benefit of their shareholders. Can someone show us an Internet that begins to respond to the civic, cultural, educational, and transnational needs of citizens? Or of artists? Or teachers, historians, curators, or (God forbid) architects? I do not mean some distant "potential"—the talk of the Net's potential is endless—but a virtual usage with these audiences actually in mind?

The new medium, the new space that will be the space in which our children and grandchildren will increasingly live their lives, has become a uniquely private, uniquely commercial, uniquely trivialized, uniquely propagandistic space. Were the state to be doing what commerce is doing we would call it totalitarian; were a church to be doing what commerce is doing we would call it theocratic. Were anyone but the "private market" to be effectively monopolizing the Web—forcing unsolicited messages into our homes on incessant pop-up and banner advertising, making it difficult if not quite impossible to get out of sites once on them, screen after screen appearing and reappearing even after the original has been exited—the American public would be crying tyranny. And the American public would be right. What we will not permit to party officials or to preachers and mullahs, we offer willingly (and for free—Bob Dole called it the "sellout of the century") to merchandisers and pornographers, without thinking for even an instant about the impact of this shaping of our new virtual space on our children, our imagination, our sense of the public and the political.

The market, of course, operates in the name of choice; but private consumer choice is not the same thing as public civic freedom. The latter must treat with the many untoward public consequences of the private choices we make as consumers. When we turn over virtual space to the same old merchandisers, in the name of freedom, of freedom from government censorship, what we are actually doing is removing the one publicly responsible authority we have to help us guarantee the diversity of that space. In the name of market freedom, pluralism is defeated.

4.

We are replicating on the Net the conceptual errors we made in suburbia. Giving developers the freedom to appropriate public space meant malls without diversity, diminished rather than enhanced choice. The curse of the new private architecture of would-be, could-be public space is homogenization—a creeping totalization of human experience. It is not suburbia alone, but the world at large that is being subjected to the market forces that create malls and destroy cities. Increasingly, the world looks more and more like a mall: the same brands, the same chains, the same apparel, the same franchises, the same fast-food eateries, the same discretionary goods boutiques, the same sneakers, the same news, the same movies, the same television programs in which news and entertainment are no longer separable—the same sameness. In the name of freedom and privacy, we are creating a world of dull, soul-crushing homogeneity in which no meaningful social choices can be made.

The one instrumentality that might guarantee us some choice is the democratic state, the keeper of our *res publica*. Yet in the "neo-liberal" ideology that undergirds privatization and commercialization, it is precisely the democratic state—the political institutions that belong to us—that is seen as part of the problem. When we dwell on coercive control or overweening censorship, we focus on the top-down state, not the bottom-up market.

Pluralism requires proactive civic allies. The market is not one of them. For the endless private choices of the marketplace result in a less differentiated and plural public space in which people look alike, act alike, and so in time think and behave alike (the Pepsi Generation, the MTV generation); and in which the civilizational markers of our individuality, our cultural heritage, our vaunted scholarship, and our creative arts have an ever more difficult time finding a place they can call their own.

If architecture is the art of designing places fit for human habitation—and so helps to define what we mean by "human"—it is hard not to conclude that architects today have either abjured their mission or are complicit in the annihilation of what it means to be human. Or perhaps they are just impotent: craven followers of trends, they might, had they the courage, be bucking. Yet the new technology offers enlivening new challenges and a perfect medium for young shapers of space to make an impact and acquire a reputation and an audience. Not that the new medium is as cheap to shape as its advocates claim. A simple home page can run a couple of thousand dollars, and outfitted with movement ("flash") and sound and a memory sufficient to hold extensive data, it can be beyond the reach of ordinary people. A Web site also represents a minimalist usage of the technology. Marketing, selling, reaching a wide audience on the Web is as inegalitarian as doing so on radio or television: those with the deepest pockets and the greatest chance for profit are powerfully advantaged. For software and content providers alike, bigger is better and richer is more successful. Doctors Without Borders (a successful NGO) is not really up to serious competition with either Bill Gates (Microsoft) or Michael Eisner (Disney); nor are Rutgers University or People for the American Way or, for that matter, the Republican National Committee. In a world arbitrated by wealth in which taxpayers are less generous than shareholders, private always will trump public and can turn a potentially public medium like the Web into one more marketplace playground for the rich and powerful.

The withdrawal of government from oversight with the 1996 Federal Communications Act, alluded to above, meant in fact the indenture of the medium to the same handful of corporations that now control the look and feel of our entertainment complexes, of our "infotainment" news networks, of our recreational and sports teams, of our book and magazine and newspaper publishers around the world.

A handful of global corporations control more than half of the networks of the world and thus just about everything called news or entertainment or recreation that we see, read, or do. And this is called market freedom and enhanced choice in the architecture of virtual space.

Should not architects be asking themselves whether these new virtual spaces are in their present form a fit environment for a twelve-year-old girl or a fifteen-year-old boy? My eleven-year-old lives in a world of screens whose shape and context have been left to the whims of those interested in making their fortunes off selling her their goods. Why are the multiplex screens, the television screens, and the computer screens regarded as private when they constitute the powerful, inescapable architecture of my daughter's daily public life? Why are their form and substance not an appropriate question for educators and statesmen and citizens rather than for merchandisers and vendors and corporate managers? The hubris of architecture portrayed in works like Ayn Rand's *The Fountainhead* has given way to a timorousness that is downright cowardly. At least the New Urbanists still dream their trivial cosmetics might modify the character of suburban life. The architects of the Web are paid hands of private corporations and do not dream at all.

For the generation whose reality will be circumscribed by cyberspace, what is on the screens and what the screens are on are questions of the first magnitude. Do we want those decisions left to a handful of telecommunications conglomerates whose only interest is shareholder profit, to people more interested in manufacturing needs than in civilizing and educating them? Are we content to watch the old ideal of one world turn into the new ideal of one global mall? Or see both the polis and the city along with their civic virtues disappear into a virtual mall of global reach?

The new world of the Web has an uncanny resemblance to Plato's cave, where chained denizens watched flickering shadows—imitations of imitations at a third remove from reality—that to them seemed like "reality." A world mediated by pixels will have a sameness that the multitudinous shapes that pixels comprise cannot overcome. Are we then fated to live in a world of flickering shadows? This question may seem far removed from what architects are supposed to be thinking about. Whether Europe retains an original flavor or is finally merely a reproduction of what parasitic imitators give back to it is not a question for which designers can have an answer. But architecture is always a mirror in which we see ourselves, a crucial part of how we shape our public lives, and if the world of tomorrow is one in which we can see ourselves only in mirrors of mirrors of mirrors, perhaps this should become an issue for architects. For it will matter to them—to all of us—that the problems facing those who craft and shape the spaces in which we live have to confront dramatic new challenges by a privatization, commercialization, suburbanization, and virtualization of our life spaces more radical than any that occurred in the several millennia of our civilization's history. The prototypes of polis, city, and city-state, and finally capital city, which for thousands of years have defined the debate, are in sudden and decisive flux. As we cross the threshold to a suburbanized and globalized world (whatever exactly that means), we must seek out new archetypes that accommodate the new while acknowledging the human essence yielded, I still believe, by variety, liberty, and the quest for justice.

There are serious commentators like Saskia Sassen who think (hope?) that globalization will take the form of new but familiar global cities, metropolises of a kind that still reverberate with the public energy and personal rebelliousness that have defined the city historically. Others write about (or hope for) a global polis, literally now a cosmo-polis, the ancient stoic ideal of the cosmopolis of ideas and ideals that could hold together a world of diversity—a reality today because of globalization. I share the dreams. But I fear the reality of globalization may point in a different direction, where suburbia's anonymous privatism and stultifying sameness take the planet by storm, carrying high its banner of liberty (private choice) even as they render democracy (public liberty) obsolete. I fear a virtual suburbanization, courtesy of new commerce-dominated, consumerist virtual technologies that have been relegated by the state to the care of shareholders, corporate managers, and quarterly profit-sheet accountants. I fear a world that is one only by virtue of homogeneity, in which cities and townships and *poleis* vanish and interaction around the ideals of common ground and distinctive values is impossible.

Surely neither citizens, nor architects, nor artists, nor even the proud denizens of suburban New Jersey will want a whole world that looks exactly like the Garden State—any more than they will want a world that is New York or Hong Kong or Paris or Bombay. Democracy demands both community and individuality, common ground and diversity; and it needs appropriate spaces in which these paradoxical combinations are possible. Who will help design such spaces in democracy's name in the coming century?

BENJAMIN R. BARBER is the Gershon and Carol Kekst Professor of Civil Society at the University of Maryland and directs the Democracy Collaborative in New York. His books include *Strong Democracy* (University of California Press, 1984) and the international best-seller *Jihad vs. McWorld: How Globalism and Tribalism Are Reshaping the World* (Ballantine Books, 1995, now translated into ten languages). A consultant to political and civic leaders, including former president Bill Clinton, he has most recently published *The Truth of Power: Intellectual Affairs in the Clinton White House* (W. W. Norton, 2001).

CAROLA HEIN teaches in the Growth and Structure of Cities Program at Bryn Mawr College, where she organized the international symposium "The Rebuilding of Japan's Bombed Cities" in 2000. She coauthored the volume *Hauptstadt Berlin* (Gebr. Mann Verlag, 1991) and is coeditor of the forthcoming *Rebuilding Japan after 1945*, to be published by Macmillan in spring 2003.

KANAN MAKIYA is professor of Middle Eastern Studies at Brandeis University. Born in Baghdad, he holds a degree in architecture from the Massachusetts Institute of Technology. In the 1980s he left the practice of architecture to write an exposé of Saddam Hussein's regime, *Republic of Fear: The Politics of Modern Iraq* (University of California Press, 1989), under the pseudonym Samir al-Khalil. His next book was an essay on the aesthetics of power and kitsch, *The Monument: Art, Vulgarity, and Responsibility* (University of California Press, 1991). This was followed by *Cruelty and Silence: War, Tyranny, Uprising and the Arab World* (W. W. Norton, 1993). His most recent book is *The Rock: A Tale of Seventh-Century Jerusalem*, published by Pantheon Books in 2001.

KENNETH MAXWELL holds the Nelson and David Rockefeller Chair in Inter-American Studies at the Council on Foreign Relations. An expert on Latin America, Spain, and Portugal, he formerly directed the Tinker Foundation and has taught at Yale, Princeton, and Columbia universities. His recent books include *Chocolate, Piratas e Outros Malandros: Ensaios Tropicais* (Paz e Terra, 1999), *The Making of Portuguese Democracy* (Cambridge University Press, 1995), and *Pombal: Paradox of the Enlightenment* (Cambridge University Press, 1995).

HAN MEYER is professor of urbanism at the Technical University in Delft. He worked for many years as a planner in the Rotterdam Department of Physical Planning and Urban Development. A member of the International Scientific Committee of Europan, he is the author of *City and Port: Urban Planning as a Cultural Venture in London, Barcelona, New York and Rotterdam* (International Books, 1999).

ROSS MILLER teaches at the University of Connecticut, where he is a professor of English and Comparative Literature. A former director of the Chicago Institute for Architecture and Urbanism, he writes frequently on nineteenth- and twentieth-century American architecture and urban studies. His writing has appeared in the *Wall Street Journal*, *Washington Post*, and *Los Angeles Times*, as well as in scholarly journals. His books include *American Apocalypse: The Great Fire and the Myth of Chicago* (University of Chicago Press, 1992/2000), *Here's the Deal: The Buying and Selling of a Great American City* (Alfred A. Knopf, 1996), and *Land That I Love: How the Jews Discovered America* (Houghton Mifflin, 2000).

JOAN OCKMAN directs the Temple Hoyne Buell Center for the Study of American Architecture at Columbia University, where she also teaches architectural history and theory. Her book *Architecture Culture 1943–1968: A Documentary Anthology* was published by Rizzoli in 1993. Most recently she edited the volume *The Pragmatist Imagination: Thinking about Things in the Making* (Princeton Architectural Press, 2001). She is currently writing a book on architecture and the Cold War.

MAX PAGE is the author of *The Creative Destruction of Manhattan, 1900–1940* (University of Chicago Press, 1999), which won the Spiro Kostof Award from the Society of Architectural Historians. He is the coeditor of *Constructing America: American Writings on Architecture, Urbanism, and Place* (University of Pennsylvania Press, forthcoming 2003) and *Giving Preserving a History: Essays on the History of Historic Preservation in the United States* (Routledge, forthcoming 2003). He teaches architectural history at the University of Massachusetts at Amherst.

ALAN POWERS is an architectural historian living in London. A trustee of the Twentieth Century Society, he has curated numerous exhibitions, including "Modern Britain, 1929–1939" (1999), "Sir Albert Richardson, 1880–1964" (1999), and mostly recently "Serge Chermayeff." He is the author of *Serge Chermayeff: Architect, Designer, Educator* (RIBA Publications, 2001).

MILAN PRODANOVIC is a professor of urbanism at the University of Novi Sad and a practicing architect residing in Belgrade. He received a doctorate in environmental design from the Bartlett School in London. The author of many articles on Balkan architecture and urban heritage, including "Mostar Warning" (1993), he codirects the Ecourban Workshop and is former coeditor of the Belgrade-based dissident publication *Republika*.

HUBERTUS SIEGERT is a writer and film director living in Berlin. He has studied history, art history, and theater and holds a degree in landscape architecture. He established S.U.M.O. Film in 1993. In addition to *Berlin Babylon* (2001), he has directed and produced two short films, *Das Sonnenjuwel* (1995) and *The Orange Kiss* (1996), as well as the documentary *Stravinsky in Berlin* (1993). He is currently working on a film dealing with the European Union's impact on national identity for an upcoming generation of young people.

RALPH STERN is an architect and architectural historian who has lived in Berlin since 1994. The author of numerous articles on architectural theory and historiography, including "Berlin: The Politics of Memory and Identity" (2001), he coedited the volume *Foreign Affairs: New Embassy Buildings in Berlin* (Birkhäuser, 1997). He teaches in the Program for Urban Processes at the Universität der Künste Berlin and has taught in the Graduate School of Architecture, Planning and Preservation at Columbia University.

"THE SWIFTER THE COMMENT, THE SHORTER-LIVED ITS RELEVANCE. NOTHING AGAINST TIMELINESS! BUT MOMENTS WHEN NO ONE KNOWS WHAT WILL HAPPEN NEXT ARE PRECISELY THE TIMES WHEN THERE IS GOOD REASON TO ATTEMPT A DISTANCED VIEW."

HANS MAGNUS ENZENSBERGER
SEPTEMBER 17, 2001

OPENING SEQUENCE

NEW YORK. WORLD TRADE CENTER SITE. VIEW NORTH FROM LIBERTY STREET, JULY 2002. PHOTO BY CHRIS BARKER

LISBON. ROYAL OPERA HOUSE IN RUINS AFTER THE EARTHQUAKE OF 1755. PRINT BY JACQUES-PHILIPPE LE BAS, 1757. COLLECTION MUSEU DA CIDADE, LISBON

CHICAGO. VIEW SOUTH FROM WATER TOWER AFTER THE FIRE OF 1871. STEREO PHOTO BY COPELIN & SON

HIROSHIMA. VIEW TOWARD DOWNTOWN ACROSS THE MOTOYASU RIVER WITH A-BOMB DOME IN BACKGROUND, 2001. PHOTO BY ANDREAS PAULY

ROTTERDAM. AERIAL VIEW OF CITY CENTER FROM NORTH, 1999. PHOTO BY DICK SELLENRAAD AEROVIEW

PLYMOUTH. CIVIC CENTER AS BUILT TO DESIGNS BY JELLICOE, BALLANTYNE AND COLERIDGE, 1960. COURTESY JOHN HINDE INTERNATIONAL

BERLIN. CONSTRUCTION ZONE IN FRONT OF THE REICHSTAG BUILDING, UNDER RENOVATION BY THE OFFICE OF NORMAN FOSTER, 1998. COURTESY HUBERTUS SIEGERT AND S.U.M.O. FILM

MOSTAR. OLD STONE BRIDGE, BUILT 1566, AFTER DESTRUCTION OF 1993

JERUSALEM. AERIAL VIEW OF THE HARAM OR TEMPLE MOUNT AREA

THANK YOU

TO THE AUTHORS OF THE ESSAYS IN THIS VOLUME FOR THEIR INSIGHTS AND THEIR ENTHUSIASTIC COLLABORATION

TO ANGELI SACHS AT PRESTEL FOR WELCOMING THIS PROJECT

TO BERNARD TSCHUMI AT THE GRADUATE SCHOOL OF ARCHITECTURE, PLANNING AND PRESERVATION, COLUMBIA UNIVERSITY, FOR FACILITATING IT

TO SALOMON FRAUSTO, FOR ALL MANNER OF ASSISTANCE, SINE QUA NON

TO CHRIS BARKER, STEPHANIE SALOMON, AND CURT HOLTZ FOR EDITORIAL TEAMWORK

TO BRETT SNYDER FOR AN EXTRAORDINARY DESIGN

TO ZOë SLUTZKY AND BOB SLUTZKY